Atlantic Drift

Atlantic Drift

An Anthology of Poetry and Poetics

Edited by James Byrne
& Robert Sheppard

EDGE HILL
UNIVERSITY PRESS

PUBLICATIONS
2017

Published by Arc Publications
Nanholme Mill, Shaw Wood Road
Todmorden, OL14 6DA, UK
www.arcpublications.co.uk
and
Edge Hill University Press
Department of English History & Creative Writing
St Helens Road, Ormskirk L39 4QP, UK
www.edgehill.ac.uk/university-press/

Design by Tony Ward
Printed in Great Britain by
TJ International, Padstow, Cornwall

978 1911469 19 3 (pbk)
978 1911469 20 9 (hbk)
978 1911469 21 6 (ebk)

The publishers are grateful to the authors
and, in the case of previously published works,
to their publishers for allowing their poems
to be included in this anthology.

Cover image:
Pete Clarke 'Ladders & Bridges',
oil, acrylic and collage on canvas, 1991,
by kind permission of the artist.

CONTENTS

Introduction / 9

CHARLES BERNSTEIN
This Line / 17
Whose Language / 17
Sunset Sail / 18
Dysraphism / 18
Castor Oil / 22
Preface to *Pitch of Poetry* / 23

SEAN BONNEY
from *Our Death* / 29
from *Cancer* / 31
Letter Against the Language / 38

ANDREA BRADY
The Fourth Call of Mr Gore / 45
All My Sons / 46
Queen Bee / 49
Men / 51
Poetics / 53

SOPHIE COLLINS
from *The Engine* / 57
Before / 58
A. S. / 59
Beauty Milk / 60
a whistle in the gloom / 61

ALLEN FISHER
from *Place* / 67
Birdland / 68
Bumblebee / 71
Jitterbug / 73
The poetics of decoherence and the imperfect fit / 76

ROBERT FITTERMAN
from *This window makes me feel* / 85
Failure: a Postconceptual Poem / 88

S. J. FOWLER
You'll find a bee and sting me with it / 95
Looper / 95
Bears attacked me / 96
Atacama / 97
from *Epithalamia* / 99
from *Minimum Security Prison Dentistry* / 100
Poetics / 102

FORREST GANDER
Evaporation: A Border History / 109
Anniversary / 110
Field Guide to Southern Virginia / 111
A Poetics / 114

LYN HEJINIAN
from 'Time of Tyranny' / 119
from 'The Rejection of Closure' / 127

JOHN JAMES
Good Old Harry / 137
Shakin All Over / 138
Stacking / 139
A Visitation / 139
Baudelaire at Cébazan / 141
A Theory of Poetry / 142

TREVOR JOYCE
SYZYGY / 147
Note to SYZYGY / 154

BHANU KAPIL
from *Ban en Banlieue* / 159
Poetics / 166

NATHANIEL MACKEY
Song of the Andoumboulou: 40 / 171
Beginning "We the Migrating They" / 174
from 'Sound and Sentiment, Sound and Symbol' / 180

D. S. MARRIOTT
Lorem Ipsum / 189
Rhapsode / 190

A Sequel / 191
Else, In Limbo / 193
Response to Race and the Poetic Avant-Garde / 194

CHRIS McCABE
555: george w. bush / 199
Axis is / 199
A 98p Voicemail Message to Blaise Cendrars / 200
Jack Straw / 201
A New Way to Pay Old Debts / 202
Changing All that is Metal in Thy House
to Gold: The Political as Personal / 203

GERALDINE MONK
Pendle / 213
The Great Assembly & Feast / 213
Alice Nutter Replies / 214
Ghost Sonnet 29 / 215
Ghost Sonnet 32 / 215
BISCAY. TRAFALGAR. FITZROY. / 216
FAEROES. SOUTHEAST ICELAND. / 217
Artemis Comes to Tea / 218
from 'Insubstantial Thoughts on the
Transubstantiation of the Text' / 220

VALZHYNA MORT
Jean-Paul Belmondo / 225
Sylt I / 226
Maria / 228
Psalm 18 / 228
Listening by the Western Gate / 231

ERÍN MOURE
from *The Fall* / 237
from *O Cadoiro: Postface* / 243

M. NOURBESE PHILIP
from *Zong!* / 249
from *Sal* / 250
Testimony Stoops to Mother Tongue / 251
from 'The Absence of Writing or How I Almost
Became a Spy' / 256

CLAUDIA RANKINE
from *Citizen* / 265

JEROME ROTHENBERG
from *The Jigoku Zoshi Hells: A Book of Variations* / 275
A Note on the Preceding / 285

ZOË SKOULDING
from *Teint* / 289
Underground Rivers: Notes Towards a Zoepoetics / 294

ROSMARIE WALDROP
from *Lawn of the Excluded Middle* / 303
from *Split Infinites* / 306
from *Blindsight* / 307
from *Driven to Abstraction* / 308
Wanting / 313
Thinking / 314
Why Do I Write Prose Poems / When My
True Love Is Verse / 315

JOHN WILKINSON
from *Reckitt's Blue* / 323
from *Courses Matter-Woven* / 325
Schlummert Ein / 328
from 'Lyric Poetry in Evil Times' / 330

About the Editors / 333
Acknowledgements / 334

Contact and conversation between transatlantic poets has been one of fluctuating relations. North American writers have always been an important presence in British and Irish poetries, sometimes physically so. Edward Dorn, who lived in and wrote about England, was aware of these relations and what he called the 'North Atlantic Turbine'. Often the traffic is reversed. Denise Levertov, a major US writer, was born in Essex, England, and lived most of her life in the United States. In the 1960s, Lee Harwood was an honorary member of the New York School; and Tom Raworth, who spent many years in the US, can be seen as a precursor to Language Poetry. Of course, sometimes the conversation is more virtual, through the exchange of publications or, today, electronic media. (There have even been simultaneous poetry readings over the Internet, connecting both sides of the Atlantic). Poets in both directions across the water have influenced, and continue to influence each other in terms of practice and poetics. *Atlantic Drift* continues this collaboration and exchange in its alphabetic juxtaposition of twenty-four contributors.

*

This anthology contains both poetry and poetics, in an attempt to establish a dialogue between the two. We have deliberately not separated them in different portions of the book, as is customary. Poetics is a term used in a number of contexts and we should like to clarify what we mean by it. Poetics at its simplest is the self-communing of creative artists, in this case poets, about what they do, what they make, and why they do it, and carry on doing it. Poetics (like the word poetry) derives from the Greek, *poesis*, 'to make'. It is often misread and we would like to suggest approaches to it.

Poetics is essentially a speculative, writerly discourse, one which might have a variety of focuses for its author: on the creative process in general or on specific works as they are written (or are about to be written). It may take on aspects of a manifesto or it may be a more mercurial affair, teasing rather than programmatic, possibly teasing for the writers themselves. Where it approaches the manifesto – the 'Projective Verse' essay of Charles Olson, for example – it may be proposing formal innovations for a creative community, either existing or hoped-for, but we are just as likely to find personal thumbnail sketches and thought experiments of an individual poet (who may even, ultimately, abandon the course of action the poetics seems to be suggesting).

One of our contributors, Jerome Rothenberg, defines the urgency and scope of poetics well, in introducing a book-length collection of his own meditations on practice, and he relates it directly to the way he sees the world:

> But the world we share, & our interplay with it, calls again & again for *discourse*: in the case of Poets, the setting forth of a poetics. I have found myself involved with that also, at first tentatively & then, once into it, discovering ways suited to my own temperament & to the sense I have… that the discourse, like the poetry, must in all events resist rigidity & closure. (Rothenberg, 1981: 3)

He also states his more general ambitions for poetics: 'At the same time – make no mistake about it – I've attempted, like other poets so engaged, to create a new & coherent poetics for our time.' (Rothenberg, 1981: 3) This rather neatly expresses the range of the discourse, the tentative nature of its utterances and yet the often communal, even global, ambition it has; Rothenberg is 'like other poets' but the writing is 'for our time', and, therefore, for other poets (and readers of poetry). Rothenberg's sense that poetics might encompass the same flexibility and openness encountered in his poetry itself (as evidenced by the reflexive, translational, re-writing of early work he offers in this anthology) leads us to imagine the formal possibilities of poetics as analogues of the poetry itself. Its own forms are often exploratory and worthy of contemplation; it is not a transparent discourse, a secondary 'commentary'. In some cases, such as that of Sean Bonney and John James in our anthology, it is *in* the poems themselves. Robert Fitterman ironically presents the text of a failed lecture as 'demonstration' of his conceptual poetics.

As these examples alone suggest, the discourse appears in many forms, and in many places: in letters and treatises, in private journals and on public platforms, in interviews and introductions, in casual asides and even in well-wrought literary criticism, though the simple 'statement', often aphoristically concise, may be its most consistent form. You will find similar range in our anthology, pieces contrasting and combining the ludic with the meditative, the specific (directed at the poems selected) or the general (involving a sense of what poetry today (and tomorrow) might become). None issues the diktats of a fully blown manifesto. (To our minds, actual manifestoes overstep the mark and damage the speculative nature of the discourse and replace it with the 'must do' of literary orthodoxies. The 'how to' of creative writing manuals is another danger to its speculative freedom.) Several of our contributors, Zoë Skoulding, and Andrea Brady to name but two, have kindly written new pieces for this anthology; for others, we have selected already extant texts. Some are formal essays, such as John Wilkinson's, or innovative ones, such as Sophie Collins', and some, such as the short pieces by Trevor Joyce and Rothenberg are nominally 'notes'. Some are even anti-poetics in their reserve in the face of possible self-commentary, but every piece demonstrates the axiom expressed forthrightly by another of our contributors, Charles Bernstein, 'Poetics don't explain; they redress and address.' (Bernstein, 1992: 160)

Given this range, we believe poetics, which is too often read as a short-cut way into the poetry it has provoked into being, as a readerly *tool*, should be studied as a unique and curious writerly discourse in its own right. However, restricting ourselves to our present collection and its arrangement, we should like to suggest *a* way in which poetics might be encountered, what mode of 'dialogue' we are proposing between the wide range of poetry and poetics we have combined here. Like Bernstein, we do not believe these pieces 'explain' the poems that they accompany. (In any case, while poets' own descriptions of their work are interesting, they may not be accurate; poetics, oddly, may function as a masking process, in the service of further innovation, stimulating creativity by *not* explaining what has been, or what might be, written.) They 'address' questions of poesis, matters of content sometimes (as in feminist poetics or eco-poetics), questions of form nearly always (and there is less 'redress' here, fewer suggestions that the poets are putting the record straight on the histories of poetic antagonisms, the so-called Poetry Wars). If for a writer, as Bernstein says, 'One of the pleasures of poetics is to try on a paradigm... and see where *it* leads you,' then a reciprocal pleasure for the reader might be to entertain creative paradigms and speculate how they operate as ideas about poetry in general, rather than searching for clues to interpretation of the adjacent particular poems. (Bernstein 1992: 161) If for the poets, their poetics denotes a 'permission to continue', then permitted continuation for a reader might suggest fruitful avenues of aesthetic encounter and repeated creative reading. (DuPlessis 1990: 156) If that reader of poetics is also a poet – perhaps a student of creative writing – then it exists as a provocation to explorative creativity, one guided by the poet's own developing poetics. Indeed, these examples suggest manners and forms which might be adopted or adapted to articulate it or, as was the case with some of the pieces collected here, to discover the poetics in the very act of producing it, in tentative and speculative drifting.

Robert Sheppard

* * *

All anthologies are as much exclusive as they are exclusionary and, in this respect, *Atlantic Drift* is no different. In a flagrant act of automatic anthologising, I could name some fifty poets who might well fit into this book, from both sides of the Atlantic. I might broaden the search to include those who do not write in English, from other countries along a deeply historical transatlantic route. Language, itself built on limitation, is one of our restrictions here.

I say this not to diminish the quality of the writing included, but to illustrate inherent difficulties within the editorial task of selecting twenty-four living poets from the US, UK, Ireland and Canada. Narrowing our list down to roughly twelve poets from each geographical space, excluding many and leaving out some of the late and great was difficult. Additionally, several poets passed away in the year or so we actively edited and solicited for the book. While they also may or may not have been included, this introduction would like to acknowledge their importance (Roy Fisher, Lee Harwood, Geoffrey Hill, Christopher Middleton, Tom Raworth and C. D. Wright, among others). It may also be worth mentioning, as often happens with anthologies, a couple of poets we approached politely declined.

It is our hope – indeed the hope of any anthologist – that rather than critique the book on its omissions, there will be a focus on the quality of the work that is published here. As Robert has already alluded to, we have included poetry and poetics together, sometimes without any clear lines of demarcation, sometimes by the turning over of a new page. Generally, the poetics text is at the end of each poets' selection, though, interestingly, there are writers featured here (Bhanu Kapil, Claudia Rankine) whose selections could perhaps be read entirely as poetics, lyric essay – Rankine's *Citizen* was subtitled 'An America Lyric' on publication – or, more simply as a creative text.

In editing this anthology, we have considered writers that either have a background in forming the discourse around poetics as well as commissioning work from younger poets who hadn't necessarily written a poetics where we wanted to read one (Collins, Fowler, McCabe, Mort). Some of these texts speak to the highly politicised times we live in or, in some way, explore the poethical-as-poetics, something which interests me. There is a better gender balance than you traditionally find, with poetics at least which, rather problematically, has been, in decades previous, overly white, middle-class and male. This feels, to me at least, emblematic of male-dominated discussion around poetics as well as literary criticism. Fortunately, things continue to change.

We have included poets who might be from the UK but live in the US and visa versa (Brady, Kapil, Wilkinson), revealing the dialogue between poets from both places to be physical and actual, as well as re-emphasising the idea that in being placed one is frequently displaced. And importantly, since this text represents over twenty years of teaching poetry and poetics at Edge Hill, we wanted to include several poets who have been key to our teaching of innovative poetry and poetics (for example, Nathaniel Mackey's 'Sound and Sentiment' and Lyn Hejinian's 'The Rejection of Closure' have been taught to our third year undergraduates for several years, books by Geraldine Monk are often assigned and Claudia Rankine's *Citizen* is taught to students in their first year). Believing poetics as important to the reading of any writer, we edited a book that we wanted to teach as much as read.

* * *

Recently I attended a conference on transatlantic poetry in Oxford entitled 'Special Relationships'. Many of the poets included in this book were discussed in a small but well-intentioned series of papers by young academics. It started me thinking how 'special' the relationship really is, or might be, between British and American poetries and how a newer generation could help towards a more meaningful dialogue between poets from both sides of 'the pond'. When I lived in New York City, every week or so, American poets would ask: 'so, what is happening in British poetry?' Awkward to be summoned as poet / spokesperson according to any national framework, I remember writing out lists of twenty or so poets and noticing how the receiver often appeared to know so few names. They were often only familiar with books that appeared through a corporatized split in mainstream publishing rights. Some of these concerns have been written about by critics, such as Stephen Burt (see 'Transatlantic Disconnections' in *PN Review*, which skilfully explores why poets from the UK / US aren't, he suggests, reading enough of each other).

The transatlantic poetry landscape is changing and will have changed again by the time you read this book. Since I returned from New York in 2011, things already seem a little better with English poets reading North American poets more widely. This has been helped by online materials being read, as well as those in print. I'm thinking of valuable archives of poetry publishing US / UK / Canadian poetries, like PennSound, Archive of the Now and my own magazine *The Wolf*. *Poetry* and *Poetry Review* now publish a transatlantic cross-fertilisation of poets, sharing work across both journals, which hasn't always published the key writers, but is an interesting exchange nonetheless since it looks to push readership forwards. If I were to be cynical about it, in times when you can buy a collection of poetry at the click of a button, I might suggest that there's still plenty of work to be done to make the relationship *special*. On the whole, the academy on both sides of the pond tends to stick close to their own waters. Some of these issues, in relation to developing a wide transatlantic sphere of influence, are down to issues of access or interest, but they also relate to our most primal behaviour: curiosity. In Britain, the Lyric 'I' still dominates over lyric musicality and this is something which appears to be shifting as more innovative writers / thinkers question lyric subjectivity and the idea of a fluid, non-fluxive self in the various forms they use in any written text. Many of the poets in *Atlantic Drift*, such as Forrest Gander and Rosmarie Waldrop, embody such approaches. Ultimately, I look forward to a more dialogic exchange between writers from the places explored in these pages. At best, anthologies are an enabler, pointing to a wider conversation, one that needs to be had. If the conversation between poetries sampled in this book is furthered, then *Atlantic Drift* does something of what we set out to do.

James Byrne

NOTES

Bernstein, C. *A Poetics* (Cambridge, Mass: Harvard University Press, 1992).
Burt, S. 2009, 'Transatlantic Disconnections, or, The Poetry of the Hypotenuse', *PN Review* 190, Vol. 36
DuPlessis, R B. *The Pink Guitar, Writing as Feminist Practice* (New York and London: Routledge, 1990).
Rothenberg, J. *Pre-Faces and Other Writings* (New York: New Directions, 1981).

CHARLES BERNSTEIN

PHOTO: LAWRENCE SCHWARTZWALD

CHARLES BERNSTEIN is a prolific poet, essayist, literary scholar and editor. He is the co-founder and co-editor, with Al Filreis, of PennSound, and editor, and co-founder, with Loss Pequenño Glazier, of The Electronic Poetry Center. He is coeditor, with Hank Lazer, of *Modern and Contemporary Poetics*, a book series from the University of Alabama Press (1998 –). With Bruce Andrews, he edited *L=A=N=G=U=A=G=E*, which was anthologised as *The L=A=N=G=U=A=G=E Book* (Southern Illinois University Press, 1984). His most recent publications include: *Pitch of Poetry* (2016), *Recalculating* (2013) and *Attack of the Difficult Poems: Essays and Inventions* (2011), from the University of Chicago Press and *All the Whiskey in Heaven: Selected Poems* from Farrar, Straus and Giroux, 2010. In 2006, Bernstein was elected a Fellow of the American Academy of Arts & Sciences. His recent prizes include: The Janus Pannonius Grand Prize for Poetry (2015), The Muenster International Poetry Prize (2015) and the Dean's Award for Innovation in Teaching in 2005. Currently, Bernstein is Donald T. Regan Professor of English and Comparative Literature at the University of Pennsylvania, where he teaches Poetry and Poetics.

THIS LINE

This line is stripped of emotion.
This line is no more than an
illustration of a European
theory. This line is bereft
of a subject. This line
has no reference apart
from its context in
this line. This line
is only about itself.
This line has no meaning:
its words are imaginary, its
sounds inaudible. This line
cares not for itself or for
anyone else – it is indifferent,
impersonal, cold, uninviting.
This line is elitist, requiring,
to understand it, years of study
in stultifying libraries, poring
over esoteric treatises on
impossible to pronounce topics.
This line refuses reality.

WHOSE LANGUAGE

No question mark

Sounds quite casual

Who's on first? The dust descends as
the skylight caves in. The door
closes on a dream of default and
denunciation (go get those piazzas),
hankering after frozen (prose) ambiance
(ambivalence). Doors to fall in, bells
to dust, nuances to circumscribe.
Only the real is real: the little
girl who cries out "Baby! Baby!"
but forgets to look in the mirror
– of a... It doesn't really
matter whose, only the appointment
of a skewed and derelict parade.
My face turns to glass, at last.

He uses a lot of plosive sounds

It's very playfulness

The poem is full of playful sounds

Collage of different voices

Conversational tone

SUNSET SAIL

Blessed are the narrow who slide
among cracks and build monuments to
slats. For long have I awaited
such news as now passes comment –
news of my comrades lost long
at sea. It was in the following winter
that word was received in a foreign
tongue that one who had refused
solace for some these fifteen months
had taken the hand of his born
foe and danced the Hokey Pokey with
the abandon of clues at
sunset. Such light that fails
me, like sticks in mission
sand, voracious melody of
hardly heard vibrations, potable
allegiance subsumed in the tube.

DYSRAPHISM

Did a wind come just as you got up or were
you protecting me from it? I felt the abridgement
of imperatives, the wave of detours, the saber-
rattling of inversion. *All lit up and no*
place to go. Blinded by avenue and filled with
adjacency. Arch or arched at. So there becomes bottles,
hushed conductors, illustrated proclivities for puffed-
up benchmarks. Morose or comatose. "Life is what
you find, existence is what you repudiate." A good example
of this is "Dad pins puck." Sometimes something
sunders; in most cases, this is no more than a hall.
No where to go but pianissimo (protection of market
soaring). "Ma always fixes it just like I
like it." Or here valorize what seem to put off
in other. No excuse for that! You can't
watch ice sports with the lights on! Abnormal fluid retention,
inveterate inundation. Surely as wrongheaded as

but without its charm. No identification, only
restitution. But he has forced us to compel this offer;
it comes from policy not love. "Fill
the water glasses – ask each person
if they would like
more coffee, etc." *Content's*
dream. The
journey is
far, the
rewards inconsequential. Heraldically defamed.
Go – it's – gotten. Best
of the spoils: gargoyles. Or is a pretend wish
that hits the springs to sing with sanguine
bulk. "Clean everything from the table except
water, wine, and ashtrays; use separate plate to
remove salt & pepper." Ignorant
I confront, wondering at
I stand. We need
to mention that this is one
that applies to all eyes and that its application is only on the
most basic and rudimentary
level. Being
comfortable with and also
inviting and satisfying.
The pillar's tale: a windowbox onto society.
But heed not the pear that blows in your
brain. God's poison is the concept of
conceptlessness – anaerobic breath.
No less is culled no more vacated – temptation's
flight is always to
beacon's hill – the soul's
mineshaft.
Endless strummer. There is never annul-
ment, only abridgment. The Northern Lights is
the universe's paneled basement. Joy
when jogged. Delight in
forefright. Brushstrokes
on the canals of the..., moles on
sackcloth. "People like you don't need
money – you breed contempt." Some way such
toxic oases. This growth of earls, as on a failing
day, gurgling arboreally. Shoes that
shock. I'd
give to you my monkey, my serenade, my shopping bag;

but you require constancy, not weights. Who
taking the lump denies the pot, a beam of
buckram. Or they
with their, you
with your. Another
shot, another stop – dead
as floor board. Pardon my declension: short
parade. "Refill platter and pass to
everybody." A
sound is a sum – a sash
of seraphs. Bored loom.
Extension is never more than a form of content. "I
know how you feel, Joe. Nobody likes to admit
his girl is that smart." "I feel how you know,
Joe, like nobody to smart that girl is his admit."
A wavering kind of sort – down the tube, doused
in tub, a run of the stairs. You should shoot! But
by the time I'd sided. Magisterially calm and pompous.
Pump ass! A wash
of worry (the worldhood of
the whirl). Or: "Nice being here with anybody." Slips
find the most indefatigable invaginations, surreptitious
requiems.
Surfeit, sure fight.
Otherwise – flies,
detergent whines, flimflam psychosis. Let's:
partition the petulance, roast
the arrears, succor the sacred. "If you don't keep up
with culture, culture will keep up
with you." Sacral dosing, somewhat
hosting. Thread
threads the threads, like
thrush. Thrombolytic cassette. "While all of this is
going on, young Sir Francis Rose – a painter of dubious
gifts whom Gertrude Stein espoused for the last decade
of her life – appears as if out of nowhere with a
painting." If you mix with him you're mixing
with a metaphor. "It's
a realistic package, it's a
negotiable package, it's
not a final package." Glibness
of the overall, maybe: there is always something dripping
through.
We seem to be retreading the same tire

over and over, with no additional traction. Here
are some additional panes – optional. Very busy
by now reorganizing and actually, oddly, added
into fractionation ratio, as you might say. Or just
hitting against, back to everybody.
Reality is always greener
when you haven't seen her.
Anyway just to go on and be where you weren't or couldn't be
before – steps, windows, ramps. To let
all that other not so much dissolve as
blend into an horizon of distraction, distension
pursued as homing ground
(a place to bar the leaks). Say,
vaccination of cobalt emissaries pregnant with bivalent
exasperation, protruding with inert material. I
can't but sway, hopeful in my way. Perhaps
portend, tarry. The galoshes are, e.g.,
gone; but you are here. Transient cathexis, Doppler
angst. And then a light comes on
in everybody's head. "So I think
that somewhere we ought to make the point that it's really
a team approach." Riddled
with riot. What
knows not scansion admits
expansion: tea leaves
decoy
for the grosser fortune – the slush
of afternoon, the morning's replay. Prose,
pose – relentless
furrier.
Poem, chrome. "I
don't like the way you think":
a mind is a terrible thing to spend.
That is, in prose you start with the world
and find the words to match; in poetry you start
with the words and find the world in them. "Bring
soup in – very hot." "You
couldn't find your way
out of a blanched potato." Silence
can also be a tool
but it is seldom as effective as blindness.
His quarter, and heir to his heart, whom he purpled
with his fife, does bridle purpose to pursue
tides with unfolded scowls, and, pinched in this

array, fools compare with slack-weary ton.
Dominion demands distraction – the circus
ponies of the slaughter home. Braced
by harmony, bludgeoned by decoration
the dream surgeon hobbles three steps over, two
steps beside. "In those days you didn't have to
shout to come off as expressive." One by one
the clay feet are sanded, the sorrows remanded.
A fleet of ferries, forever merry.
Show folks know that what the fighting man wants
is to win the war and come home.

CASTOR OIL
for Emma

I went looking for my soul
In the song of a minor bird
But I could not find it there
Only the shadow of my thinking

The slow sea slaps slow water
On the ever farther shore
And myself pulled under
In the uneven humming
Of the still wavering warps

Tuneless, I wander, sundered
In lent blends of remote display
Until the bottom bottoms
In song-drenched light, cradled fold

PREFACE TO *PITCH OF POETRY*

Here's the pitch.

Black and thick.

The confidence man's selling, but not a bill of goods: the pitch itself.

Only this and nothing more.

Pitch is the foul stain, the skank and stench of a viscous taint. The kind of poetry I want is when you can't get the pitch out.

Poetry's the thing with feathers (tethers) tarred on, as in Poe's "system" of Tarr and Fethering (fathering). The kind of poetry I want gums up the works.

A tangle of truths.

This is the scandal of poetry. Not the one but the many. Not the many becoming one but the one becoming many. (Appearance precedes essence the way purpose is a perfume and being late to school a blessing.)

"I'm not a helluva poet but a poet for the hell of it," Diego Maquiera tells me one sunny spring day in Santiago. "I'm self-untaught," I replied. Back home in Brooklyn it's deepest fall.

The politics of poetic form is no politics at all. But it's the only politics that can't be taken away, the cartilage of the body poetic.

Who'm I kidding?

Mostly myself, that's *whom.* So come on let's beat that dead horse until we're blue-faced or green with envy or just whistling old tunes that we make up in the pitch dark of night. Until the rhythm becomes alive if not to us then to that part of ourselves we no longer recognize.

No man is himself, even to an island.

Nor woman neither.

(Obviousness is the hobgoblin of common sense.)

You can't represent what you can't think, and thinking is nothing near what it's made to do. What's done's undone in the twist of a phrase or a catchy image. The past is just as lost as our love is, our love was. Ontological pitching (a metaphysical lurch or stagger): here / not here; heard / not heard; taught / untaught.[1] Gently rapping and then it's all you can make out. Abstraction is the dream of figuration just as lines are a way of marking time till the sentence is over.

Unheard melodies are celestial demographics. Even if you can't put your finger on it you can still pretend to count.

You go the club in the evening only to be clubbed at dawn. How long has this been going on? There's more than one way to fleece a sheep but only one way to stop.

Echopoetics is the nonlinear resonance of one motif bouncing off another within an aesthetics of constellation. Even more, it's the sensation of allusion in the absence of allusion. In other words, the echo I'm after is a blank: a shadow of an absent source.

A network of stopgaps.

Even my explanations need explication; my commentaries, elucidation; my prefaces, glosses; my shadows, shadows. (Truth be, I'm afraid of my own shadow.)

This book starts by interweaving threads, from metaphors for abstraction and representation to the poetics of cultural dissent. L=A=N=G=U=A=G=E gives a historical and archival ground for the often speculative essays.

Pitch is the sound of poetry. But pitch is also the attack or approach. The angle.

Pitch in the sense of register.

Poets catch my ear because of their pitch: I prefer live wires to retread tires. In the second section of the book I provide a set of accounts of such "more perfect" pitches. (The poem as conceptual scheme, poetics as scam or scum.[2]) This is followed by a series of conversations that echo and extend (ravel and ruffle) my threads until, in the final section, they end in a kind of threnody. (Echopoetics is dialogic critical encounters. Pataquerics is the arena of the excluded.)

The book concludes with a wild pitch (low and outside) for the aesthetic, which, still, I hope strikes responsive chords.

The value of a poem's pitch is not in the words but in what the words allow for a reader. As valuable as poems are for themselves, this value is eclipsed by what they may foment in intensified perceptual / conceptual experience.

So let's pitch in.

You and I may be referring to the same thing, but the thing's not the same. (We'll bridge that cross when we come to it.)

Let's take play into our own hands rather than become its plaything.

For instance, what happens when you realize that the devils underfoot might not be the problem, that Satan is dressed as if it were St. Michael? The issue is not identification with the downtrodden but recognition that even the best angel is a diabolic (dialogic) angle.

But some would rather curse the light than put it out!

Is it an error to think my reliance on error is an error?

A mirror is better than most art.

I like poets who are clutch hitters. Who can knock the ball out of the park.

Score tied... Bases loaded... It's the windup... It's the...

NOTES

[1] In his "Overture" to *A Pitch of Philosophy* (Cambridge, MA: Harvard University Press, 1994), Stanley Cavell speaks of pitch "as a determined but temporary habituation and an unsettling motion", p. ix.
[2] See Middleton, Peter. "Conceptual Schemes: The Midcentury Poetics of Muriel Rukeyser and Charles Olson," in *Physics Envy* (Chicago: University of Chicago Press, 2015).

SEAN BONNEY

PHOTO: AUTHOR'S ARCHIVE

SEAN BONNEY was born in Brighton and brought up in the north of England. He lived in London for twenty years, and is now based in Berlin. His selected poems, *Letters Against the Firmament* was published by Enitharmon in 2015. His work has been translated into several languages, and he has performed it at occupations, on demonstrations, in the back-rooms of pubs, in seminar rooms, on picket lines and at international poetry festivals. He edited the micropress 'yt communication' with Frances Kruk and for a number of years helped run the reading series Xing the Line with Jeff Hilson. His current work in progress, *Our Death*, will be published by Commune Editions in 2018.

from **OUR DEATH**

3. A NOTE ON MY RECENT POETICS

I stopped smoking pot a few months ago because it was making me paranoid, but since then most days I've been taking potentially fatal doses of amphetamine. It's almost certainly making me psychotic, but it does at least have the advantage of saving me from the vast cataclysm that sleep has become. Most mornings I feel uneasy, visible and invisible at the same time, trapped between the proverbial *two worlds*, neither of which I'm prepared to accept or even tolerate. I can't tell them apart anyway - everything's functioning at some kind of stroboscopic level, where the invisible world is populated by a gaggle of flesh and blood insomniacs staggering around after a shipwreck, and the visible one by a weird star-map, a network of knots and tumours that up until now have been locked somewhere in the centre of the earth, a hell of alphabets and spectral injustices that we can summarise as a string of cysts arranged in strings along the chronology. Lets see. There was the poll tax revolt. There were punk houses. There was ecstasy and acid and free parties. The criminal justice bill. Britpop. The rise of the ironic wank. The phrase zero tolerance. The boredom of enforced hedonism. The skeleton of Tony Blair. The flames of humanitarian intervention. The inevitability of jihad. And that's just one more or less arbitrary little cluster, a hall of various mirrors that every morning I chop and snort increasingly gargantuan lines from until, in the words of Ernst Bloch, "years become minutes, as in legends where, in the apparent time span of a single night, a witch cheats her victim out of a long life". And I don't know whether I identify with that witch or not, but I do know that there are some mornings when I consider the possibility of powdering Blair's bones, and then casting them at the feet of various monuments – say for example the statues that encircle Trafalgar Square – so as to transform them into real demons. The crisis, or whatever it is we're supposed to call it. The ruins of the Ritz, for example. The broken glass of Millbank. The jail terms of the rioters. Ah shit. The smell of blood is overpowering. See you later. It is becoming increasingly clear that Thatcher faked her death.

22. Georg Trakl's Psalm
as I imagine it spoken by the ghost of Anita Berber

It is a light gone out forever.
It is a bar that's never opened never closed.
It is a vineyard it is a black hole it is a mouth full of spiders.
It is an abandoned room, sprayed with burning milk.
The maniacs have died. It is an undiscovered island
It is the sun as it is in nightmares. They are smashing the drums
They are inventing war.
Here they are wriggling their hips here they are buying smack
Oh the screaming ocean. Paradise is catastrophe.

It is all porn especially the fairytale forests.
Here they are they have buried the refugees. Oh my its raining again.
Nasty old gods are digging the ditches
They are all asleep in the boring city squares and bombs are
    falling.
It is chemical rain it is little girls it is poverty and celebrity and
    crocodile tears.
It is rooms filled with impossible chords it is your tedious record
    collection.
It is shadows it is Airbnb it is mythological mirrors.
Here are the inmates they have burnt the hospital down.
Here is your favourite dealer, here are the latest plagues.

An invisible person has appeared in everyone's simultaneous
    dream.
Oh look here I am. Fuck the police.
It is the surveillance laws. All ages are not contemporaneous.
We are outside this century. We are very glamorous. We are
    waiting in the hall.
Somewhere near Moritzplatz the adepts are getting sick.
It is the stupidity of gardens. I love the tiny sparrows.
The janitor's kids are not playing they are digging up gold.
It is the last song you will ever hear. It is horrible blind children
    waiting in the alley
Their shadows are climbing the wall, it is poisons and fascists and
    fairytale roses.

It is a tourist boat on the Landwehrkanal.
It is the building where I live, it is valium and speed.
Here are the dead refugees, piled up inside the walls.
It is our smug little rooms it is our wings stained with shit.

It is the western border it is what you want it to be it is England
   controlled by maggots.
Here I am, in love with this city. It is peaceful like my childhood
   dreams.
Here we are choking our memories to death.
What if this year never ends.
Here are the experts being fed to the dogs.

In America a very boring lunatic opens his eyes.

from **CANCER**

POEMS AFTER KATERINA GOGOU

let's drink with the unemployed
with all sun and silence
with all dust in the sun and silence
and sun and cognac and dust
and cigarettes and sun
no, lets not go on about our health today
pills and drink and snot
don't worry
I feel very calm
there are nails there is hair there are years
dirty
the pills are great. the party, you know which one I mean
impossible to tell who's a cop these days
music
the cognacs shit
no, I haven't heard anything for quite some time
you know I'm thinking I might want to, you know
there's a room upstairs
I want to see you without your pants
kind of curious about your dick
music, for chrissake
you take a solo
"they took a stick and beat me"
cognac
music
silence

you pullout your switchblade start slashing
The Bonnot Gang were right.

*

There are four cardinal points.
The first is the sky, it is where they have buried us.
The second, the earth. There they question us. It is very silent.
The other two points were recently taken out of commission.
No explanations were offered

one day I'll come out from the houses
I did it yesterday
no thought for anything
one small shred of my father
a tiny piece of the sea
no-one can take them from me
the city they fucked like a dead friend
so many dead friends
one day I'll come out from the houses
straight into powder and flames
I did it yesterday
you fascist bastards
you pig bastards
red banners barricades black banners
a new city a new kind of sun
one day I'll come out of the houses
and listen I need to tell you
don't think I'm afraid when I tell you
they got me. don't do it. they got me.
reinvent time. reinvent violence. then
listen, go at those bastards like the furies.
only then will you disappear
only then will you learn the magic
a tiny shred of childhood and ocean
one day I will come out from the houses
a strangers language of rags and dreams
and the loneliness, the disappearance
oh god the loneliness. I mean
what do you think I am
some kind of cop

Someone has taken our knives. We go down like the sun. Place of birth. Unknown. They have scratched away our slogans. Colour of eyes. Unknown. We go down like hail and rain. Year of birth. Fuck it. Next time they shoot us, we'll refuse to die. It's raining again. Give me a cigarette.

we'll cut ourselves down
they hung us yesterday
no escape from the massacre
this whispered 'no'
liars. informers. murderers
squealing 'yes'
always 'yes'
no escape
always 'yes'
>   *this whispered "no"*
>   *this rotten world*
>   *this world we loved*

Fearful we'll abandon our history or steal it. Fearful we'll set up borders around that history. Fearful we'll drive up the rents on that history and talk and talk about the old days in meter and rhyme while the pigs close the borders. Fearful we'll be those borders. Fearful we'll confuse those borders with songs and sit inside those songs as if they were the scars on our veins. Fearful our scars will become a lullaby and that we will turn into dogs. Fearful we'll confuse dogs with doves. Fearful of doves and swans, of corpuscles, of medical robes, of silence and smack. Fearful we're doing what they want. What silence wants. We police their borders. They know how it is. Fearful bastards. Fearful of everything. All of us. Fuck it. Do it tomorrow. No escape from the massacre.

We are being followed. They are hunting us, are mostly silent. Lines of them, they are hunting us. Their sentences, relatively simple. Our hunters, our educators. It is very simple. We don't mention the silence. What we keep inside our whispers. In our signals, in our silence. As each of their faces change. As each of their cells divide. In great procession, the faces. Their lessons are endless. Silence, in circles, our hunters. As if we were dogs. As if we barked at strangers. And now they will murder. There is safety in murder. Somewhere are angels. Angels have claws. Dogs are everywhere.

*

music, I don't talk about it
my eyes. seriously. where are my eyes

every day there's something to reject
I will not scream when I die
Marx Lenin Trotsky Luxemburg
The Kronstadt Massacre and the dream of Sisyphus
there are flowers there are colours
revolvers and homemade bombs
I'm going crazy, why aren't you
my dreams my friends' dreams
all these dreams are the same dream
repeated breakdowns endless weeping
this is measure
you and me
up and down
and back and down
there is a false symmetry separates us
lets not laugh
if we don't sign the paper
they won't be able to act on their decision
night falls
the central committee
night falls
they want to know if I have a television
night falls
I'm still kind of keeping it together
I won't sign
Long like the 204th International

*

and we collect little pieces. of resistance etc.
don't talk to me about fragmentation. it is
rain. talk about rain. Durruti had it right
transubstantiation. rain. metallic burning rain.
red rain. crowbars. the richter scale is
a calendar. bones piled like rain beneath the earth.

*

40 degrees in the shade. 40 below.
No-one was ever born here.
Fascists and charitable organisations
have made an agreement. They have bought up the city.
They have poured oil on us.
They talk about rats. And houses. The contractors

And the cops, of course
like voyeurs
Fucking them. They talk about the houses.
They are breaking up the houses
They have tied you to the bed with your legs and face.
It's how they put up the rent. How they get us out.
They change our names. Elect us. Pour oil on us.
The streets names. Our names. They burn our names.
40 in the shade. 40 below. Our mouths are swollen.
No-one was ever born here.
A stone. Beneath it, that liar the sun.

*

that there are houses
on grand roads, we know that
and we used to know
in the silence and dawn
of bottles, and passcodes
never would we live there
hating the roses, fearing them
we knew the address of each one
we had the blueprints, everything
we talked
minute to minute
we talked
wire to wire
of what we would say
at the pre-ordained moment
class vengeance, we understood
futuristic and ancient, as
all of history, as
one click, as
some kind of message
left on the table
          like a packet of fags
in an overheated kitchen
not even the ones I used to smoke
squealing, yeh, thanks a lot
you destroyed the wrong world
pack up your roses, asshole, get out

*

Today they cancelled the carrion birds
and we are in love and sleep in peace.
There are cops inside our pillows.
Try and say their assassins work for us.

*

Every day I wake up everyday inside the wage system
inside all its houses, never paid rent on even one.
Sleep nowhere. Every morning inside my wages
I lie in wait for those who sleep, I sleep
on their chests and never speak. Never
Take this as spectral evidence. Meaning. Fuck death.

*

Our houses are packed so close
They are no longer houses. Get that.
These our beds these our scraps of food
We eat with the same mouth. We no longer
Use our bones. We are desperate we are fabulous
we are possibly dead.

       4 in the morning. Sleep fuck get high
and that monster in the sky taking our details.

Ghosts walk at noon. Everyone's a weapon.

*

this is me puking in the metro

my name is Katerina I have been dead
for all your life. you can buy my clothes
if you like, in the vintage stores, in the
renovated flats, you will find them, in

my senses, enraged, form cracks
the cities I sleep in no longer there

LYRICS FOR KRUK

Fuck it. The sun is doing whatever suns do
The citizenry all creeping like flowers.
Idiots. The sky is grey on further grey and
The haunting, its sharpened hail, never stops.

*

Oh wow. A single life-time. We crawl about the earth
As if the sky were an image, or something special, as if
Never mind. Flowers for example. Try eating one. But
Don't get me wrong. I'm just like everyone else.
They keep their gold in me, the dullness of riches. Beware it.

*

What did we really expect. I mean, we look at clouds
Are impressed by thunder and

                                        The invisible.
People eat it like they do famous persons.
Carbon. Indigestion. Property. Watch that shit.

*

But it was only pills made me queasy. That
and flames underfoot.
                        The cities have almost vanished
we list them like molecules. Lesions. We list them
every morning like describing a shadow is mania
To inhabit a name. To eat human flesh.

*

You think its imaginary. Maybe so. Try telling that
to the fortune tellers. You know the ones. Those
who never think or say an original word. Their
vocabulary is monstrous.
                        Ours too. I love the cities
as they so predictably burn, the sound of ash and
yes this talk. Of music. Of soul. This so brief life.

LETTER AGAINST THE LANGUAGE

> God has chosen precisely what does not exist in order to reduce to nothing what does exist
> ST PAUL

> The criminals of the Vision are a totally different matter
> PASOLINI

So I moved to a new country, a new city. The effect is not dissimilar to tearing your name off your face, to finally stumbling onto the secrets of archaic techniques of invisibility. Or at least that's what I tell myself when I've been awake for several days. Invisibility being, in its simplest meaning, visibility amplified to the max. Anyway, when I first arrived I walked everywhere, at absolute random, sometimes with eyes closed, sometimes open. When you feel that alive, meaning not alive at all in any sense that you've become used to, meaning absolutely and utterly lost, well, the distinctions between dreams and sight, between whatever it is that waking and vision are supposed to be, become pretty much meaningless. For a long time I was simply scrambling around in the more popular parts of town. Not really sure why, to be honest – I mean, they're popular for a reason and its not necessarily one I'm particularly sympathetic with. So I started venturing further out to the strange external circles with the weird unpronounceable names – and by that I don't mean unpronounceable simply to a person who doesn't speak the language, but even to the people who live there. There are some strange red doors out there. Some pretty strange landscapes. For some reason I started thinking about Pasolini. To be specific, the scene at the end of *Theorem*, where the father – having given his factory away to the workforce, and then having tried and failed to pick up a boy at a railway station, takes off his clothes and wanders off into some strange volcanic or desert landscape and, as he enters that landscape, he screams. I was ranting on to a friend a few days ago that I take that scream to contain all that is meaningful in the word 'communism' – or rather, whatever it is that people like us mean when we use that word, which is, as we both know all too well, somewhat different to whatever it is the dictionary of the visible world likes to pretend it means. You know what I'm saying. A kind of high metallic screech. Unpronounceable. Inaudible. I'm obsessed with Pasolini. I stuck a naked picture of him on my office wall earlier on today – it helps, it helps when I'm trying to think about that scream, about toxicity and audibility, about the weird silence I live inside right in the middle of the deafening din of this city. Some academic once wrote of Pasolini that we "should turn down the volume on his political sermons and listen to what he whispered in his work", which is obviously pretty stupid because the politics are precisely within those whispers or, rather, those barely audible screeches. I guess you must be familiar with his unfinished St Paul screenplay – the bit where he quotes Corinthians on "hearing inexpressible things, things we are not able to tell". I got really obsessed with that for a while. Don't get me wrong. I'm not about to disappear into some kind of cut-rate Cloud of Unknowing, or worse, some comfortably opaque experimental poetry. I mean, fuck that shit. In one of the last essays he wrote, Pasolini made it pretty damn clear what might be implied by "inexpressible things", things "we are not able to tell". It is names. "I know the names", he wrote, in that essay published in 1974. The names of those who sit on the various committees. The "names of those responsible for the massacres". The names of power. The forbidden syllables. The names of those whose names it is impossible to pronounce in certain combinations and continue simply to live. And obviously, this has very little to do with what certain idiots still call "magic", which means it has everything to do with it. But anyway, I was thinking about all of this and all the while I kept walking further and further out of town, in wider and wider circles, until my own interior dialogue, if I can even be accused of having such a thing, seemed to come at me in a language I could no longer commit to, or comprehend, or even hear. Perhaps I could smell it. But anyway. Things we are not able to tell. Inexpressible things. Accountability. Transparency. Blah blah blah. Hölderlin called it the nefas. You know? Mystery cults and so forth. Revealing the secrets etc. The saliva of judges. Chewing on gristle and bone. And we could, if we wanted, I thought to myself, spinning round and round in 920 degree circles, we could translate that whole thing into geography, so those spittle-flecked unpronounceable syllables would become the sheer disks of unliveable landscape. The deathcell. The plague-pit. The city of the sun. Utopia. All of the dreams of all of those dry fuckers who neither believe nor remember their dreams. "For that is the tragic with us", wrote Hölderlin, sometime before he wandered off into the mountains and had his head split apart by god knows what infernal statistic, "to go away into the kingdom of the living in total silence packed up in some kind of container, not to pay for the flames we have been unable to control by being consumed in fire". Quite a metaphor, yeh? And one whose implications go further than anything Hölderlin would have been able to recognise. I mean, right now. "The kingdom of the living". "Packed up in some kind of container". "In total silence". As the borders are going up. As the teeth are being sharpened. And as I walked I wondered whose "the kingdom of the living" was, and whose was that "total silence", and if the inexpressible names that

Pasolini had almost uttered were of that silence or not, and if those who had, or possessed, those names, were of the living, or not. Because sometimes in Pasolini's work, in the late work, it seems as if utopia itself is the necropole, a ring of slums, a circle around the city, a "force from the past", tearing up the present, a fever-desert, coming from the future, at inexpressible distance, inconsolable. And that screaming factory owner, in the last scene of *Theorem*, was he screaming because he was entering the "kingdom of the living", or because he was leaving it. I don't know. It isn't even a scream, not really. More a dead thing, a powder-rasp. And as I was thinking this I suddenly realised I was no longer walking, because there was nothing to walk on, or through, or anything. Vague impression of a ring of houses or bones. Vague sense I could enter into any one of them. That no-one would stop me. That I would be as invisible as any living person, as any corpse. That's right. Rimbaud. Anyway. Like the bourgeois I am I went looking for a bus-stop. But I couldn't find one, so like the person I used to be I lay down in the filth of the road and did my best to ignore whatever conformist signals the stars were trying to throw my way. As in, none whatsoever. Like a rough and aged bedlam sheet. The wage relation. The pennies on my eyes. And the sun coming up. Or maybe it wasn't. Maybe someone had smashed it. Like the blinded eyesight of the living has been smashed. Like the 'total silence' of Hölderlin, ecstatic and packed with noises, has been smashed. But whatever. It seemed I was sitting on a bench somewhere, with some old guy, sharing a beer with him, all thin and vacant bone, and the language we were using wasn't English or German or whatever the fuck language a person is supposed to use in this the kingdom of the living or this the kingdom of the dead and, well, I was ranting on to him about Pasolini, about how in the last interview Pasolini gave, just hours before he died, he did admit to a belief in magic and how that magic was not simply to be found from knowing how to pronounce the so-called unpronounceable names but, more to the point, from knowing how to translate those names into sheer anger, which means the knowledge of how to inhabit the word "no", its landscape and its geography. Not of course the pinched "no" of border-guards and the rest. But "no" as in the opposite of the sun. And I don't know if I was even using words at all, or just some kind of structure of barely audible squeals, but I was still going on about Pasolini, about his poem "Victory", where he has the bodies of the Partisans crawling out from their graves and marching, with all the silence of that simple word "no", into the cities below. Horrified by what they find there, by the residue of what they thought they died for, they turn around, clamber back into their holes in the earth. And though its a poem of great bitterness and defeat it still carries within it a sense of how to continue, of how not to capitulate, in the face of whatever it is that is breaking our names apart, our names, shattering them, until their meanings change into something terminal and alien, alien as the pitiful groan I mumbled as I stood up and staggered back to my temporary flat in one of the more fashionable areas of this hopelessly gentrified and haunted city. I did a shit-load of speed, stared into space for a while, then wrote you this. Hope you don't mind that I haven't been in touch for so long. We are not completely defenceless. We have not yet been consumed in fire.

ANDREA BRADY

PHOTO: AUTHOR'S ARCHIVE

ANDREA BRADY's books of poetry include *The Strong Room* (Crater, 2016), *Dompteuse* (Bookthug, 2014), *Cut from the Rushes* (Reality Street, 2013), *Mutability: scripts for infancy* (Seagull, 2012), *Wildfire: A Verse Essay on Obscurity and Illumination* (Krupskaya, 2010), and *Vacation of a Lifetime* (Salt, 2001). She is Professor of Poetry at Queen Mary University of London, where she runs the Centre for Poetry and the Archive of the Now (archiveofthenow.org). She is also co-publisher of Barque Press.

THE FOURTH CALL OF MR GORE

All of us can walk on water,
salt our degrees in the stripes on our backs
turn the air on silent as turpentine breaks
wave painlessly all our metal goes black.

Likeness is kindled by a civic bonfire, all of us
applaud the release
of history bubbling in pulp,
the waves we break insidiously against hold back

nothing to open the glass down our necks
until the Target on fire is a corporate memory,
a drafting charcoal, and prison hulks
char the silky bases of the harbours.

In excited delirium we can return
that all of us are subject
to terry stop, all liars whose degrees
of harm cool against the boy's face whitening

under glass. Are we treading on water, alive
and barbed in our driveways, or when will we
know we trade ceremonial release
for the overthrow of wave over wave.

We need to see
who we can become in each other's company but
being spooked by our reflections start
to sink.

Shame charges specific
skin into the likeness of a creature. We look at each other
like committees struck by lightning:
scorched, electrified, bewildered that we are still alive.

ALL MY SONS

The invisible Marcus
is painting the ceiling. When we slept together
he was painting the walls
the shade of a number problem, a veil,
he lingers on the adult side where television
is not a ration and the poem is a manner
of holding it together. Do you think it's right

that only certain people can be famous?
To extend the definition and give us each
half a chance would keep us from getting ancient.
We climb elephant-coloured branches,
the air is free like us in the entire world under
a state dept. travel warning.

It's given out that a wild boar has seized a train,
the hoof prints lead to Calais.
When its blood is up it has a blind stamina
the rough edge of its hair rubs off its skin,
the skin keeps it from sliding into the hole
of a carnivorous tree into slavery,
if it is silent it will soon be laughing
burning like a herd of suns over the fields
of Fukushima.

The girl must be a Peshmerga
boar-spear or dragon, she chooses
the blue and white sail and circles indefinitely
above the Angolon. These fierce and slender limbs
climb jugs and divots, she flies
breaking nuance among the pine tops
but would be the child I lost,
her lungs scissored by an epoch
or she goes out drowned in scarlet.

The boys are also ones I would have lost,
and may yet, the pitiless front
of their jammies maps every place
that is not a target, it is the single dinosaur
who might have evolved into a man but is now
a relic they dig out of bricks for fun.

The box overhead shows a heaven made in ash.
They grow towards it forcing a trope of fear
as a thing to be managed or blamed.

I saw the heavies of special branch
in the departure lounge guarded by seven gates
and seven crowns. They chose the boys
for their ballistic look and the girls as slaves
who fell through that fabled hole in their bodies.
Waking up with a sword, smashing the wrist with trucks.
I snatch him away

he has been flipping his brother his whole body
shakes and can't be held in fear
of my outrageous discipline. He asks only for special time
riding the 38 in a loop, London's carbolic sky
full of canaries and cancer, we agree
each chapter must end with 'boobytrap'.
At night his head rests on owls.

There are only four people in this room. We
threaten to leave the table
in Vienna as a sandpit full of fox piss,
leave the children by dying off to
pick each other up under the arms,
make a catenary arch on Hatterall ridge
and subsist as best they can forever.
Their skin is still dripping; putting the head
through the hole is doubly impossible,
how can they make food or lodging?
He consoles himself picking out carbine stars
and multiplying them by larger numbers, sketching
out groups

of fish and cupcakes and imagining filling the toad.
What is the number before infinity?
What does produce mean? That the art of holding
is palliative, and no one need live
having lost her sparkle.

Tonight it's claw club, the lesson
Gothic mathematics,
each werewolf sleeps in a cubicle where in the daytime
it does some clerical work.

In combination they produce feelings
which take the place of the sum;
the tv is full of spying numbers,
they shoot out of the arm of the sofa,
the brain quivers with disco as a rubiate x marks
their zone of landing.

You are a bonkenger called rhubarb.
That means fighting but then holding
hands with strangers at soft play,
crying when asked to be sorry as if
your entire personality was on the spit
at the despatch
box. The fox
fought with the breakfast till it turned into dinosaurs
and was cleared away. He doesn't want
to be born. If he was born,
like a little born boy, when he was two,
he had nothing but weapons in his head. And maybe clothes.
We water-board amoxicillin,
owning the good we claw back his shut face.
To make up that good with sweet
night gardens believing
we are rescuing their ears. The analyst
saw this child

as an artist whom the mother records
shouts into oblivion
wishes to repair sometimes
like a clock whose singular complexity she keeps,
is shoved off, anxiously needed.
But he recoiled from being fed on too.
Retreated into the hollow trunk of a tree
where none could command him to communicate,
a prince of lost countries.

Smiling over the field
of poppies like a good witch their mothers
feed them with their own images
which is the lie of their harmlessness,
which puts them to sleep
instead of killing them.

That is a strong place. Like Socrates
the baby tied to his pushchair waits
in his bedroom with a blanket covering his head
for death; the child drifting in and out of reality
in his bedroom
with pythons and rats,
his wrists held by wires
to the fire-guard, and nothing will save him.
The sky bulges with giant bullets,
but only an individual retches bringing
nothing up but the desire to know nothing again.

I must get back to my own.
The only consolation
of mornings like this one is that their damage
can be so easily held.

QUEEN BEE

I love you, leaning over: he nods his head,
even dead asleep. The magnetism of loss
pulls me very near,
it pours over the barrels of the armed police
and the junkanoo of these casual people
scrolling their bodies towards oblivion
amid cupcake stands is washed off
by the possibility of the minute.
Enquire not what with Isis may be done
Nor feare least she to th'theater's runne
where girls dance in cages enflamed by sex.
What to say to them who survive
your addresses and take them for ransom?
To say nothing you must sacrifice
the only human-delineating thing
which has been permitted to proliferate,
here in the nest of wire wool
which is bigger than your life.
The tower blinks a milky eye
you put out

The footage shows a Soviet experiment
in which the severed head
of a dog was reanimated by an infusion,
it nods, yawns, and blinks away a serum dropped in its
cadaverous eye. Shining in the face of the ejected
pilot was the sudden disapparition of the idea,
like the octopus head-down inside my tooth
which makes his way into my body. My son
draws his friend's stomach full of engines,
with markers he traces his own path through them.
We expected to be slaves to these machines
but not to be so excited by them
singing them aubades
        against the broken-winged motors
            infested with red lights
        against the crows' wet call, the mouse's dry one,
shit which smells of smoke. Your brain
created in the image of an oyster
you reach inside it for a memory
which slips off the grabber like a stuffed
toy you have already paid too much for
to stop now, feeding the machine with coin.
The house is held together with ribbons
a way for the child to protest our ignorance
the one to which we insist she will be superior,
held on capital charges, held on

The perversity was not imagining money
as a yellow fluid but in contradicting Aristotle
and forgetting the sterility of metal, its cursed
extraction
wounding the musculature
of the earth of the body on the table,
sleeping through her aspiration,
her eggs rinsed and cultured. Danae so grabby
with this she must part

gold, randy species of punctuation
no less coveted in Nice or Aleppo.
Form is a vehicle
ploughing through multiple checkpoints
to hold something in my mouth

is a reminder that I am a poor animal,
my forepaw extended toward you,
    bathing my wounds in royal jelly
    gathering my offspring furtively around me

MEN

        I wanted
to describe the single man,
living perfectly in a common happiness,
the infant draped around his neck.

He suffers no compulsions,
his work is good, he eats well and carefully rests.
He is for others

a stage in a history which began with germs,
much better than he could have been,
holding his peace, weatherproofing his fence.

Drawing on his military training
but these days he specialises in logistics.
The movement of packages is an art of war.

At home he respects us, the bricks
and chairs thrown in sunny countries have nothing
to do with him, reading

in the shade. On occasions he is an ultra
leftist, knowing he will never have to give up the bike.
He disdains all forms of ribbons. His violence

is theoretical.

        He threatened me with an axe at a Halloween party.
        He stuck his hand up my skirt while negotiating to buy
            the neighbour's car.
        He broke into my dorm and circled me on the highway.
        He questioned my account as if it were rhetorical.
        He pushed me into the bus shelter, screaming insults.
        He waited until I was drunk then kneeled on my hands.

He left me scarlet roses and a card saying 'Sorry'.
He shot me with an AR-15.
He crept up behind me and made sucking noises in my ear.
He put something in my drink.
He texted everyone at school my photo.
He got me to sit on my lap and slipped his hand up my skirt.
He lost his appetite for steak.

You are also the man I know. How can anyone imagine your decency?

POETICS

It's January 2017 and my mind won't settle. I am supposed to be writing this statement of poetics, and another essay about love. I want to find the possibility that we can refute catastrophe and finish death in that rare form, the poem of happy love. But I have deadlines to finish, the business plan for a cultural strategy at the institution where I work, and through which I contribute to the extraction of more labour at lower costs. I also have to butter up some students with Foucault, Aemilia Lanyer, and the NSS. All our feeds are laced with hate. Civilisation, I say, was once associated with sacrificing the infantile pleasures of self-destruction in order to control or destroy the other. Our governors, I say, now recall those pleasures too and there is no limit to their biting, burning, and eviscerating. So there's no point now in mythologizing poetry as the exhalation of the organs of breath and mind, *phrenes*, and the Empedoclean theory that the universe is a breathing, emanating organism in which each object touches the other. The blue sky over London is full of poison, particulates swerve into my children's lungs as they wait at the green man for permission to cross.

A poem may be written under compulsion, but a poetics always under duress. To stand apart from the object, generalise it as a topic of reflection, is a kind of temptation – to expose an intimate act and devolve it into a principle. Anyway, what can poetry, which was post-truth *ab initio*, teach us about killing fascists? Walking around the reservoir, plotting this little speech for you, I decided instead to say that I began writing primarily as a way of Getting Out. As a small girl in a web of violence, I consoled myself that if the people near me were unreliable, bad or stuck, at least I had poems, their better, immense and empowering unreliabilities; my poems were a sign that I could not be contained, and a method for escape.

The critique of white supremacist, patriarchal capitalism that I found in college slipped some inexplicable persons off the hook, and allowed me to continue to feel the love that was required for individuals in situations of harm. But if intellectualism was a prompt to sympathy and reconciliation, it might also be an excuse for the lavish expenditure of feelings. The poem begins life as an uncontrollable desiring machine, which outruns my habits of shame, particularly the shame of being too loud or too female or too American in this tightening island context. It comes on in a rush, a grandiose assumption, a connection which feels rooted in the broad female power of the earth, the unmistakeability of the world's presence ferried over to a representation which is both an excess and a total absence of attention. The object slides off, the work of revision begins, the work which is already obsolete. I haven't even begun to speak of the imaginary relation to you, reading this, as some subversion of that neoliberal order of production in which the work of writing this very statement of poetics is an interlude, a box on the infinite to-do list ticked.

But I want you to know that, even now, a bad day, when I am a walking edge, unable to do anything but fear and rage, trying to shut every portal to our house against the horror which is the product of people choosing to make death in order to get a little bit of money, against the sound of that gilded voice from the podium – even now, I believe that poems are the only thing big enough to contain everyone I cherish, and my hopes for their lives. I sit down to write about these hopes. The particles swerve through catastrophe, the infinite space between is cold, I end up somewhere I don't recognise. But I have kept my hopes with me, and turn to face the people I love, not having made a machine which will carry them to safety, not going anywhere at all, but knowing they are still with me, and the possibility that we might finish death is there too, a great kinetic fiction, kept in mind, near at hand, never achievable because it cannot be spoken and therefore cannot be denied.

It has made things a little better, setting it down. Outside the window the sky is the same blue.

SOPHIE COLLINS

PHOTO: JOSH GORDON

Sophie Collins grew up in North Holland and now lives in Edinburgh. She is co-editor of *tender*, an online journal promoting work by female-identified writers and artists, and editor of *Currently & Emotion* (Test Centre, 2016), an anthology of contemporary poetry translations. She won an Eric Gregory Award in 2014. Her poems have appeared in magazines, anthologies, newspapers and art books, and in *Penguin Modern Poets 1: If I'm Scared We Can't Win* alongside work by Anne Carson and Emily Berry. She has been an Associate Poet at the Institute of Contemporary Arts in London, and is currently an artist-in-residence at Glasgow Women's Library, where she is researching and writing a text on self-expression, self-help and shame; *small white monkeys* will be published by Book Works at the end of 2017. Her first poetry collection, *Who Is Mary Sue?*, will be published by Penguin in spring 2018.

from **THE ENGINE**

Small white monkeys stretch around in the dirt beneath a tree but do not get dirty. They pick themselves up and dash away across the concrete plane, bobbing out of sight. They are silent.

I see faces in objects so frequently. Is this empathy? A door handle, a gate, a bony rock, a refuse sack, a tree, a church, a glove, a button, an icon...

On an oriental lamp base a floral design becomes a kind of ugly peony bonnet baby, petulant and saccharine.

*

'Finally I'm happy,' I think. I eat some supplements, drink some coffee and for hours everything is interesting.

I take over two hundred photos on my phone. Everything is poetry. Everything is trompe l'oeil.

I try to think objectively about the individual elements required of a masterpiece. I become itchy. I fall asleep.

*

The following evening is my dinner with the curator. I wear a fresh white gown.

During le plat principal my left bell sleeve slides through a rich sauce as I reach for my glass, but when I retract it the sauce slides right off.

I bother the sleeve edge with my fingers for the rest of the evening. The white monkeys watch me from a pylon, far away.

*

The dinner is ultimately disappointing. I had nothing to say, barely knowing any of the names the curator mentioned, and, on the few occasions I purported to recognise one, further discussion revealed me to be inept. I feel terribly guilty after the drink wears off.

I remember at one point noticing in my behaviour that I was more or less pretending to be the curator's daughter.

The next day I am offered an interview with a contemporary art magazine. I accept the invitation, and they never email again.

*

I wake up a day not long after covered in milk. My nipples are leaking warm stuff all over. I get up and notice that I am pregnant; my belly is huge.

I update my social media profiles with the news. The curator stops contacting me. The editors stop contacting me. Only one or two of my peers continue to send me emails and they have so little to say. They ask for updates on me and the pregnancy but the interest is all feigned. I cry and smoke packets of white cigarettes and don't tell anyone.

I tell everyone I'm not pregnant anymore. They have even less to say to me. Soon, I have a baby.

BEFORE

In 1239 the Mongol leader Batu Khan led his hordes
in a full-scale invasion of Rus'
His chief khatun Borakchin meanwhile
was at home, knee-deep
in mutiny
The servants had
in the absence of the fearsome khan
begun to rebel in small but unacceptable ways
making eye contact

& addressing the khatun directly
representing just two misbehaviours
in this stream of noncompliance that culminated
in their spitting at her hair & body as she rose
from bed
They had always despised her shallow breathing (*Pretentiouùs!*)
the pale crown of her head
visible beneath an odd number of thin hairs (*Sick!*)
& permanently covered in beads of sweat, necessitating
the near-constant application
of some powder of dubious origin (*Abomïnable!*)
One late afternoon
after finding a pornographic etching on the inner lid
of her family box
Borakchin escaped the court unattended
to the North Gate
where she straddled an outsize stone turtle
& picked at the uneven skin surrounding her left thumbnail
wondering at the politics of transmission
until she became so furious that she began to resemble a little white
     monkey
What followed was a long period of rain
a yearning for empirical consequence
& an influx of anachronistic beetles
escaping time
Somewhere in the present
a table of sisters became silent the moment
their food was placed in front of them
Two trees were similar but not the same
they were sister trees
A Fiat Panda carrying a team of cleaners with dark hair
approached a Russian cathedral via a backroad
marked out by a low fence of dead reeds

A. S.

And what was it Anna Sofia couldn't say? That all had started
with Arlo, when she had started up with Arlo, who had been nice
enough, but whose presence had turned her into herself. And so
first the faces, then mainly the eyes, but, in the end, all of it really.

And what was it she couldn't say she was after? To smash to pieces the earthenware jug on the stove top? The sound of a veil tearing? Both were nice ideas, but she couldn't stick with them. She walked around a bit and started to blurt things out. She told old men just how much they smelled, that their breath smelled and more, and this got her into some real trouble. A white old man, pale lizard face, small teeth, paper neck, hat the colour of yellow dog shit...

He came at her in an alleyway with the red tie just as bad, and, quick as she needed to be, A. S. had pulled out a razor knife – could have been Arlo's, could have been anyone's – and flicked it at his papery neck.

She would tell them she had been where she had always intended to be that day in September 2013: the Mushrooms and Health Summit, Washington D. C. And if it didn't get her off (it wouldn't), it didn't matter. Powerful, she can cook.

BEAUTY MILK

[handwritten annotation: Doesn't seem like a person]

I don't matter.
I am a blemish,
a fragment,
an apartment.

[handwritten annotation: It feels like i coherent voice]

I am a multiplication
and a made up belief.
I am nothing for days afterwards.

[handwritten annotation: Seems quite non-human]

[handwritten annotation: An element of unsaying in the poem]

They say 'sum' about me
because they believe I am expanding.
Really I'm too clean cut.

[handwritten annotation: Seems to be distancing as the poem goes on]

This one time I was owned
but he wouldn't pay the charges
at the German border.

Russia is the pits.

[handwritten annotation: May be a political element]

a whistle in the gloom

The feeling of inauthenticity under certain linguistic circumstances, of not being able to tell the truth, however strenuously one struggles to reach it – isn't this feeling commoner than is usually acknowledged?

[...]

The very grammar of the language of self-reference seems to demand, indeed to guarantee, an authenticity closely tied to originality. Yet simultaneously it cancels this possibility. Any I *seems to speak for and from herself; her utterance comes from her own mouth in the first person pronoun which is hers, if only for just so long as she pronounces it. Yet as a human speaker, she knows that it's also everyone's, and that this grammatical offer of uniqueness is untrue, always snatched away.*

[...]

My autobiography always arrives from somewhere outside me; my narrating I *is really anybody's, promiscuously. Never mind the coming story of my life; simply to enunciate that initial 'I' makes me slow down in confusion.*

*

Pauline Réage's *Story of O* follows the title character as she submits herself to the sexual predilections of a secret society. At the novel's outset, O's lover, René, takes her to a château on the outskirts of Paris where she is trained to serve the society's associates. O is flayed. She is manhandled and chained to the château's walls for hours at a time. She is instructed on matters pertaining to the society's sartorial customs and preferences. She is penetrated by one man after another in regular orgiastic sessions. René looks on. During one such session, an associate has difficulty entering O and demands that she have her anus stretched, which she does (after René approves the modification), in increments.

Subsequent trials follow at various locations as René's initial ownership of O is passed on to one man after another. O's second owner, Sir Stephen, has one of her labia pierced and adorned with a series of rings that form a heavy chain. To the heavy chain is attached a small disc engraved with a motif that signifies O's subjugation.

O consents to everything.

*

My own copy of the book, a cracked black paperback with a spare, cursive font that dubs Réage's text 'The Erotic Classic', offers readers two distinct endings.

In the first, O, wearing nothing but a highly realistic bird mask, is led into a ball where she is made a strange attraction for its guests. Two children, a boy and a girl, are among those who engage with O. The boy forces the girl, who is wearing a white dress (indicating that this is her first ball), to sit down next to O and touch her breasts, to run her hand over O's labia, her piercing, its chain and tag. The young girl complies in silence, and then listens in silence as the boy tells her how, one day in the very near future, he will have the same thing done to her. Once the ball's attendants disperse, O is led to a stone platform where she is once again penetrated by multiple men.

In the second, alternative ending, O kills herself (or asks to be killed) when Sir Stephen makes clear his intention to relinquish her.

*

'Pauline Réage' was a pseudonym for Dominique Aury, a journalist, translator and editor for renowned literary publishers Gallimard. When she was willingly 'unmasked' in an article in *The New Yorker*, in 1994 (fifty years after *Story of O*'s initial publication), the disparity between the book's author – Aury's professional, public persona – and Réage's narrative (its sadomasochistic content) was relayed in tones of surprise.

In the article, Aury relates having begun writing the book hotly and privately, at night, in bed, ostensibly for her lover, Jean Paulhan, in an effort to revive what she perceived to be his waning interest.

Already a well-known intellectual and Aury's superior at Gallimard, Paulhan saw to it that *Story of O* was published, and tried to improve its chances of commercial success by contributing a preface. In this text, titled 'A Slave's Revolt', Paulhan professes again and again his ignorance of the true author of the book, stating that the manuscript has the look 'of a letter more than of a diary'. 'But to whom is the letter addressed?', he continues. 'And whom does the discourse aim to convince? Whom is one to ask? I don't even know who you are.'

*

Aury was herself not sure. Asked about the book's sex scenes, she was adamant that the fantasies were neither her own, nor something that she particularly imagined would stimulate Paulhan, but belonged to an entity whose origins and shape she could not trace. 'I saw, between what I thought myself to be and what I was relating and thought I was making up, both a distance so radical and a kinship so profound that I was incapable of recognising myself in it,' she explained. 'I no doubt accepted my life with such patience (or passivity, or weakness) only because I was so certain of being able to find whenever I wanted that other obscure life that is life's consolation...'.

Of the 'childish' chains and whips she said, 'All I know is that they were beneficent and protected me mysteriously.'

*

In a reading of Réage's text, the symbolism of O is impossible to resist, despite the author's consistent attestations as to the letter's arbitrary nature.

Here I will purge the associations by listing them; zero (none); an exclamation (archaic); a lament (archaic); an interjection (archaic); a circle; a ring; any body orifice, including a gasping mouth or gaping anus; and, more tenuously, the grand rooms and dungeons to whose walls O is fixed; a mirror; an eye; a wound.

O was originally named after a friend of Réage's, Odile (a moniker shared by Pyotr Tchaikovsky's Black Swan and Odile of Alsace, patron saint of good eyesight). Shortly, however, Réage found herself unable to inflict on her friend O's experiences, and so she erased the majority of the name, rendering her protagonist an initial – a conspicuous lack.

'Initial', from the Latin for 'standing at the beginning'.

At the beginning of the book, O is not standing but sitting, in a car (a cab), her skirt gathered up in order to allow her bare genitals to rest directly on the vehicle's leather upholstery.

*

Before I know the details of its origins, Story of O is a book I treat as an artefact, a ruin I explore for its beauty, its strangeness, its shattered intimidations. I touch its scaly parapets while looking out at the developing world I usually inhabit from inside this one, whose decay is caused by both external factors and inherent flaws.

During one such visit, O seems to effect its own modality, to constitute a part of speech other than its designation as a proper noun.

'O heard a whistle in the gloom',

'O placed a new log on the fire',

'O listened and trembled from happiness' –

I type out these disembodied phrases and read them again and again until, whimsically, and for moments at a time, I allow myself to comprehend O not as an initial, but as a personal pronoun; a Rubenesque alternative to *I*; an innovation in grammar signifying a tacit acknowledgement of the paradoxes of self-expression; a room to live and breathe in, with some honesty.

*

I recently read, in another poet's poem, a passage that claimed apparently impersonal poems as the byproducts of trauma.

I witnessed, noiselessly, a thought forming; I watched it take shape as one watches a small movement in the distance: with a fleeting sense of calm.

I read the passage again, and I understood it. I understood it, and I felt the shame rise; I knew that the poet was right; I knew that she was absolutely wrong.

NOTES

The initial italicised text is excerpted from Denise Riley's *The Words of Selves*.

Dominique Aury was in fact itself a pseudonym (chosen for its gender neutrality). Aury's given name is stated elsewhere; I don't use it here.

My edition of *Story of O* does not credit a translator.

The phrase 'its beauty, its strangeness, its shattered intimidations' is borrowed from Rose Macaulay's *Pleasure of Ruins*.

ALLEN FISHER

PHOTO: ROBERT EDGE

ALLEN FISHER is a poet, painter, publisher, teacher and editor who currently lives in Hereford. He is Emeritus Professor of Poetry & Art at Manchester Metropolitan University and has exhibited paintings in many shows, including one-man shows in London in 2003 and in Hereford, 2013. His most recent publication is *Imperfect Fit* (University Alabama Press, 2016) which focuses on modern and contemporary poetics, since 1950. His two major works are *PLACE* (2005) and *Gravity as a consequence of shape* (2016), both published by Reality Street Editions. He has produced more than 150 chapbooks, books of poetry, graphics and art documentation and is also the editor of *Spanner* magazine.

from **PLACE**

I & VII

the earth spins too slow for us
the day's come-and-go   directs our tiredness
                    this is new to us

                            This place
it wasn't yesterday
    but soon we will recall why the land governed us

how we continue we cannot know
                            the sun is not stationary
            the days' passing amazes
                        it must amaze us
        how much we can fill our day
                    the day spends all we/
the earth wont wait
            the loci of a sphere   i have seen it
            I, not Maximus, but a citizen of Lambeth
                        cyclic on linear planes
            the construction of parallels along a water line
            where the intersections are our mistakes
return we will not   we have come

                            all this way
to return
            lovers never meet the same again

out from here   get out from here   stay
    the only process we can know is what we can deal with
in the oneness our bodies can merge us   lost
            but gripping the process we will survive

to get the facts right
                    under our feet are crushed carbons of our knowledge
we have only to stay
                and eat our carrots raw

    *

Shut that violence
                    STAB! STAB!
          the blood comes through teeth tasting of metal
                    poisoning our giblets
          swelling our nerves into holocaust
          the holocaust that will follow
                the one we have ignited
          that will throw our thinking into the vault
                the despair   we have tempered
                with our own acids

below me from here
                dogs circling the verge
          slowly we blind them in tetrachloride lead
if we spoke
          we would tell them what is unproven doesn't exist
what their bodies know   we will help them forget
          even their paths follow the roads we have torn
haemorrhaging their senses into factual non-sense
                              that some call intelligence

BIRDLAND

1

An image of the Engineer's model
shudders in a basement
as sand stabilisers are loaded.
The left arm bright gold, the ears glow green.
Out of its head energy spatialises
overlappings of spirallic fields.
A figure appears to attempt flight,
it may have wings, yet held to the floor
accelerates towards an openness through liberation
of its partner, unseen from the pit entrance.
Is it male? What is there to say
concerning child birth?
Its presence takes place
between table and pasture, at this moment
takes space between road and underground river:
it is named jouissance :
The arrival.

It brings experience of radical separation of self,
like child birth, produces an object of love.

2

In the morning television I carry
a cylinder of heat in my embrace
down a garden path labelled by the placing of stones,
Hey Bellman, someone shouts,
puts a match to a felled lime
lengthways in the walkway
with meanderings of drama
thought I was moving forward
lost ground
in mistakes, with grinding gaps in what I know about
fidelities or reproduction. By chance, it seemed,
back to the path I had opened
Its trace visible in footmarks and
potential infinity to an unknown fold.
On certain days, this morning is an example,
I remove my helmet cross the path
with a slight intoxication
to check the lime has been properly extinguished.

Endless destruction
makes Brixton
Call it the coexistence of prohibitions and
their transgression
Call it carnival and spell out jouissance and horror,
a nexus of life and description, the child's
game and dream plus discourse and spectacle.
On the edge
of death High Road, the Busker
starts up a reel, it begins as dance interlaced
with anger. I guess at the ridiculous partners
that perform. The Busker dances with
her saxophone
'Ideas of Good and Evil' are subsumed into this nexus,
production knots and
unknots paranoia
Blake stands his ground
on the Common asks, Are
          Her knees and elbows only
                    glewed together.

3

A woman came down the walkway
lost in transport
exploded her language at a kid
with a stick
restrained by another who breaks
the rod across his leg,
We've had enough, got it! We've had enough!
One hour later someone has dragged
a felled lime onto the walkway
Its leaves make a green path
A pack of dogs surround this, yelp
out of phase. Down the High Road
a new siren on a police weapon
fills the walkway
It leaves a burnt fizz overhead
grooves the mud plane on the roof.
Next door fits an extension to his aerial
changes tone of CB interference
in loudspeakers makes audible
amplified pulses from a geranium
in a Faraday cage. A poster snaps the letterbox,
Come to Paradise in Brixton's Coldharbour.

4

Beneath helicopters
Brixton abandoned
challenges the closure of meaning
so far removed, nothing will have taken place but the place,
flattened housing for ecological reasons,
fuses with a beyond, a successive clashes in
formations, memories of bodily contact, but
warmth and nourishment do not underlie the air.
The Mathematician
gets on the subway in a pinstriped
with a microchip blackboard. A spotted handkerchief
matches his tie. On the back of his head someone
has singed a domino it
matches his ear rings. As he starts to leave
his accounts, he pulls the arms from his jacket,
sets them alight.

The effect is laughter,
an imprint of an archaic moment, a threshold of
spatiality as well as sublimation.
Suddenly a path clears Sleep relates the squeezed
State to a lack of community He leans
towards me, Last night, he insists,
I had a strange dream.

5

The imaginary takes over from laughter,
it is a joy without words, a riant spaciousness
become temporal.
The demonstrative points to an enunciation,
it is a complex shifter straddling the fold of
naming it, and the autonomy of the subject.
Wearing four tones of grey soap I
read photocopied pages on lighting effects,
the Mathematician battery-shaves and makes
notes on squeezed light using a notation
echoed by remnants of beard clung to hydrogen
on his trousers. Subjection to meaning gets
replaced with morphology. I become a mere
phenomenal actualisation moved through a burning gap.
The irrational State insists on control.

BUMBLE BEE

Fatigued by his attempt
to reach
Blake falls in Kennington Road
before a half-open gateway
Puts into question
the subjectivity of weight;
prevents its gather.
She falls and rotates about
a canvas on the floor
there tries a variety
of orientations
for hanging it.

What is positive in Blake's weight
sinks
Held on while losing
his balance, or the Painter
becomes vertigo
felt as insinuation
finds herself over a void. It breaks
open an absence of place.
A mirror fastened across the posts of the gateway. No,
it's not a mirror, it must be an
effect of the light.

She stretches out of Repose
and lifts from a couch
Their bodies are not clarified
as arrivals of consciousness.
Understanding,
perhaps made of sensations,
events in patterns of connectedness
that constitute it, which
give their processes recognition exposed
to fields of sensations,
can change the connectedness
without altering the emphasis of
the pattern.

Their experience of materiality not lost.
Not lost and persists
given duration,
like but not actually
eternity, Not yet immobilised by malnutrition,
simply jags of pain from toxics
that prevent some movements.

In different angles, weathers, the colours move,
the reflections suggest, light from greens
then from blacks.
Inscriptions made by gains of momentum
underfoot in the walkway pansied mosses
checkerboard the right of way.
I am irremissible, as if free
with respect to the past, but
birdcaged watch the flight
outside. I breathe the gravity

of where I am. It is not
the ballast of hereditary weight;
I weigh myself.
Never long anguished by things done
stricken by what has not been.
Memory doesn't
replace the felt the paving stone
unless relieved in
some temporary anæthesis
or complete relaxation.

From vertiginous heights to a sludge
her arrogance breaks the gate
Humiliation by the windmill
at the next curve of the switchback, blinks.
At each section different attributes
of the image, intensity colour space.
Each switch reduces her metabolic requirement
doubles her dynamic range.
In the reflections diffidence
fragmented into abstraction and thoughtlessness

until the balance locks
awash in shadows and noise, the heterochrony
of existence as the suspended cage
swings.
Blake's fatigue
gave his momentum gain
unseated his load
His shock from quick recovery
greater than the effect of his fall.

JITTERBUG

1

When you can't sleep you make choices
Between staying awake or feigning sleep
Until the differences between the imaginary
And the real blur or become distinct.

In the City at the end of the century
Evil flees the Earth, writes González de Eslava
Before 1600, Now comfort is come.

Uniformly large embalmed travellers on the ground
Smashed aubrietia
Bourgeois security, self-absorption, destroyed community.

In the streets a turbulence of waves
Interferes with Music
Imitated by a bird. This must
Be fifty years ago, or four centuries past.

A leopard's shadow moves over my eyes
And I begin to express terror
Locked onto a vocabulary of telos and beauty
That perpetuates mystery in number.

2

I climb over a disruption pile of basalt rocks
Each holds a machined part in a bed of warmth and creation.
Each holds fossilised light and regenerates.

Rights spring directly from understanding who we are
But there is no agreement or
Belief that such is in principle possible.

There is a conference in the air
Concerning time and whatever couples with it.
Before spacetime could be perceived
Perhaps this is what some call eternity.

The Artist returns a drilled out cone to its extraction place
The headlight child sieves regeneration in a bed of
Felt and clay, warmth and creation

There never will be autonomous moral choice
No superior dignity entitles anything
Not even intelligence and the experience of pain.

3

It is the dawn of a hundred rabbits
It is the end of a millennium
How is it possible for some survivors to reach new, similar,
Worlds and thus perpetuate the species is still a mystery.

At the end of the century death keeps me awake
Recognition made universal
Birds alight aubrietia in the garden.

THE POETICS OF DECOHERENCE AND THE IMPERFECT FIT

1 ART AND AESTHETIC FUNCTION

While art has many functions, the predominant function is aesthetic. The aesthetic function involves understanding frameworks and their interaction with disruption or, put another way, a complex activity of setting out a particular structure and using that structure as a basis for improvisation and innovation or change. Art production involves two processes. The first is the facture by the artist. The second is aesthetic reception when patterns of connectedness are discovered within the work and in the comprehension of the receiver (the reader, viewer, listener). There are two alternative outcomes: one proposes a perfect fit or match between the work and the receiving consciousness, which would promote a boredom; a second proposes an imperfect fit that encourages efficacious activity in which comprehension is a complex of the facture and the reception.

The whole matter can be further referred to what could be named as *work*, that anticipates a contemporary collectivity of response, a cohesive tropology[1], as if these ideas were part of the historical conditions, a mutual struggle with and in opposition to other tropologies, other ways of attending, in the societies named as England. This becomes a consciousness economically dependent upon the system it ideologically and politically opposes. Adorno states only that art is radical which subverts both the traditional, incorporated forms of art and the commodity nature of the contemporary production of art. Otherwise art, whether highbrow or popular, retains its affirmative character.[2] It is in effect what pertinence means. (Impertinence would simply affirm values; it is pertinence that subverts them.) Simply expressing or depicting great inequalities and suffering, as Marcuse states, affirms the existing social relations, discourages critical thought, 'pacifies rebellious desire.'[3] What 'The poetics of decoherence and the imperfect fit' proposes is an aesthetics that is critical of the status quo.

2 DECOHERENCE AND AESTHETICS

Imperfect fit is the machine to engender an active aesthetics. In the classical world of refined proposals and clarity it might seem strange to bring matters of truth, and thus beauty, into question, but questioning is what this poetics continues to propose. Anglophile poetics have moved some distance from the archaic modernist proposal for 16 definitions of beauty in 1922.[4] The ideal proportions of the golden mean and the Fibonacci series continue to obstruct contemporary thought. But reliance on these particular measurements and values can now be shown to be ideal, approximate and rudimentary.

When in 1966 John S. Bell and others made it known how the world understood through phenomena no longer holds up. This proposal gathered a considerable comprehension of poetic dilemma.[5] Humankind may appear to be two centuries away from non-Euclidean geometry and John Keats' 1817 position of negative capability, yet continues to be in his position, capable 'of being in uncertainties, mysteries, doubts, without any irritable reaching after fact and reason'.[6] The different context with Werner Heisenberg's work published in 1927 on quantum physics that he characterised as 'uncertainty'[7] and the different situation from Kurt Gödel in 1931 who brought these ideas together when he proved that truth was not demonstrable,[8] led poetics into a new realisation, that there is a tangible world of things and experiences, and there are worlds beyond our experience, which can only be accessed remotely by tools and traps. These can provide evidence that both the micro-sub-atomic and the macrocosmic levels exist and perform and are part of and thus affect our existence, but this evidence is not quite available to perception except as artefacts.

This is a dialectic about the local and the problematic, larger world. In quantum mechanics part of this dilemma has led to naming the situation *decoherence*.[9] Beyond the state of coherence fought for by twentieth-century modernists like Ezra Pound and W. B. Yeats, Georges Braque and Pablo Picasso, Walter Benjamin and Theodore Adorno, to an understanding that part of our existence cannot be realised, is beyond perception, has a proven actuality and is typically experienced indirectly through artefacts. Physicists and biologists working on these actualities use laser and gravity traps and digital tools to make observation possible, but precise measurement remains out of the question. Instrumentation is itself part of the effect on measurement and its disposition. John S. Bell's proposition partly reiterates earlier statements, made by Max Born and others, that the observer interferes with the observed and thus consciousness affects measurement.[10] This has metamorphosed into understanding the role of the spectator, the measuring physicist, the viewer in art, the reader of poetry and listener to music, as a participant and an effect on the completion of the aesthetic production.

Measurement thus becomes an ethical issue; ideal structures and golden proportions must be displaced and this position is in confluence with three other significant appraisals of truth in twenty-first century poetics: (1) that energy concomitant with momentum (*momenergy* [11]) together with consciousness are discernible in wave-packets or quanta and thus change in step-like shifts and develop in four dimensions with a direction and not in an uninterrupted continuity or stream of thought; (2) that time and space (*spacetime*) are intricately affective and not usefully separated; (3) that extended and apparently smooth behaviour, such as experienced in the growth of an embryo, the mixing of more than one chemical or the loss of breath in a runner's stride, always rely on catastrophic jumps, phase shifts, sudden stepped changes. These 'jumps' are often unpredictable in terms of *momenergy* and *spacetime*, but often predictable in terms of quality.[12]

3 Poetics in action

Most of these ideas came together in 1982[13] in preparation for the work that has been underway since then and until 2007, *Gravity as a consequence of shape*.[14] In 1981 I had brought to a close two ten-year projects. One of these, named *Place*[15], had tackled the consequence of spacetime in terms of location, history and situation using a method of composition by 'field' and with points of access that could be determined by the reader. The location of South London, chosen in 1970, was used as the *Lichtung*,[16] the opening from which to research into local histories and the actuality of contemporary situations in the street, so to speak, both responded to and instigated. The subsequent poem, 'Gravity as a consequence of shape' uses a book factured in 1982, *Ideas on the Culture Dreamed Of*,[17] which drew from the vocabularies of contemporary physics, biology and chemistry and combined these with a selection of jazz dances into an A-Z array that formulated an alphabetical framework and structure from which to improvise and facture. The compositional procedures used in *Place* were radically reappraised for the *Gravity* work, taking into account the critique of the classical and ideal models of preparation and existence. The overall plan, conceived as the loci of a point on a moving sphere in *Place*, was replaced in *Gravity* with the looser diagram of a cylinder marked off in Fibonacci ratios and then crushed, thus leading to a new set but of damaged proportions. The text 'Traps and Tools and Damage' then comes rhetorically into the fore.[18] There may be many ramifications from the image of the crushed cylinder, rhetorical and pragmatic, but for these poetics the image aligns with the damage perpetuated and now escalated against the planet, once thought of as home[19] and now beyond repair, as well as the continuous need for organisations like the Medical Foundation for the Care of Victims of

Torture.[20] The image's display of numbered rows crushed into each other, causing geological shifts in and out of sequence due to stress and strain, produced unexpected patterns of connectedness, thus unexpected consciousness, and thus the need for proposals for an aesthetics that would seek to help solve the traumas, the damage of the situation. During the process of this work, variously published in the period 1983-2007,[21] this damaged structure has led to the need to constantly reinvent compositional conceptualisation to overcome or, so to speak, repair the damage perpetrated against humankind by humankind, and of course prepare not to repeat it. This process could also be thought of as a ploy to maintain personal homeostasis and homeorhesis.

4 THE POETICS OF THE IMPERFECT FIT

Consciousness and aesthetics share the summary of their activity as patterns of connectedness, which are patterns necessary for life.[22] They are patterns that provide the structures for ethical, moral, and social understanding and efficacy, and they change, can be changed. Loss of renewing and changing capacity of this patterning... amounts to loss of significant life.

The concept of imperfect fit involves the relationship between consciousness and aesthetics. In this relationship a pattern of connectedness between an object and its image in the perceiver's perception can almost match, and where this near-match has the capacity to produce a more significant aesthetic effect than, for instance, a perfect match and identity, or a complete mismatch and distinction. That fit is part of the viewer or reader's production.[23]

The poetics supporting this thesis are developing and this indicates the need for a follow-up. The openings proposed through Michel Foucault's last lectures regarding *The Government of Self and Others* and *The Courage of Truth* contribute to this development,[24] where *parrhēsia* (truth-telling) is a virtue, a duty, and a technique which should be found in the person who directs others and helps them to constitute their relationship to self. In *Milton*, William Blake proposed 'To Annihilate the Self-hood of Deceit and False Forgiveness.'[25] In *Proprioception*,[26] Charles Olson interrogated the singularity of the self, contemporary with his debate in *The Maximus Poems*. This poetics, first manifest in the aesthetics of collage and later in the dream theories of Surrealism and work of William S. Burroughs and others,[27] came to a new understanding in Olson's proposal through the 'Big Traum,' elaborated 'between chanting and letting the song lie in the thing itself and there canting off what the poem turns out to be, or to put the same in the words of another dream which makes sense to me as disclosing the scheme of discourse which my own persuasion – or the conviction of the dream – strikes me as being the truth of discourse: / of rhythm is image / of image is knowing / of knowing there is / a construct.'[28] He extended this proposal through his practice and theory of the performative in poetry led by his ideas of the breath, parataxis and proprioception, or that activity of stimuli arising from movement in the body's own tissues as they are affected and bring about a complexed spacetime.[29] This is the spacetime where the self is other; Foucault in his final lecture stated, 'there can be truth only in the form of the other world and the other life.'[30] The poetics of this are still in the process of being lost and found, as the poem *Place* noted in 1973, through 'a general movement of ideas.'[31]

NOTES

[1] From the root *tropos*, to turn or bring about change.

[2] Theodor Adorno writes, 'The uncalculating autonomy of works which avoid popularisation and adaption to the market involuntarily becomes an attack on them,' in Arato, Andrew and Gebhardt, Eike (eds.). *The Essential Frankfurt Reader* (Oxford: Basil Blackwell, 1978) p. 314

[3] Douglas Kellner (ed.). *The Collected Papers of Herbert Marcuse, volume 4 Art and liberation* (London: Routledge, 2007) p.104.

[4] Ogden, C. K., I. A. Richards and James Wood. *The Foundations of Aesthetics* (first published 1922, London: Routledge, 2001)

[5] Bell, John S. 'On the Problem of Hidden Variables in Quantum Mechanics,' *Reviews of Modern Physics*. 38, 1966, pp. 447–52; Bell, John S. and M. Nauenberg., The Moral Aspect of Quantum Mechanics' in De Shalit, A., H. Feshbach, L. Van Hove (eds.). *Preludes in Theoretical Physics*, Amsterdam, 1966.

[6] John Keats letter to George and Thomas Keats, December 21, 1817, *Letters of John Keats*, selected and edited by Stanley Gardner (London: University of London Press, 1965) p. 68.

[7] The more precisely the position of some particle is determined, the less precisely its momentum can be known, and vice versa. Heisenberg, Werner. *The Physical Principles of the Quantum Theory* (Chicago: University of Chicago Press, 1930) and Heisenberg. *Physics and Philosophy. The Revolution in Modern Science* (London: George Allen and Unwin, 1959)

[8] Gödel, Kurt. 'Über formal unentscheidbare Sätze der Principia Mathematcia und verwandter Systeme,' *Monatshefte der Mathematik und Physik*, 38, 1931, pp. 173–198.

[9] Omnès, Roland. *Understanding Quantum Mechanics* (Princeton, New Jersey: Princeton University Press, 1999); Zurek, Wojciech Hubert. 'Sub-Planck structure in phase space and its relevance for quantum decoherence,' *Nature* 412, 2001.

[10] The uncertainty principle (that measurements of certain systems cannot be made without changing aspects of the system being measured) is inherent in the properties of all wave-like systems and all quantum objects. The

principle states that the product of the noise in a position measurement and the momentum disturbance caused by that measurement should be no less than the limit set by Planck's constant as demonstrated by Heisenberg's thought experiment using a gamma-ray microscope. Masanao Ozawa showed that this common assumption is false: a universally valid trade-off relation between the noise and the disturbance has an additional correlation term, which is redundant when the intervention brought by the measurement is independent of the measured object, but which allows the noise-disturbance product much below Planck's constant when the intervention is dependent. A model of measuring interaction with dependent intervention shows that Heisenberg's lower bound for the noise-disturbance product is violated even by a nearly non-disturbing, precise position measuring instrument. Ozawa. 'Universally valid reformulation of the Heisenberg uncertainty principle on noise and disturbance in measurement,' *Physical Review* A, 67 (4), 042105, 2003 and subsequently see: So-Young Back, Fumihiro Kaneda, Masanao and Keiichi Edmatsu. 'Experimental violation and reformulation of the Heisenberg's error-disturbance uncertainty relation', *Scientific Reports* 3, article number: 2221, 2013.

[11] Wheeler, John Archibald. *A Journey into Gravity and Spacetime* (New York: Scientific American Library, 1990).

[12] It might be too rigid to call these paradigm shifts, as Kuhn would, but this is what they could be articulated as; see Kuhn, Thomas. *The Structure of Scientific Revolutions* (Chicago: University of Chicago Press, 1996).

[13] This is correct with the exception of *decoherence*, which came to the fore in the 1990s during new experiments in quantum mechanics. See Omnès, 1999 and Zurek, 2001, *op.cit.* 10.

[14] The three volumes of *Gravity as a consequence of shape* were published as: *Gravity* (Cambridge: Salt Publishing, 2004), *Entanglement* (Willowdale, Ontario: The Gig, 2004) and *Leans* (Cambridge: Salt Publishing, 2007) and then in a single volume as *Gravity as a consequence of shape* (Hastings: Reality Street, 2016).

[15] Fisher, Allen. *Place, Book One* (London: Aloes Books, 1974, reprinted St. Paul, USA: Truck Books, 1976). The complete *Place* has now been published by Reality Street, Hastings, 2005. The other project was *Blood, Bone, Brain* (London, Spanner, 1981-2).

[16] *Lichtung* a neologism from Martin Heidegger meaning lighting-clearing or opening. David Halliburton. *Poetic Thinking. An Approach to Heidegger,* (Chicago and London: University of Chicago, 1981) pp. 42-43.

[17] Fisher, Allen. *Ideas on the culture dreamed of* (London: Spanner, 1983). A reprint was published by The Literary Pocket Book in 2016, www.literary-pocketblog.wordpress.com/books/

[18] The text has appeared in many forms, most recently as a chapter in Fisher, Allen. *Imperfect Fit: Aesthetic Function, Facture, and Perception in Art and Writing since 1950* (Tuscaloosa: University of Alabama Press, 2016).

[19] For example, J. H. Prynne. 'What was most familiar [to Olson] was home. And what is home? Home is the planet on which you live. Nowhere have I been more struck, oh more passionately struck by the notion that the planet, the whole globe, the earth upon which we live, is home to us.' From Lecture at Simon Fraser University, 27 July 1971, 'On Maximus IV, V, VI' [transcribed by Tom McGauley], *Serious Iron* [*Iron*, 2] (Vancouver, 1971).

[20] The initial image recalls the experiments carried out by the National Aeronautics and Space Administration (NASA) on spacecraft and space station cabins subjected to zero gravity and high impact conditions.

[21] All the poems now appear in *Gravity as a consequence of shape* (Hastings: Reality Street, 2016).

[22] Fisher, Allen. *Imperfect Fit: Aesthetic Function, Facture, and Perception in Art and Writing since 1950* (Tuscaloosa: University of Alabama Press, 2016) p. 112.

[23] A first elaboration of the concept of *imperfect fit* appeared in Fisher, Allen. *The Topological Shovel* (Willowdale, Ontario: The Gig, 1999).

[24] Foucault, Michel. *The Government of Self and Others: Lectures at the College de France 1982-83*, edited by Frédéric Gros, translated by Graham Burchell (Basingstoke: Palgrave Macmillan, 2010) and Foucault. *The Courage of Truth: The Government of Self and Others II, Lectures at the College de France 1983-1984*, edited by Gros, translated by Burchell (Basingstoke: Palgrave Macmillan, 2011).

[25] Blake, William. *Milton*, plate 15.

[26] Olson, Charles. *Proprioception* (San Francisco, Four Seasons Foundation, 1965).

[27] For example, William S. Burroughs noted, 'Cut-ups make explicit a psycho-sensory process that is going on all the time anyway. Somebody is reading a newspaper, and his eye follows the column in the proper Aristotelian manner, one idea and sentence at a time. But subliminally he is reading the columns on either side and is aware of the person sitting next to him. That's cut-up.' Burroughs. 'St. Louis Return' and 'The Art of Fiction' interview, *Paris Review*, 35, 1965, p. 27.

[28] Olson, Charles, 'The Bezel,' *Io*, 8, Cape Elizabeth, 1971, p. 81.

[29] The important discussion of parataxis not included here, develops from Eric A. Havelock. *Preface to Plato* (Oxford: Blackwell, 1963) p. 251, n. 7, where he refers to James A. Notopoulos, 'Parataxis in Homer: A New Approach to Homeric Criticism,' *Transactions and Proceedings of the American Philological Association*, Vol. 80, 1949, pp. 1-23.

[30] Foucault, 2011, p. 356.

[31] Fisher, Allen. *Place* (Hastings: Reality Street Editions, 2005) p. 9.

ROBERT FITTERMAN

PHOTO: AUTHOR'S ARCHIVE

ROBERT FITTERMAN was born in St. Louis, raised in nearby Creve Coeur, and now lives in New York City. A leading conceptual poet, he is the author of more than a dozen collections of poetry, including *Nevermind* (2016), *now we are friends* (2010), *Rob the Plagiarist* (2009), and *Metropolis*, a long poem of city life in four volumes. He often builds poems through appropriating and recontextualising found text, ranging from photo captions in the United States Holocaust Memorial Museum (*Holocaust Museum*, 2013) to expressions of loneliness posted on online message boards (*No, Wait. Yep. Definitely Still Hate Myself.*, 2014). As Nick Thurston notes in a 2014 review for *Flux*, "Robert Fitterman's *Holocaust Museum* is a relentless re-presentation of how social histories are constructed [...] His poem is a linguistic memorial to the objectification of modern life. It is not *about* the Holocaust even though it is."

from **THIS WINDOW MAKES ME FEEL (2002)**

This window makes me feel like I'm protected. This window makes me feel like people don't know much about recent history, at least as far as trivia goes. This window makes me feel whole and emotionally satisfied. This window makes me feel like I'm flying all over the place, gliding and swirling down suddenly. This window makes me feel like I count and I enjoy knowing my opinions are heard so that hopefully I can help change the future. This window makes me feel like I'll find the one thing that makes me feel like I want to feel. This window makes me feel like I can tackle any problem anytime. This window makes me feel like I have energy again and it refreshes my brain cells and makes my feet move. This window makes me feel like I'm the only person who can do something

*

as cool as drumming. This window makes me feel like it's better to hear that other people have gone through it – it's like a rainbow at the end of the storm. This window makes me feel good and grounded and peaceful all at the same time. This window makes me feel like the year I spent campaigning was worth it. This window makes me feel like the artist really knows something about *the truth*. This window makes me feel really good and also makes me feel like it heightens the sex when it finally happens. This window makes me feel like I'm walking along a creek behind a super-market. The window makes me feel like I did when I went to a heavy-metal hair stylist who wore a swastika belt buckle and I didn't say anything. This window makes me feel like violence is around every

*

corner. This window makes me feel like there is a part of the news story that I missed. This window makes me feel like I'm a rabbit being hunted. This window makes me feel like I have a tangible, relevant role in some ongoing process. This window makes me feel like I've won a prize, like I got a part in a movie. This window makes me feel like I do when I hug my dog. This window makes me feel like I want to travel there and find out for myself. This window makes me feel like a special person to have them take a personal interest in my life. This window makes me feel like I'm on the ship in Ben-Hur. This window makes me feel uncomfortable like when people judge other people's sexuality. This window makes me feel like I'm giving back something to the place that gives so much to me.

*

This window makes me feel like I've always been somebody outside looking in. This window makes me feel more Jewish. This window makes me feel like I do when I take care of other people. This window makes me feel like people rely on me to get the job done. This window makes me feel like she's a nice girl who makes mistakes. This window makes me feel like it's raining outside and I feel dizzy and I like it. This window makes me feel blessed that I will be living in America for another year. This window makes me feel weird like I know what happened on that visit couldn't happen and it makes me feel good to see how things have changed for the better. This window makes me feel good about myself to be able to paint because my artwork helps me to show my feelings that I

*

couldn't show before. This window makes me feel like I cannot be responsible for what other people say or do. This window makes me feel rich as I engage in this non-essential and expensive habit. This window makes me feel good to know that my company cares enough about its employees to even consider going for a program like this. This window makes me feel good knowing that the little things that I do can make such a positive difference in others' lives. This window makes me feel like I really shouldn't take extensive lie-ins on Sundays, that I've wasted most of the day, which makes me feel like I'm cheating. This window makes me feel more mature like when I volunteered at the hospital. This window makes me feel good and lets me know that I'm a pretty good player. This

*

window makes me feel like my disappointment is a rock in my chest – it makes me feel hard inside. This window makes me feel like I'm actually doing some good and besides I get to sneak in a lesson on life. This window makes me feel like I have knocked down some pretty thick walls for others. This window makes me feel like I have a front row seat at the world's most ancient and mysterious show, that I am witness to the dawn of time. This window makes me feel unwanted and ugly and sometimes it makes me feel dirty when we make love because I don't know what he's thinking about. This window makes me feel rich but what a contradiction because I loathe capitalist hullabaloo yet still crave Vegas. This window makes me feel closer to God by worshipping through song. This window makes me feel like I should return those purchases at lunch.

FAILURE: A POSTCONCEPTUAL POEM (2013)

If the artist changes his mind midway through the execution of the piece he compromises the result and repeats past results.

Sol LeWitt, *sentences on conceptual art*

I have failed miserably, over and over. In fact, this reading, about my failed presentation, will be a complete failure. And by choosing this form of a quasi-essay – a form that I am neither comfortable with nor practised in, I am more or less guaranteed to fail. The presentation of this failure might uncover some ideas about the nature of these poetry events and other aspects of our poetry institution, but I doubt that. My guess is that this presentation will fail at doing any of that work in a serious way. I was planning to present an awkward slide presentation from *SPRAWL* – the latest installment of my poem 'Metropolis'. This presentation would have included random online images of shoppers in conjunction with my voice reading a text appropriated from online shopping chat rooms. But this idea would have failed miserably. It would have failed to say something, anything, more useful about the very consumerism it points to. It would even fail, believe me, at exposing the emptiness that continues to get filled as I speak. *SPRAWL*, even as a text, fails because it is ethically suspect – it seems to make fun of the shoppers who are being duped by the very corporations they chat about. And then, if I did show the images – which I'm not because I failed to get that together – there is the ethical problem of association – e.g., is it random that the Southeast Asian woman is linked to *Payless ShoeSource*? What kind of responsibility am I taking for this association? Clearly not much. The failure, here, cannot be rescued or excused by randomness. If it is a purposeful association, that's a worse failure. And what if, somehow, she were directly linked to a *Payless ShoeSource* site? Would that make a difference, would that be justified by some sort of authenticity? No way! But I have failed miserably to get that technology to work – so you're not seeing anything. This is an especially unfortunate failure given the fact that technology is so central to my whole thing here.

As a corrective to this problem of how appropriated images and text from people online could be viewed as condescending, I thought to write about the ethics of appropriation in the parking garage section of *SPRAWL* (because while parking we do ask a lot of questions). But this text also fails because it explains too much and compromises the conceptual frame of the whole project. At the very moment that I'm hoping to deconstruct this practice of appropriation, my own concession fails because it sounds too self-righteous and too obvious. It fails to bring home any of the complexities that sympathetic practitioners also face in their own practices to catalog or document mass information. One might argue that this is a non-issue and that I fail to grasp the dimension of this no-win situation or that I fail to recognize the blatant fact that appropriation is ubiquitous in all aspects of contemporary culture – both in a general, historical sense and specifically in the use of found materials from the Internet. Had I not failed to present the powerpoint, you could be looking at the woman in the V-neck tennis sweater photographing herself in the mirror. But you don't need to see this image because it's a complete failure – it doesn't challenge the viewer to look beyond the role of spectator – we see these images all the time and we may get some creepy feeling of the appropriator exploiting the subject here, but do we, as viewers, feel complicit? Do we think about our own roles as appropriators, culture makers, consumers? Not here we don't. I've failed to push the reader beyond his or her sympathies and into the space of complicity. From a more theoretical angle, I have even failed at suggesting new ways to destabilize the authority of the author. Some writers and artists may argue that this whole dialectic of the "I" and the authority of the author is an outdated or misguided dialectic and that there is no radical shift in the reception of our works if we destabilize the authority of the author. But my text, here, does precious little to further this debate on either side. In fact, it fails at destabilizing the authority and it fails at carrying out any authority of its own.

When I realized the dead-ended-ness of this failure, I thought the best way to rectify the dilemma would be to go online and join a shopping chat room myself. In this way, my hope was to create some equal ground and encourage a conversation even as I was making an intervention. What a waste! The idea was doomed to fail, because the poems that I posted were already appropriated from previous postings by other online authors, and then reformatted as poems and re-posted by myself. The result was a complete and total failure. Here's what I posted:

GNC

Most of us
are trying to get the best

out of our bodies everyday
through work

and play. Mine is mainly
through work.

Getting older
my body tires faster and my

joints and muscles take longer
to recuperate.

And here is the first response to my post:
Dear Iggy Z – What da fuck?! Is there something way
wrong with your word processing program or is this
some kind of poem – which would be cool – Either way,
GNC sucks!!! don't trust anybody who works there.
Dan the Man.

Dan the Man seems to sniff me out as either a poser or a loser
or both. My aim to confuse identities here is way off the mark – a
huge failure. To think critically about my own identity in relation to
these other identities is also filled with fundamentally failed thinking. Even when I am not entering the dialog of the chat room, but
only appropriating the language of online anonymous authors, one
might argue that these identities are also shared, and that, somehow,
the Internet offers us the possibility to feel like we are engaged in a
collective identity. But this, too, is a failed premise and the act of borrowing online identities is more like Identity Theft than a meshing
of subjectivities. I am a failed avatar just waiting for the delete key.

So, my failed text and failed powerpoint presentation travels the
flawed road about the proposed ethics of appropriation, but it's like
a service road to the main road because it fails all over again at vi-
sioning a larger worldview. The demarcation between the appropriated and the authentic is an obviously failed distinction; failed because in "real" life we don't make such distinctions, so why would
we do so in art? I could imagine someone coming to my defense
here to explicate the notion that these empty, appropriated texts in a
consumer context reverberate differently in a new context. But, right
now, I fail to see why that is meaningful.

And with this failure in mind, I have the messy job of returning
to the ethical question which I failed to respond to in any satisfac-
tory way. I've tried to consider how I might borrow this language
without having a superior relationship to it. I've even considered
removing or avoiding online language that could make my relationship to the text seem condescending, but this too fails because I am

intervening with a heavy editorial hand. By presenting a more sensitive, more PC or PG version of what anyone could read on the web, I've failed to minimize any of the superiority that troubles me. This dilemma is best exemplified in the conflicted decision of whether or not to correct grammar and spelling of online found text. If I leave in the original errors, I take the risk of making fun of the online authors who might be less privileged in class or education, and if I do correct the errors, then I run the risk of controlling and purifying the found text. Either way points to failure all over the place.

There are issues, too, about labor and craft – all that work that did or did not go into the presentation and the labor of choosing or not choosing the right borrowed texts in the right combinations? If I had completed the powerpoint that I failed to produce, the viewer might notice the amateurish quality of the web images and the presentation, but since I have no real powerpoint to show you, the example is failed and my point about the amateur is ridiculously failed. In fact, the very notion that I'm talking about a visual example that you can't see and wasting a considerable amount of time on this explanation is a more prime example of the kind of failure we're talking about here – total, far-reaching, and unmistakable. Of course, one could even argue that those adjectives I just used failed to describe the depth of this failure.

And yet this particular failure of presentational skills could have been an important failure to point to because it could illuminate something about the democracy of skills that one sees on the web: everyone and everyone's grandpa can be a consumer critic, or self-help advisor, or photographer or video artist or archivist or boardroom presentation specialist. Where does this leave poets and other skilled artist? I don't know because I fail to think through the ways in which this challenges our ideas about the materials we use and the skills with which we use them. I fail to do any significant investigation into how this plays out. There are compelling issues to consider here about labor, production, artists' skills, authenticity and reproduction... isn't there a rich theoretical body of work that might intersect these concerns? I'm not sure... that's the kind of failure I'm up against.

But it is a failure too, maybe a deeper failure, to then explain these paradoxical uncertainties. So, by explaining the project here, even in failed terms, I have failed to let the reframing do my talking for me. In effect, what we have here is a triple failure: once for failing to create a more direct critique; twice for a faulty commitment to letting the object be and speak for itself; and thrice for over-explaining these self-defined failures. In terms of conceptualism, where the idea itself might have steered the text through these troubling

waters, I have failed by my own editorial hand – fixing and doubting and reshaping the found text instead of letting it to perform its
conceptual duty towards the larger idea, without the interference of
my authoring. So, as a conceptual poem, this work fails miserably
because it does not resonate a compelling idea that stands outside
the text. As a crafted poem, this text is an obvious failure in that the
materiality is not at all carefully composed – where's the rhythm,
assonance, consonance, etc? As a result, I'm in a kind of conceptual
purgatory. In other words, I might have once thought it was enough
to reframe the language in order to shift the conversation to a discourse about network culture, but I keep intervening and so the
text then fails over and over again. Let's not forget, too, the ways in
which this text and the non-presentation itself has failed independently of the text it refers to. What we are left with is a presentation
about a failed presentation of a failed text with the hope, I guess,
that such a discussion might bear fruit – but don't count on it.

I had hoped that I might write a conclusion to this short piece – it
even fails at achieving a respectable length – that brings together
these ideas in a meaningful way so as to not to waste your time and
my own, but that convention, which offers the hope of resolution,
has also failed me miserably, again and again.

S. J. FOWLER

PHOTO: AUTHOR'S ARCHIVE

S. J. FOWLER is a poet, visual and performance artist and playwright. He has published several poetry collections, including his most recent title *The Guide to Being Bear Aware* (Shearsman, 2017). Previous books include *Enthusiasm* (Test Centre, 2015) and *The Rottweiller's Guide to the Dog* (Eyewear, 2014). He is the curator of The Enemies project, which has led to collaborations between hundreds of poets from across the world. He is director of Writer's Centre Kingston, Lecturer at Kingston University in England and teaches for Tate Modern in London, where he lives.

YOU'LL FIND A BEE AND STING ME WITH IT

> I'll book myself a bee-hunting bee
> PETER RILEY

The length of bodies, stacked end to end,
allows more room
for the numbers to be known by many.
Bodies become rides across the sand.
They get icy.
They become the brick in walls
splitting the lands of a baron,
dividing the museum from the living quarters.
In the court,
there are still those who kneel for mercy.
Still robes becoming entangled in stirrups.
Still people falling from horses.
They land in the mud,
into the ether, namely, that which is not
          and need not be.
That which was once a vision and is now reality.
Knowing that, I tell you,
is a wholly untrustworthy path
for you cannot know what is not.
Our universe with no other purpose
          than its own existence.

LOOPER

> Why hurry, life, why chivvy on the hour?
> You'll soon have time to sew my mouth right up,
> stitching with iron threads.
> OLGA SEDAKOVA

There are troubles conceiving,
and whether it's exciting anymore,
when it has a purpose
and such fearsome consequence.
Girls in the street look up
and away

even though I'm only looking
because they're dressed as mummies.
Or maybe I look disgusting,
feeding myself apricots
like a pharaoh.
But they were grown from wings
and soon rot on the feather
if you don't eat them in bloom.
Maybe they look away
because I'm ugly,
like a lizard.
Or because I live in my underwear.
Or because of my fertility.
Or because I can regenerate limbs
Or because I insist on tickling everyone.
I'm a good lover though,
I get really nervous.

BEARS ATTACKED ME

They're so delicate,
that's why they're those above,
who can't be loved,
asking *why can no one love me?*
Like a blind bear biting my crotch
this evening is a letter of correction.
Mole follows water,
compulsion follows nature
into a magazine.

There have been two marathons to suffer.
One was running
the other a poetry reading.

With two dogs, two female dogs,
I collaborate.
So if we could have quiet debate
for the letter of the sun
that burns permanently
into my brain,

I can say it was a bitch,
surrounded by the suffering
of museums.

Sometimes the story
    like the man who imagines
he is special
to the prostitute,
      like life,
    goes on and on and on and on so long
you wonder if it's a parody of its own length.

ATACAMA

like with women
the desire for multitude
leads to a certain solitude

   *

does this work support me in what I truly wish to do?
or does it paralyse me, promising the achievement of a spectre
while maintaining conditions of that paralysis

   *

chacabuco foam, they took to take her teeth
deprived of her enemy
she shucks dust

   *

if it's still human
& fine weather, in the admin. of stars
on the clarity that isn't the bottomless
of rather a dead mother – by tractor
those contests of dead chests
proudly thrust out forward

   *

and the gasps of love, after all, had got him
ready. john berryman

*

the made comes like a swelling vision
an eye cracked beneath, good stoppage
the past are taking over
from the time it takes for my eye to see
the light that it has been agreed
will be let go

*

chilean watches are the best movement
like a rat that was scorched by flame
and filled, rowed up in old slaveminer's houses
tranquill waterless mountains
many a man here lies, holding holy shit
only the sin that laid them low
knows how they forgot life

*

the tractor digger furrows
the sand & in so did
get to doing
the devastation of the skeleton's integrity
bits as in teeth chics
fingertips and bone chips
spilled out the side thresher

*

an unfortunate
accident for the searching
mothers

from **EPITHALAMIA**
> *for livia dragomir*

The Roman Wife

a horrible love that ends a massacre
burn ours as the twin to a jungled war
imply the notion of a kind end
smothering a poem about the high end
the tower of escape into hours
get it for all it means before it was
that we won't be lonely again until one of us dies

Memling

there have been depictions
of skeletal horses still animated
ready to drag a carriage
through the night
a simple calculation – our
marriage is a kind of dead horse &
I have spent my life preparing
the nest

Unicorn Baby Shower

unison singing future family folkbank
a herd of buffalo's trying to fly is AIDS apparent heir
we'd never go to marry new york when it was enough for mexico
heat & even the women said she looked beautiful dressed
as curbs of terror
are all the more risk of horror now
DON'T RUIN it

from **MINIMUM SECURITY PRISON DENTISTRY**

COB

what prison bars do not
is what a spider web does not
bars laid upon stones
on stones & stores
empty, elbow decoration, by bars.

climb a love below the granite line to lock with the
locking sound. The setting lock, the frozen sea of
granite. The smoke of prison bars shape trees

Each bar is a virgin. Each door a flock of
joists & atoms. I am the filament of granite. I
have become the child of filter & filigree. I am a
prisoner at the feet of the dark house. Its sons
are architects

CAHOOTS

I read schopenhauer inside
he tells of a man in tangier
who tore another man's jaw
clean off, of a mother who
drowned her baby, of the hunger
of man for misery. I read
Nietzsche inside he tells of a
man who brooked the damn
who cut down the lion in its
prime. I read spinoza inside
I am a little bubble of oxygen
I am gypsum fantastic

TATTOOS

I have atatattoos shaped
like a Whistle
a cock & a weathervein

& a warbird screaming
tearing talons at coy carp scales
the fish swims south
& is unsullied
I am Britain
& in Britain we don't bugger
the weakbirds against their will
our resolve is far more resolving

POETICS

> "Ambivalence is what all ordering activity is sworn and set and hoped to eliminate. Ambivalence is the *cause* of all ordering concerns: life-business needs clarity about the situation and certainty about the choices and their consequences, and it is precisely the absence of that clarity and that certainty which rebounds as ambivalence, triggering an effort to introduce order – that is, to clear the mess: to confine every object and every situation to a category of its own and only the category of its own – and so to make the obscure transparent and the confused straightforward. But ambivalence is also the *effect* of ordering bustle. The production of order has its toxic waste, a vain attempt to impose discrete classes upon non-discrete time / space."
>
> ZYGMUNT BAUMAN

My poems are toxic waste.

Any *explanations* I might offer do feel quite tired, like homework, precisely because they come after the fact of writing. Before all of which will follow I can only say I'm selfish. I write for myself. This takes two forms, outward and inward, social and intellectual, and all this, I would guess, comes from my engagement with poetry coming later than many and through pure chance. As such I'd suggest I'm constantly confused by the assuredness of many of the declarations around poetry and its culture. My poetics are a self-centred exploration of inevitably unanswerable questions through trial and error, hypothesising, aiding and opposing towards nothing but more of the same. I hope too they are an expansion of this practise through poetry into daily life, happily relegating poetry to a vehicle or vessel, that might be replaced (with gardening? cooking? kite flying? chess? dog breeding?). I look forward to the day I am asked to contextualise my dog breeding practice.

My poetics can be, superficially, divided into a number of concerns. All of which arise from a fundamental sense of inquiry / curiosity / confusion. They might be listed, knowing the irony of this systemising, as:

> A fundamental wonder before the possibility of language itself and an ensuing interrogation of its always approximated character through active linguistic texts and poems.

> An underlying attempt to engage with inherent failure of language to cohere to its meaning, and how this process is aberrant in the mind, and even more so when spoken or written from the mind – never settling, never really conveying its essential purpose, an always failing and approximating

and being inspiring / intriguing precisely because of this impasse. An attempt in ape sounds and markings to reflect very certain universes of these idiosyncratic language cultures. A fundamental awareness that context completes content, and never the two can be separated.

Often, an attempt to utilise fragmentation, disjunction, juxtaposition as means of provoking equally complex responses and run on meaning in the mind of the reader / listener. Often running toward mishearing, misgiving, ambiguity, misspelling, mispunctuating, as normative language is everything else, everywhere else. Worrying about that which is not normative at its root, not just when allied to arbitrary genetic traits. Using poetry for what it can do that other artforms can't.

Engaging with tradition in poetry with both legitimate wonder, and irony, both of which it needs. Deploying *I* carefully, showing my reading deeply in my works, but (I hope) quietly, in hiding, knowing I will not get to any end of reading and writing, and reflecting even this confusion in my more traditional poetry.

In all this (so far) happily prolific, methodological, energetic, workmanlike, as seems to be perfectly acceptable and not detrimental (in principle) for the visual artist or filmmaker or actor or musician or novelist, but not the poet(?). Confronting suspicions about productivity. Engaging with each subject with mindful method and rigour and actual hard work and time investment.

Responding to the challenge of changes in language and expression in the world in general, not happy writing the poems of twenty, fifty, or two hundred years ago when my world is really new, and really wild. The internet is new, and made of language. The world population has doubled since the mid 1970s and language has been assailed and devalued by advertising, political rhetoric etc... Trying to be in league with an awareness of poetic traditions with future facing ideas, which are known as the avant-garde, but just those with invention in their core mode, to steal strategies for solving my own problems.

Further methodological worries about the visual character / composition / meaning of language, through concrete, visual, asemic poetries, as well as the sonic character of language through performance literature, sound poetry and improvised vocalisation. A general further exploration of the potential of performance and liveness in poetry, again context meeting content.

An engagement with collaboration, but not a preoccupation, as some would suggest (just because it appears unusual?) as a way of marking life in friendship through creativity, and a way of learning. My first pedagogical revelation, learn through doing, do through collaboration, working with intelligent / warm hearted people makes you more intelligent / generous, or so the theory goes.

The mixing of arbitrarily divided artforms in the service of myself, what can be gleaned methodogically and culturally from the music, art, film worlds etc? Both aesthetically and practically. The latter, seeking commissions, new routes of making time for further work (and joy?) Making a living in poetry as a daily concern.

Actively organising or curating to discover new worlds and works on my own terms, and to create social / living artworks in the event. To create a poem in the reading order. To have no utopian goals, no long term vision, to be as invested in the happening as it occurs. To create a welcoming environment that facilitates the fermentation of difficulty / difficult work. To provide a space for like-minded, independent humans to meet, collaborate, build friendships. Paulo Friere's notion that organization presents the antagonistic opposite of manipulation, that it is a natural development of unity.

A practical internationalism, cosmopolitanism, travelling to festivals to read and write and make new relationships which will undoubtedly grow my poetry, and lead to a more generous life, gaining perspective, realising my life's (and my work's) fundamental smallness, pointlessness, meanness, fear, and keeping on writing anyway, because this is so essential and obvious to not be a revelation. Then, in turn, welcoming poets to my home, offering hospitality through poetry and events.

And beside or beneath all of this, a concern about complex and pragmatic ethics that might surround poetry (or trying to know my lack of knowing, knowing limitations), most especially against contemporary reductive ethics that are bafflingly self-defeating, judgemental, hypersensitive, hypocritical and parochial. A poetry against small things, small ideas, small folk, small souls, that I hope can't be immediately understood, reasoned with, consumed quickly. That which will please only the few who give it its time, not trying to please everyone, comfort, satisfy, console. Poetry for each individual, not for a group, not for a collective understanding I can never understand / reach when I can barely understand myself from one day to the next, let alone a single other human being.

When asked about a boat one is using to sail should we speak about the boat, the water or the act of sailing? Poetics are the boat, which doesn't matter too much to me as long as I'm not sinking (which is quite feasible).

I have resisted poetics and criticism, writing almost none, for a myriad of reasons. All my higher education was in philosophy, very much in the analytical tradition, which leads to a certain burn out and suspicion. But also because I have seen it deployed as the stilts on which many a rotten house is built, smothering invention with a literal-mindedness that's most often restrictive, or I've found it deployed after the fact of writing, a retrospective justification made to get an academic position or something to that effect. And I've never found it to be anywhere near as illuminating as the text itself.

FORREST GANDER

FORREST GANDER is a writer and translator with degrees in geology and English literature. His book *Core Samples from the World*, published in 2011, was a finalist for the Pulitzer Prize and the National Book Critics Circle Award. Other collections of poetry include *Eye Against Eye* (2005), *Torn Awake* (2001), and *Science & Steepleflower* (1998). Among his many translations are *Fungus Skull Eye Wing: Selected Poems of Alfonso D'Aquino* and *Alice Iris Red Horse: Poems by Yoshimasu Gozo*. Gander's latest title is *The Trace*, a novel. He teaches at Brown University in Providence, Rhode Island.

EVAPORATION: A BORDER HISTORY

Paisanos they call
       roadrunners, brothers of the land. A dozen
Mexican corpses maroon
          under desert sun.
    In cottonwoods by the river,
zone-tailed hawks squeal. Visible
      from the air, the craquelure of
an abandoned runway
            overlies
         toxic waste and unexploded munitions.
    Bordered by purple and yellow
bloomstalks: lechuguilla.
         Volcanic chimneys up-thrust
           from barren flats. Agleam
    in a basalt outcrop, fist-size
          feldspar crystals. The old raiding trails
    from Comanchería converge
in a path packed by hoofprints.

      Alarming *ki-dear ki-dear* of a
         Cassin's kingbird on the
            barbed fence. 150 miles
        surveilled by a white aerostat
     shaped like a whale. Between those peaks
    sits Panther Laccolith. Both vaqueros
        staked-out naked, left screaming on an ant hill.
Female katydid waving her foreleg tympanum
         at the stridulating males. The fine-
           grained intrusion that veined the mountain
         also silled Paint Gap Hill.
        His horse quivers in agony, pinned to the ground by a lance.
     Hovering over the field, a flock of crested flycatchers.
        The border patrol dog lifts its leg
at the tire of the Skywagon. Coachwhip
          fences parallel the dirt way. Chihuahua
Trail following Alameda Creek. They call it
        horse-crippler cactus.

Vietnam-era seismic probes
buried across private lands. Lava rock rims the sides.
Give it a break, mockingbird.
El Despoblado. Giant yucca and bunch grass.
And what ventures into the afternoon heat? Only Pharaoh ants.
Only the insulated darkling beetle.
On either side of the pavement, magnetic sensors
record movement and direction. Evening
cicadas eclipse tree crickets.
A thousand head of cattle
driven below the trachyte hoodoos. It nibbles
a prickly pear. Cottontail at dusk.
Human contraband at dusk. Famous
for their dwarf fauna, these fossil beds. Depositions of
carnage, catches
of light. Our legacy
mission. A carcass of
the unspoken
howling.

ANNIVERSARY

Not, not to be known, always,
not to be known always by my wounds,

[handwritten: Quite dark, violent connotations]

[handwritten: A physical action but abstract idea]

I buried melancholy's larvae
and followed you. Gathered

[handwritten: Human element of desire]

myself like dusk
to the black tulips of your nipples. (Tulips, tulips).

For seven days we locked the door,
we scoured the room with bird's blood.

[handwritten: Ritualistic, animalistic]

[handwritten: Carnal]

And for a little while
in the hollow where your throat rose

from between your splendid clavicles (rose, rose),
our only rival was music,

[handwritten: Music could be the ultimate beauty]

[handwritten: Who can be louder?]

the piano of bone-whiteness.
Nor did the light subside,

It is very musical (handwritten)

But deepeningly contracted.
The rawness of the looking.

Filled with romantic imagery (handwritten)

The quiver.

FIELD GUIDE TO SOUTHERN VIRGINIA

*   *   *

True as the circumference
to its center. Woodscreek Grocery,
Rockbridge County. Twin boys
peer from the front window, cheeks
bulging with fireballs. Sandplum trees
flower in clusters by the levee. She
makes a knot on the inside knob
and ties my arms up
against the door. Williamsburg green.
With a touch as faint as a watermark.
Tracing cephalon, pygidium, glabella.

*   *   *

Swayback, through freshly cut stalks,
stalks the yellow cat. Can you smell
where analyses end, the orchard
oriole begins? Slap her breasts lightly
to see them quiver. Delighting in this.
Desiccation cracks and plant debris
throughout the interval. In the Black-
water River, fishnets float
from a tupelo's spongy root
chopped into corks. There may be sprawling
precursors, descendent clades there are none.

*   *   *

The gambit declined was less
promising. So the flock of crows
slaughtered all sixty lambs. Toward the east, red
and yellow colors prevail.
Praying at the graveside,
holding forth the palm of his hand
as a symbol of God's book.
For the entirety of the Ordovician.
With termites, Mrs. Elsinore explained,
as with the afterlife, remember:
there are two sides to the floor. A verb
for inserting and retrieving
green olives with the tongue. From
the scissure of your thighs.

*   *   *

In addition, the trilobites
were tectonically deformed. Snap-on
tools glinting from magenta
loosestrife, the air sultry
with creosote and cicadas.
You made me to lie down in a periGondwanan backarc basin.
Roses of wave ripples and gutter casts.
Your sex hidden by goat's beard.
Laminations in the sediment. All
preserved as internal molds
in a soft lilac shale.

*   *   *

Egrets picketing the spines of cattle in fields edged
with common tansy. Flowers my father gathered
for my mother to chew. To induce abortion. A common,
cosmopolitan agnostoid lithofacies naked in the foothills. I love
the character of your intelligence, its cast as well as pitch.
Border wide without marginal spines. At high angles
to the inferred shoreline.

*   *   *

It is the thin flute of the clavicles, each rainpit
above them. The hypothesis of flexural loading. Aureoles
pink as steepleflower. One particular day, four hundred
million years ago, the mud stiffened
and held the stroke of waves. Orbital motion.
Raking leaves from the raspberries, you
uncover a nest of spring salamanders.

A POETICS

I

Neither Jewish, Christian, nor Buddhist, when I write I am cloistered, nevertheless, in my own imagination. The basic gesture of my writing is a listening. Perhaps this attitude resembles that of the religious. But my credal source is worldly. Faith, for me, derives from the most common revelations. *What is* stands revealed. Yet, like Edmund Jabès, I have found no Truth but truths and interrogative, no reality but feeling and interpretation.

We shall all be changed, the Bible promises, though for most of us it is momentary. Love unseats us, but we thread ourselves slowly back into the dull wood of our egos. It is hard to sustain a constant awe, as Lao Tzu importuned, and so tragedy befalls us. We fail to construct a lifelong state of wonder. And yet artistic and spiritual endeavors inspire our efforts to do so, as though the efforts themselves were all important.

If the language practices commandeering world history are increasingly standardized, utilitarian, and transcriptional, poetry offers a different order of relationship with the other. Because poetry's meanings are neither quantitative nor verifiable, because they are distinct from those meanings obtained by rational and calculative processes, they might well be considered miraculous.

How else can we account for acts of language that communicate coursing emotional registers and instigate insights and so articulate the world that we see as though for the first time? Poetry can be an ecstasy of words spindling perceptions. The meaningful dialogue between poem and reader is as much a sacred manifestation as I hope to encounter.

I come to consider language by how it uses me. Poetry offers a transformative summons. It enacts my own felt need to engage emotional, aesthetic, and intellectual experience in forms neither self-serving nor predatory. When, in an interview, Rosmarie Waldrop says that "The one transcendence that is available to us, that we can enter into, is language," she implies that language houses all of us together, shaping human experience. The great capacity of language is to bring us into proximity with one another. We fill with recognitions. In my own encounter with poetry, I approach the imagined possibility of an attentive mode of being. Shifting my perspective, poetry reconstructs my relationship to the world and to the future. I am torn awake.

II

...but I was more declamatory in my twenties.

In college, I majored in geology. I spent four years learning to recognize crystal forms, using an x-ray diffractometer to make structural maps of minerals, tracing the archaic mammalian radiation, cracking open black shales to study graptolites so compacted they were hardly more distinguishable than pencil marks and I was careful not to inhale them.

Sometimes I begin poems with a structural penchant, but my architectures deform according to what they come to contain. A long poem in *Deeds of Utmost Kindness*, 'The Faculty for Hearing the Silence of Jesus', started as mimetic enthusiasm for a rhetorical motif in a section of the *Bhagavad-Gita*, but in the final version of my poem, no approximation of the original pattern remains. Overriding musical and semantic concerns transformed the poem. "Feel pattern, be wed" goes Robert Creeley's gnomic verse, and so I do.

Whether form or cadence triggers the poems, measure always conducts my composition. Writing, I pass from time to space, from succession to juxtaposition. I write the poem in all directions at once, emphasizing not the stability of single words but the transition that emanates between them, or between a word and its rings of association, rings of silence. My idea of meaning derives from the continuity of the transition, which is, for me, erotic.

I was raised by women and among women; we communicated in a way that rendered men's minds – when later I came to think I knew them – strange to me. Maybe this has more to do with my family than with gender, though gestation and birth are metaphors I continuously associate with writing. I have always believed my body is involved in my thinking as a locus and means of perception and its arousal, that pen and paper transform the hand into the mind.

What I want is simple enough: to combine spiritual, intellectual, emotional, and technical elements into a resistant musical form. To summon the social and political meanings of sound and rhythm as well as meanings whose truths lie beneath or above semantics. And for it to have the fillip of implication. As Thelonius Monk put it succinctly: "Just how to use the notes differently. That's it."

Among other poetries, I am interested in those that find in sensual experience not a supplement to the rational intellect but a different, even incommensurable form of insight. I distrust definitions and homily and life insurance. And I follow those poems whose rhythms and syntax draw me away from what is already familiar, secure, agreed upon. The thorn-bug and her nymphs clustered on a green stem, the woman at the nursing home stirring her tea with a frozen Charlotte, the twin flight attendants deadheading back to Pittsburgh, the boy in the dog's bed curled into a question mark, starlight bending near the limb of the sun, coffee cut with honeysuckle, lagoons of coal slurry leaking into an abandoned strip mine, the faces in foreign newspapers of those we have bombed, tomatoes ripened with ethylene gas, two 300-plus pound men in a canoe fishing for alligator gar, fingerling birches, the thrushes already quiet at mid-morning, and my dead friend and his dog Charlie Parker peeing together in the snow: these are the insurmountable a priori of my poems. Exposed, I close my eyes. Listening. Open. Torn awake.

LYN HEJINIAN

PHOTO: AUTHOR'S ARCHIVE

LYN HEJINIAN is a poet, essayist, translator and publisher from San Francisco Bay Area. Her most recent publication is *The Unfollowing*, published by Omnidawn in 2016. *The Book of a Thousand Eyes* was also published by Omnidawn in 2012: a collection of poetry that began as a homage to Scheherazade, the heroine of The Arabian Nights. *Description* (1990) and *Xenia* (1994) are two volumes of her translations from the work of the contemporary Russian poet Arkadii Dragomoshchenko and have been published by Sun and Moon Press. She is the recipient of a Writing Fellowship from the California Arts Council, a grant from the Poetry Fund, and a Translation Fellowship (for her Russian translations) from the National Endowment for the Arts; she received an Award for Independent Literature from the Soviet literary organization Poetic Function in Leningrad in 1989. She currently lives in Berkeley, California where she teaches Contemporary Literature at University of California.

1

Anxiety, ambition, energy, and sleep are caretaking
fish in the deep black sea, my sweet, the black deep sea. Yes
and I tossed a twig
the x, y, z of unrest and loss of privilege
they never had, the vanquished Inca
at the sharp angle of a perfect rainbow and afterwards Jupiter appeared
of which the Rocky Mountains are like mules hauling oats
perceived by senses words a set of names
in music. All this should scare the legislators
noble and real and we are crazy and smell smoke
for entertainment, social bonding, and great anxiety,
that trinity of apricot, scalp musk, and gas
of life where light falls on the passenger seat
first upright and like a cornflower, but slow.

2

I'm not too old to dance meadowlarks: great punctuation
locks in black and blocks, crepuscular and vain the sun
in its descent. "You kicked up dust"
of which the Ural mountains are but dim reminders
through a wooded alley loud as if disturbed
in the unbuttoned fog that grays a pedestrian's silhouette
while the passport picture reaching out to me is true or false
to tetrahedral nation-states dead in winter water, enzyme ice.
I cannot fear to be forgotten
a child born another book the dust at dusk
of skilled blind sculptors whose cities sink
the swollen toad, her pride
flamingoes, lilies, and boy flowers
the center of a blue-black vault, an apron, history on it.

3

Language is a victim of its own success
while into the carriage comes a louder lyric me
of which the Cockscomb Mountains are like apples rotting in the dust

that none of us would be content to leave unlifted
from a caterpillar's cud to chew. Poor tucks
can kill, pour tanks, and call. People are forced
to live, work, yearn with bourgeois linearity to change
this rake-wielding life upon row upon row upon row
of the river pulled further and further apart
under the unswallowed elegy of a collared stork.
Then productivity as reproductivity ends. Motion
gets immobilized by perception into things perceptions get
but perception gets it wrong from quantum habits
of sadness, the hem of a sack wet under a hen.

4

Doing is highly thought of and frequently abandoned
as at a bus stop beside a stunted gingko, and time is tossed
a laundry pile large as the crown of a tree
or the gravid animal of Pythagoras, and every mathematician dies
while runnels vacillate or do nothing astrophysically speaking.
Let's go for eggs and to the bakery. My kid wants to be
a puppeteer. But someone must polish glass and since then the refugees
weep wax and travel over agate pastures and gag.
But we have to trust philosophy – and deny the property
where depiction most perfectly depiction depicts.
In a faux chateau of finance the proposition is a picture
of corn cakes, last crumbs, weapons passing from hand to hand.
Let's rest. Life is fast. As the city rat, resuming, says: "Rudeness
is rude." What kind of ego would utter that demand?

5

Runts have their tools and outlive lust and age
with introspection rewritten one word at a time of
humility with notes descending. Music goes to hell
to cruise that heavenly neighborhood with a strong wing,
the horse a ruby roan. Patterns of judgment, chess
of text, respect that cannot sleep as night falls on the shores
before an infant knows of time that there is something
in mathematics shorn of ideology. The public
does not need to be convinced. An idiom
like Kierkegaard on Halloween gathering twigs
and fathering eggs while a stunted thorn

frolics in the shade now dead inconsistently down the large white sea
does what a poem does, making itself
understood. Yet none of these things contented them.

6

Every situation can be taken as subject to a proposition
at stake at this stage of the state. Rejection of a context
need not be of one's own hoeing
of the sun, one's head a building site. Say I rode in on a vicious mule
surrounded by leaves under the northern star, the eternal conflict.
Say I beat my brow and only put on shows, withered
webs, a rigmarole, an atrocity to which I'll give no words. I refuse it
representation. The janitor is innocent, autumn is ill, and cruelty
will be the rule until I die from a flea bite or while beating
a metal drum, eating honey and corn like a girl again
with an umbrella under a redwood tree with all of which I am
in a certain sense one. The roof on trust of hover can't render love
pathetic. I claim too much and yield to the Bighorn Mountains
of which the truth of history is but an indifferent silence.

7

Because we refuse to personify the gaping east or deformed west
or cranial north or sacrificial south we must accept this box
and these panoramas to which we were led through sliding doors
just as certain Alpine cliffs reproduce the "head" variants of Mayan "script"
with an impersonal cluck to the jeweler.
Wherever a human is to be found, there you will find
occupation, a skyscraper, a 9-foot copper weathervane, imperial pickles
a force plundering an unarmed ceramic bowl.
Urban greenbelts lift a feisty allegorical vegetation in human voice
above an opium fish, a dime in cinders under the wind
and there are wealthy men, skin not yet charred. They are popular
as hardware, music, poached eggs, modesty, multicolored snapdragons
and the alphabet sacrificed in times of need. I live under the authority
of a stucco beehive and a soldier speaks affectionately to me.

8

We think, we approach, we exist
sweep and speak, on ziplines or not.
Sayings spread as amusements for children women and men
by pony-poets, beetle-poets, crow-poets
are voiced by the words themselves and not by anyone speaking them.
I dab fingernail polish on six croquet balls.
Which of the names of Hercules do you hear and in which of your ways
of which the hill behind the soldier bathed in sweat is like a general's nose
or the yellow bowl upturned beside the kitchen sink
to dry. It's now a wedding finch a reference to whistling rain
a great honesty in the far sacerdotal south.
Do they piss on the spider,
the aged face of the great organizer on slender evidence,
the rising sun that hangs a puppet from my hands?

9

The mountaineer rappels at midnight the wall a wall
a wall a woman recalls: a contingent object – it might never have existed
then you look at your fists and there are the letters o
in admonition, odor, foot. A dog shakes premonitions from its coat
lovers of time – time of all kinds –
winged insects, mosquitoes mostly but also moths.
Welcome, unwelcome, buffeted? Who can make durable wax?
Who can knot? The baker is a man and brutalizes wheat
and all attempts recall a textual residue of celebrating rats
a game of backgammon with dancing kissing getting drunk
hugging singing crying when we were leaving war
a stumbling block reconstructed and constructed
o xank history thistle e tspung hatchet
corvid head over human heels, facing a direction wrong or right.

10

Pity combatants on the line who self-concretize, becoming paving stones
but I say too loudly that of which I don't know how to say enough
borrowing transcription from a local pebble held in a palm
from which a puppet tugs as if pulled by the revolutions of the planets
Mercury Saturn or Mars over nearly twelve and a half million days
marking time, which is the subject matter of history

in which the sun itself bakes the bread then drawn from the oven
and cooling under the proprietary nakedness of the caustic trees.
So, asked a bee of experience, "How is it that umbrellas are raised
against the future of the sun?" Remnants of the past
don't expect us, remnants of the past didn't foretell us.
Our songs are sonically shattered over shortwave by a scop
singing the praises of his patron, the racist acquitted – he nods
and flees the derelict pattern.

11

People work under the clouds and are direct
inheritors of the things that happen every twenty days.
What saddle do we use? A wolf has been caught
and it sweats. My own sleeps do not unfold in easy procession
which is called lustrous, erect, major, and will in some field cease
altogether. Then tell me what you have to say.
The chains obey, the dogs piss under glass, voracious
fish leap from the beams, we do arbitrary things – appear
and disappear as leonine as dogs. The first person
is made for oneself, denizen of a cult or rubbish heap
ready for the evening show in the cavern of centuries. The second
is made for you, a respectable human of greenish hue.
We had a drink and it cost a house
into which we moved, music coming from stone.

12

Drift of grief a feather that scarcely seems to fall
or feature. Future a chair standing on a counter with Cuisinart
quietly in its nest. We sniff our underarms and sing at intervals
and nail captions onto facades, we are like corn kernels clapping
on their cob under the eyes of the neofascists who have always been
among us, ascending bougainvillea onto roofs
in the dark. No – that's unfair to rats. Neofascism is subcutaneous
slime. Subtlety is not neofascist. Neofascism is
like fascism blunt. Under the stars there are many things
with capacity to collide or combine with other things
in our vicinity (that gravitational field of monsters). Affections
are cruel, tortures sociable. Do they stop
there, the sun brown and impossible, the female *per se*
illicit, sulphuric, and fucked?

13

Words hang from his tongue which he has bitten
saying "territorial terrarium" because it is a joke he says
"wolf" to alleviate the tongue pain it makes him
walk between dots on circles shoveled
in a corner where desire has deliquesced
into very windy surly foulness newly built
with deviant speech and sins of the tongue
and of the impoverished poplars, American beside my coffee,
an army major at once in an eternal army
stationed on a perennial battlefield for an undying cause
whose every combatant in her or his monotony
is pumped from a boom box
hot, exotic, and able to do something *really* well
and be a presence in the present tense of rain.

14

The name of which the name pops sorrowfully and labor-filled
from the 365 days of the true year, the first, would be of something
in white shoes sipping lemonade and dead in his tracks
and there would be budding dust small flies: they
totter: female, and female relatives, dodging
bees in orbit, captions composed by tyrants extolling tyranny
of broad appeal to individualists always arrogant always
afraid of which the Appalachian mountains are only inconclusive
tales. Palomino centaurs more horse than human become geraniums
of church under clotheslines monumental now in their failure
it's all too linear I thought the popinjay
some kind of bird injustice speaks assertively
of its identity – or claim to identifiability – of blame
the tyrants were too drunk to remember what they'd watched halfway.

15

A charity-performing pepper-jay leaves curves
unholstering his or her unconcealed carry grille
on which to barbecue rivers and rivers us some blackberries
both feet fortunate handsome kind entire and strained trees
approach the city, wild horses are miserably bad
from 8 am to 8 pm and then they trot to excellent oak or laurel

madrone water in a semantic way performing livelihoods
passing the waterfall and sword ferns and a gnat
laughing at a great beast's despair at something minute
of which the Ural Mountains are but that great beast's despair
breathing disdain laden with salt but sparing the rat
under the insubordinate brambles which are Babylonian
or Antipodean or formerly Soviet or French with which
I dare not wittily uncurl the irregularly torrential morning.

16

The foreman of the regimental puppet show
hissed at me and I could only hang my head
a gray stone encircled by a band of white sedimentary
stone signaling yes, that's it, stone
signaling a day, the first
of a future year mathematically proven
by latching calcium onto a congruent cog over a 52-year period
of war awaiting critique waged by the week, hour, minute
we force to act, we force to micturate, we force to gadgetize
instantiate, frame, monetize, grade
the chord which takes us into a room left dangling by the puppet
so that rain flow will not flaw
the road along which orchards order shadows claiming distance
controlled by the familial near and domestic dear. I stop.

17

Faces are long streaks emphasizing repetitive round ties
but temporal destinations – all endpoints – make
no sense. I am bound unequal to a screen
the task and show a drone dove grey in nervy clutches going
back and forth from one house to the next front over the leafblowers, o
the leafblowers: they monitor the orange colors of the solar system
and its textures and its magistrates overseeing poverty
or make that property doing its shedding of blood red shells
and shields and, too, sine qua non par excellence the pantry shelf
is better versed in math of which the Atlas Mountains
are like the mythological remains of the darker dead corpus
of humanity that (though logical) was strange. Round as time
and character but not as fate is the first date on the unbroken calendar
of the mouthed language, contralto.

18

The days of the seven almonds have passed out of the public sphere
of a great number of sheep in the field of which Mount Shasta
is the only one standing like a winter sycamore, a scrap
of orange peel, till we serve our mothers with money in the life
to come and their glossy green leaves are somewhere
down an alley, short and morally blind. How could we know which
if any is a radiant number with lucky energy? And I will
fucking do so not too old for fucking that
too well when the kids on the dance floor are boys and girls with M27 IARs
and great and guileless national pride with which peace of mind
is incompatible. Time is ingenious, impatient, dulling, never
dull that of the heart. I speak of my own. I demur. I go
and come in black sweater and skirt from an obsidian blade
of a macuahuitl left dry by the sea.

from **THE REJECTION OF CLOSURE**[1]

Two dangers never cease threatening
the world: order and disorder.
　　　　　Paul Valéry, *Analects*

Writing's initial situation, its point of origin, is often characterized and always complicated by opposing impulses in the writer
and by a seeming dilemma that language creates and then cannot
resolve. The writer experiences a conflict between a desire to satisfy a demand for boundedness, for containment and coherence,
and a simultaneous desire for free, unhampered access to the world
prompting a correspondingly open response to it. Curiously, the
term *inclusivity* is applicable to both, though the connotative emphasis is different for each. The impulse to boundedness demands
circumscription and that in turn requires that a distinction be made
between inside and outside, between the relevant and the (for the
particular writing at hand) confusing and irrelevant – the meaningless. The desire for unhampered access and response to the world
(an encyclopedic impulse), on the other hand, hates to leave anything out. The essential question here concerns the writer's subject
position.

The impasse, meanwhile, that is both language's creative condition and its problem can be described as the disjuncture between
words and meaning, but at a particularly material level, one at
which the writer is faced with the necessity of making formal deci-
sions – devising an appropriate structure for the work, anticipating
the constraints it will put into play, etc. – in the context of the ev-
er-regenerating plenitude of language's resources, in their infinite
combinations. Writing's forms are not merely shapes but forces; formal questions are about dynamics – they ask how, where, and why
the writing moves, what are the types, directions, number, and ve-
locities of a work's motion. The material aporia objectifies the poem
in the context of ideas and of language itself.

These areas of conflict are not neatly parallel. Form does not
necessarily achieve closure, nor does raw materiality provide openness. Indeed, the conjunction of *form* with radical *openness* may be
what can offer a version of the "paradise" for which writing often
yearns – a flowering focus on a distinct infinity.

For the sake of clarity, I will offer a tentative characterization
of the terms *open* and *closed*. We can say that a "closed text" is one
in which all the elements of the work are directed toward a single
reading of it. Each element confirms that reading and delivers the
text from any lurking ambiguity. In the "open text," meanwhile, all

the elements of the work are maximally excited; here it is because ideas and things exceed (without deserting) argument that they have taken into the dimension of the work.

Though they may be different in different texts, depending on other elements in the work and by all means on the intention of the writer, it is not hard to discover devices – structural devices – that may serve to "open" a poetic text. One set of such devices has to do with arrangement and, particularly, with rearrangement within a work. The "open text," by definition, is open to the world and particularly to the reader. It invites participation, rejects the authority of the writer over the reader and thus, by analogy, the authority implicit in other (social, economic, cultural) hierarchies. It speaks for writing that is generative rather than directive. The writer relinquishes total control and challenges authority as a principle and control as a motive. The "open text" often emphasizes or foregrounds process, either the process of the original composition or of subsequent compositions by readers, and thus resists the cultural tendencies that seek to identify and fix material and turn it into a product; that is, it resists reduction and commodification. As Luce Irigaray says, positing this tendency within a feminine sphere of discourse, "It is really a question of another economy which diverts the linearity of a project, undermines the target-object of a desire, explodes the polarization of desire on only one pleasure, and disconcerts fidelity to only one discourse."[2]

"Field work," where words and lines are distributed irregularly on the page, such as Robert Grenier's poster / map entitled *Cambridge M'ass* and Bruce Andrews's "Love Song 41" (also originally published as a poster), are obvious examples of works in which the order of the reading is not imposed in advance.[3] Any reading of these works is an improvisation; one moves through the work not in straight lines but in curves, swirls, and across intersections, to words that catch the eye or attract attention repeatedly.

Repetition, conventionally used to unify a text or harmonize its parts, as if returning melody to the tonic, instead, in these works, and somewhat differently in a work like my *My Life*, challenges our inclination to isolate, identify, and limit the burden of meaning given to an event (the sentence or line). Here, where certain phrases recur in the work, recontextualized and with new emphasis, repetition disrupts the initial apparent meaning scheme. The initial reading is adjusted; meaning is set in motion, emended and extended, and the rewriting that repetition becomes postpones completion of the thought indefinitely.

But there are more complex forms of juxtaposition. My intention (I don't mean to suggest that I succeeded) in a subsequent work,

"Resistance," was to write a lyric poem in a long form – that is, to achieve maximum vertical intensity (the single moment into which the idea rushes) and maximum horizontal extensivity (ideas cross the landscape and become the horizon and weather).[4] To myself I proposed the paragraph as a unit representing a single moment of time, a single moment in the mind, its content all the thoughts, thought particles, impressions, impulses – all the diverse, particular, and contradictory elements – that are included in an active and emotional mind at any given instant. For the moment, for the writer, the poem *is* a mind.

To prevent the work from disintegrating into its separate parts – scattering sentence-rubble haphazardly on the waste heap – I used various syntactic devices to foreground or create the conjunction between ideas. Statements become interconnected by being grammatically congruent; unlike things, made alike grammatically, become meaningful in common and jointly. "Resistance" began:

> Patience is laid out on my papers. Its visuals are gainful and equably square. Two dozen jets take off into the night. Outdoors a car goes uphill in a genial low gear. The flow of thoughts – impossible! These are the defamiliarization techniques with which we are so familiar.

There are six sentences here, three of which, beginning with the first, are constructed similarly: subject – verb – prepositional phrase. The three prepositions are *on, into,* and *in,* which in isolation seem similar but used here have very different meanings. *On* is locational: "on my papers." *Into* is metaphorical and atmospheric: "into the night." *In* is atmospheric and qualitative: "in a genial low gear." There are a pair of inversions in effect here: the unlike are made similar (syntactically) and the like are sundered (semantically). Patience, which might be a quality of a virtuous character attendant to work ("it is laid out on my papers"), might also be solitaire, a card game played by an idler who is avoiding attention to work. Two dozen jets can only take off together in formation; they are "laid out" on the night sky. A car goes uphill; its movement upward parallels that of the jets, but whereas their formation is martial, the single car is somewhat domestic, genial and innocuous. The image in the first pair of sentences is horizontal. The upward movement of the next two sentences describes a vertical plane, upended on or intersecting the horizontal one. The "flow of thoughts" runs down the vertical and comes to rest – "impossible!"

The work shifts between horizontal and vertical landscapes, and the corresponding sentences – the details of each composed on its particular plane – form distinct semantic fields. (In fact, I would like each individual sentence to be as nearly a complete poem as possible.)

One of the results of this compositional technique, building a work out of discrete fields, is the creation of sizable gaps between the units. To negotiate this disrupted terrain, the reader (and I can say also the writer) must overleap the end stop, the period, and cover the distance to the next sentence. Meanwhile, what stays in the gaps remains crucial and informative. Part of the reading occurs as the recovery of that information (looking behind) and the discovery of newly structured ideas (stepping forward).

In both *My Life* and "Resistance," the structural unit (grossly, the paragraph) was meant to be mimetic of both a space and a time of thinking. In a somewhat different respect, time predetermines the form of Bernadette Mayer's *Midwinter Day*. The work begins when the clock is set running (at dawn on December 22, 1978) and ends when the time allotted to the work runs out (late night of the same day). "It's true," Mayer has said: "I have always loved projects of all sorts, including say sorting leaves or whatever projects turn out to be, and in poetry I most especially love having time be the structure which always seems to me to save structure or form from itself because then nothing really has to begin or end."[5]

Whether the form is dictated by temporal constraints or by other exoskeletal formal elements – by a prior decision, for example, that the work will contain, say, x number of sentences, paragraphs, stanzas, stresses, or lines, etc. – the work gives the impression that it begins and ends arbitrarily and not because there is a necessary point of origin or terminus, a first or last moment. The implication (correct) is that the words and the ideas (thoughts, perceptions, etc. – the materials) continue beyond the work. One has simply stopped because one has run out of units or minutes, and not because a conclusion has been reached nor "everything" said.

The relationship of form, or the "constructive principle," to the materials of the work (to its themes, the conceptual mass, but also to the words themselves) is the initial problem for the "open text," one that faces each writing anew. Can form make the primary chaos (the raw material, the unorganized impulse and information, the uncertainty, incompleteness, vastness) articulate without depriving it of its capacious vitality, its generative power? Can form go even further than that and actually generate that potency, opening uncertainty to curiosity, incompleteness to speculation, and turning vastness into plenitude? In my opinion, the answer is yes; that is, in fact, the function of form in art. Form is not a fixture but an activity.

In an essay titled "Rhythm as the Constructive Factor of Verse," the Russian Formalist writer Yurii Tynianov writes:

We have only recently outgrown the well-known analogy: form is to content as a glass is to wine.... I would venture to say that in nine out of ten instances the word "composition" covertly implies a treatment of form as a static item. The concept of "poetic line" or "stanza" is imperceptibly removed from the dynamic category. Repetition ceases to be considered as a fact of varying strength in various situations of frequency and quantity. The dangerous concept of the "symmetry of compositional facts" arises, dangerous because we cannot speak of symmetry where we find intensification.[6]

One is reminded of Gertrude Stein's comparable comments in "Portraits and Repetitions": "A thing that seems to be exactly the same thing may seem to be a repetition but is it." "Is there repetition or is there insistence. I am inclined to believe there is no such thing as repetition. And really how can there be." "Expressing any thing there can be no repetition because the essence of that expression is insistence, and if you insist you must each time use emphasis and if you use emphasis it is not possible while anybody is alive that they should use exactly the same emphasis."[7]

Tynianov continues:

The unity of a work is not a closed symmetrical whole, but an unfolding dynamic integrity. ...The sensation of form in such a situation is always the sensation of flow (and therefore of change).... Art exists by means of this interaction or struggle.[8]

Language discovers what one might know, which in turn is always less than what language might say. We encounter some limitations of this relationship early, as children. Anything with limits can be imagined (correctly or incorrectly) as an object, by analogy with other objects – balls and rivers. Children objectify language when they render it their plaything, in jokes, puns, and riddles, or in glossolaliac chants and rhymes. They discover that words are not equal to the world, that a blur of displacement, a type of parallax, exists in the relation between things (events, ideas, objects) and the words for them – a displacement producing a gap.

Among the most prevalent and persistent categories of jokes is that which identifies and makes use of the fallacious comparison of words to world and delights in the ambiguity resulting from the discrepancy:

—Why did the moron eat hay?
—To feed his hoarse voice.

—How do you get down from an elephant?
—You don't, you get down from a goose.

—Did you wake up grumpy this morning?
—No, I let him sleep.

Because we have language we find ourselves in a special and peculiar relationship to the objects, events, and situations which constitute what we imagine of the world. Language generates its own characteristics in the human psychological and spiritual conditions. Indeed, it nearly *is* our psychological condition.

This psychology is generated by the struggle between language and that which it claims to depict or express, by our overwhelming experience of the vastness and uncertainty of the world, and by what often seems to be the inadequacy of the imagination that longs to know it – and, furthermore, for the poet, the even greater inadequacy of the language that appears to describe, discuss, or disclose it. This psychology situates desire in the poem itself, or, more specifically, in poetic language, to which then we may attribute the motive for the poem.

Language is one of the principal forms our curiosity takes. It makes us restless. As Francis Ponge puts it, "Man is a curious body whose center of gravity is not in himself."[9] Instead that center of gravity seems to be located in language, by virtue of which we negotiate our mentalities and the world; off-balance, heavy at the mouth, we are pulled forward.

> I am urged out rummaging into the sunshine, and the depths increase of blue above. A paper hat on a cone of water. ... But, already, words. ... She is lying on her stomach with one eye closed, driving a toy truck along the road she has cleared with her fingers.[10]

Language itself is never in a state of rest. Its syntax can be as complex as thought. And the experience of using it, which includes the experience of understanding it, either as speech or as writing, is inevitably active – both intellectually and emotionally. The progress of a line or sentence, or a series of lines or sentences, has spatial properties as well as temporal properties. The meaning of a word in its place derives both from the word's lateral reach, its contacts with its neighbors in a statement, and from its reach through and out of the text into the outer world, the matrix of its contemporary and historical reference. The very idea of reference is spatial: over here is word, over there is thing, at which the word is shooting amiable love-arrows. Getting from the beginning to the end of a statement is simple movement; following the connotative byways (on what Umberto Eco calls "inferential walks") is complex or compound movement.

[...]

In the gap between what one wants to say (or what one perceives there is to say) and what one can say (what is sayable), words provide for a collaboration and a desertion. We delight in our sensuous involvement with the materials of language, we long to join words to the world – to close the gap between ourselves and things – and we suffer from doubt and anxiety because of our inability to do so.

Yet the incapacity of language to match the world permits us to distinguish our ideas and ourselves from the world and things in it from each other. The undifferentiated is one mass, the differentiated is multiple. The (unimaginable) complete text, the text that contains everything, would in fact be a closed text. It would be insufferable.

A central activity of poetic language is formal. In being formal, in making form distinct, it opens – makes variousness and multiplicity and possibility articulate and clear. While failing in the attempt to match the world, we discover structure, distinction, the integrity and separateness of things. As Bob Perelman writes:

At the sound of my voice
I spoke and, egged on
By the discrepancy, wrote
The rest out as poetry.[11]

Notes

[1] "The Rejection of Closure" was included in *Writing / Talks,* ed. Bob Perelman (Carbondale: Southern Illinois University Press, 1985), and, following suggestions from Barrett Watten, in revised form in *Poetics Journal* 4: "Women & Language" (May 1984). More recently, it was anthologised in *Onward: Contemporary Poetry & Poetics,* ed. Peter Baker (New York: Peter Lang, 1996), and extracts appear in *Postmodern American Poetry: A Norton Anthology,* ed. Paul Hoover (New York: W. W. Norton and Co., 1994). The essay has been translated into Serbian by Dubravka Djuric, and that version appeared in *Gradina* 2-3 (1991; Nis, Yugoslavia).
[2] Irigaray, Luce. "This sex which is not one," tr. Claudia Reeder, in *New French Feminisms,* ed. Elaine Marks and Isabelle de Courtivron (Amherst: University of Massachusetts Press, 1980), p. 104.
[3] Grenier, Robert. *Cambridge M'ass* (Berkeley: Tuumba Press, 1979); Bruce Andrews, *Love Songs* (Baltimore: Pod Books, 1982).
[4] At the time this essay was written, "Resistance" existed only in manuscript form. A large portion of it was eventually incorporated into "The Green" and published in *The Cold of Poetry* (Los Angeles: Sun & Moon Press, 1994).
[5] Bernadette Mayer to Lyn Hejinian, letter (1981).

[6] Tynianov, Yurii. "Rhythm as the Constructive Factor of Verse," in *Readings in Russian Poetics,* ed. Ladislav Matejka and Krystyna Pomorska (Ann Arbor: Michigan Slavic Contributions, 1978), pp. 127-28.

[7] Stein, Gertrude. "Portraits and Repetitions," in *Gertrude Stein: Writings 1932-1946*, ed. Catharine R. Stimpson and Harriet Chessman (New York: Library of America, 1998), pp. 292, 288.

[8] Tynianov. "Rhythm as the Constructive Factor," p. 128.

[9] Ponge, Francis. "The Object Is Poetics," in *The Power of Language,* tr. Serge Gavronsky (Berkeley: University of California Press, 1979), p. 47.

[10] Hejinian, Lyn. *My Life* (Los Angeles: Sun & Moon Press, 1987), pp. 14-15.

[11] Perelman, Bob. "My One Voice," in *Primer* (Berkeley: This Press, 1981), p. 11.

JOHN JAMES

PHOTO: AUTHOR'S ARCHIVE

JOHN JAMES was born in 1939 in Cardiff, Wales, and was educated at Saint Illtyd's College. He was founder of the poetry journal *The Resuscitator* in Bristol. He was Arts Council Creative Writing Fellow at the University of Sussex, 1978-79 and, for many years, the Head of Communication Studies at Anglia Ruskin University. In 2002 his poetry was published by Salt in a *Collected Poems. In Romsey Town* was published by Equipage in 2011.

GOOD OLD HARRY

we go to sleep like anybody else
though some awake like bullets
like Romans
munch munch

we aren't Romans
we aren't Americans either
we drink a lot of beer
every nation has its own greatness

we are the English
easy-going & lazy
we sleep pretty well
& when we wake

we are usually pretty thirsty
but not for anything too drastic
you can trust us to be
wooden & quietly proud

of our larverbread
our dumplings
a tomato or two
does no one any harm

& if there did happen to be a bullet amongst us
it would never find anywhere to go
it would just keep travelling through the air
without hitting anything

we have thirty-eight rulers
which is very economical
& they are well protected from
tomatoes on the whole

we call them the cabinet
& cupboard is the name of the land
where everything is in its place again
the natural rulers

behaving like proper gentlemen again
eating a bit of cabbage
& sausage now & then
like the rest of us no doubt

when Edward goes for a walk
we take off our caps & wave them in the air
England is a mature nation
& is not a bit like America

SHAKIN ALL OVER

dip your head in the basin & go
walking the early morning streets late March rotting
from the inside out leather under
dog-tooth green check tweed   Change of Pace
lathering the aching in the rib-cage just got to be
got up & gone I'm not turning away I'm
not looking down I'm puzzling over
the influence of the Stickies I
freely enter your special unit I
don't look down
light drapes flap at the covered windows
touch at the hairs at the back of the hand
the shackling of trucks in the sidings rattle of
curtain rings & soon I hear that crazy fluttering sound
cut through an otherwise absolutely silent room
it's the undertones
of your vibration rattle of pink noise
the poise with which you set your arm alight
our mutual pride &
randomly chosen limited isolation

oh baby what a place to be to disregard
the giant hoard of wounds this tress
in the creaking of copper ear-rings
strands pins & hair-slides & drinking Black Bush
a wave of dark air rolls through the barley
& then you can recall it all &
jet discs rattle as you walk

close to the shifting metacentre
that stripe in your wrist where
the heat is still fresh &
reckless of the edge your face as pale as
quartz or gypsum you're turning backwards
to a new scene as the lozenge dissolves into
crossover & he leisters the jumping thigh
with whatever comes to hand a beer-can amber or zip
the flax caught in the teeth of the comb
& she cries out for once & for all
churning the mud in the pool

                    & later
in the studded augury of bar-tables in the Midland
the immediate future appears strictly female there
will be somebody to talk to & I like to look at you
without somebody watching over us happy &
glorious & even under close escort
the narrow band of pouncing
will be hidden in the skin
                    & we'll be
lapping up a sleek pony
eye rolling over a speckled back zigzag
the stun-shot sways you as you stay on top
they say you'll never be free
but give me your hand here
under the duress of sliding straps
the tang of the white bush
the linen spattered with honey & lager
the dawn spouting with little birds & pressing
a shoulder-blade to the mattress
& there's not so much as a bit of boiling pig
left to be eaten the coverlet hoods you
squinting into the sunlight the talk
twirls at your throat & your hard green
is painted with flashing white
emulsion disinfectant as you apply an orange
towel to the stomach the neck the
perforated magma warm & moist & groaning

STACKING

a little Benzedrine to clear the airways
night gathers itself towards the dawn
the stars zap through my room again

the head was of some importance in all this
though sometimes I think I'm just another little bit
of River Avon driftwood well who isn't?

You are called Michael who is like God
a big sulking bruiser like yourself
o dark lovely phantom we wake again in our separate nations

A VISITATION

driving through softer light south of the Thames
in March the gorse in yellow flower on Ashdown Forest
where lovers kiss in summer time among the bushes

check-in complete the engine cools & the glass flows over
supping alone for tonight on Harveys Best in the Lewes Arms
where once a diva called to slake a thirst in aid of opera

now clerics dispute the way to write the time so out of joint
as far away the rushing air beyond the Severn
rocks the tolling bell beyond Nash Point

a child on the shore scrambles over blue cobbles
looking up to the light above the bivouac in the clearing
before coal slate farm & quarry close

& now a darker figure hunches home against the rain
oh Simone o sea moan

BAUDELAIRE AT CÉBAZAN

your text is traced in burnt sienna
across the span of ochre wall in the old Co-op at Cébazan
& tells me now as it did in my youth
of how the wine sings in the bottles
of the toil & poverty to come of deprivation
calling out to all the honest people of the earth

but even in its glass & vermilion capsule of lead
the wine offers up a song full of light & solidarity to those
who know the solitude between the vines in winter
who know how much it takes on the blazing hillside
who know recurring trouble sweat & pain & the burning sun
bringing to life the vision of their hope not full of hate
but flushed with delight in the throat of a man worn out by work
    at the end of the day
knees under the table deeply reassured & breathing quietly
content to raise a glass he looks into the smiling eyes of his companion
as the echo of the Angelus beats out the song
a little girl is singing in the road outside
weariness falls away at each fresh vegetable sip
something precious returns like a seed cast again
& reaches toward the heavens like this scarce flower

A THEORY OF POETRY

it's very important
to make your lines
bands of alternating colour
running from one side to the other

these will bind
your poem together
like an egg
& make it exist

a reticulated broken edge
the positive ingredients of
banality & repetitiveness preferable
to histrionic virtuosity on most occasions

indeed be dogged
it's better to be expressively dumb
than full of mediocre elegance
& bullshit

& though expensive paper will provide
the physicality your poem needs
you can also apply a bit of boot polish
to transparently tinted over-painting

& in this act of obliteration
performed in a fusion of
calculation cynicism & fervour
the poem will suddenly realize itself

this will subvert any/ deny any/ positive/ negative
narrative reading
& stress the written surface
with all its openings windows apertures leaks

& the incongruity of this literalness & frivolity
will induce in the reader a greater objective awareness

reading is often a big help
but wherever you turn
you are surrounded by language
like the air

you will find the difficulty of working this way
makes you long to be

another kind of poet
however try to be stringent & lean
as well as luscious from time to time

assert the bodily means
by which your poem is written
after all
as the man said
thought
is in de mouf

standing out
luxuriant & mundane
against the subtlety of English light
which is the foil

you can afford to be less cerebral
less intellectual less brilliant less clever
less locked-up-in-your-room-at-night-ish
less reticent & deferential

& more programmed flatter
more all-over more environmental
always
on the prowl

for the materials
of your existence
in the city
which is sometimes what is meant by spirit

get as much as possible into
sitting-rooms bathrooms bedrooms
kitchens & hotels
gardens parks & streets & saloon bars

there you will discover
particular people at a particular time
& in a particular place
these people are the others
without whom you would not exist

avoid the countryside unless
you are going to do something there
like ascend Helvellyn
or shoot a brace of partridge to take back to your kitchen

useful activities include
eating talking & dancing
listening to music (preferably live bands
looking at paintings & undressing
dressing & undressing

do not be too overawed
by wide open spaces
love France by all means
but love your own language first

that way it will be of your own
as well as your own
& will be trusted by neighbours
& summer visitors alike

& thereby your formal relations
untempered by such vulgar considerations as taste
can adjoin
crude broken ridges

overlaid by sluggishly dragged bands of the drab & blaring
can adjoin
delicate smears & caresses
that

TREVOR JOYCE

PHOTO: AUTHOR'S ARCHIVE

Born in Dublin, Ireland, in 1947, TREVOR JOYCE founded the New Writers' Press. His first book was published in 1967 and his *Selected Poems: 1967-2014* was published by Shearsman in 2014, offering a major retrospective of his work. He has lectured in Dublin and Oxford on Classical Chinese poetry after visiting China in 1983. A volume of his translations, *Courts of Air and Earth*, was published by Shearsman in 2008. Trevor Joyce lives in Cork where he founded and directed the Cork International Poetry Festival.

SYZYGY

The Drift

and then there is this sound
that starts with a scarcely audible
rustling inside gold the whisper
echoing within the diamond
grows to take in snatches
from high stars from elsewhere
the disintegrating actions
of clocks so that eventually
you attend to the infinities
of numbers shattering
the shriek that is the change
of several millions

*

the red fish leaping from the mouth
up the cold fresh stream
to the empty source
spilling down
through stars and through
the watching courses of stone
until the fixed mesh abstracts
unerringly each hour
with all its clamouring brood
jerking routinely to the tune

*

noise of concerns sequestered
ultimately will get out
states sundered bleed
surely each to each
by breaking bounds ghosts
traffic through the empty squares
stay mum and the child will answer
even what it must not know
which you realize cannot
but end in an exposure

*

bones may well
bring meat to market
on the road voice lodges
in the fine apparatus
of the throat
there to recount
the exaltation of the source
disclose the system
shock of close attention
and to the distracted hearing
it sounds a history
of all the ordinary
aches we suffer

*

when the thieving
that was well advanced faltered
the imperial presence surveyed
the ordered territories
and declared in measured words
nothing there is savage any more
intelligence and griefs are tamed
rage is reduced in parks
only perhaps along the furthest bounds
may be some dirt a little ghost
and these are even as we speak contained
in three quart jugs

*

sea will fit full of fish of many orders
these will be my varied meat
then surface craft with manifests
for relish weed for bread
abyssal waters for cold broth
though scarcely yet begun
finished already
and to follow
garrisons brief zones
of time and influence
the tempting metals of the air
do not they fly and last of all
bright asterisms will fit in

*

in three quarters now you lie
lacking a fourth
of your voice that flew at once away
not a tremor breeds within the marble orchard
and is it that this simply is either finished or not
or not yet begun
perhaps truly not begun
twig of bone empty still
until there come the words
now quite forgotten whats the air
the sun leans down
and lifts the sea

*

jugs standing sealed and safe exhale
intoxicating the rare earths
dark matter in the air
there is nothing either
fishing the empty grounds
the heavy elements
turn over in their sleep
uncertain ever
when the filling
when the thieving

*

millions are too vast
cruelly they hunt the fields
and bring down awkwardly
the quickening in its course
behind their staggering weakness
leaves devastation and impersonal rage
but even these may be attended to
outside the foundries where they sleep howling
as sometimes fierce and weary
one will sprawl and rest
its harsh throat on your arm
and then there is this sound

*

the tune of several mysteries
what brought this on
the sand whispering
in your veins
what wind of knives could
buzz the nodding headbone blind
what soft amends
the clock disintegrates
the sun does not rise
the dream is mistaken
pulse of sand is
roaring obliterates the red

*

exposure to the extreme
stillness of fire
the flickering rock
disturbs
all night across an empty sky
the high frosts creak
and strike the clumsy sun
leaves on the grass
the shadow of the vaulting white
beyond the bounds
no silence no noise

*

we suffer an old vertigo
that strikes with the first dream
of irresistible winds
across these settlements
thats how the unhinged
thrones and dominations fell
attending as joints lost their grip
throughout the deadlocked centuries
as new wood broke
disordered from old stock
voices were joining
in a round of bones

THE NET

and then there is this sound the red noise of bones
when the thieving sea will fit in three quart jugs
we suffer an exposure to the tune of several millions

fish that concerns may well bring
full of fishers now you lie that was well standing
the extreme old mysteries are too vast

starts with a leaping meat sequestered
lacking sealed and advanced of many orders these will be
vertigo that strikes stillness cruelly what brought this

ultimately scarcely audible from the mouth up to market
faltered the imperial my varied meat then safe a fourth
on the sand with the first dream of fire they hunt

the cold rustling on the road will get out
surface of your voice exhale presence
the flickering of the fields whispering

inside gold states fresh voice
that flew at once intoxicating craft with surveyed
irresistible winds in your veins rock and bring down awkwardly

lodges in the fine the whisper stream sundered
the ordered away not a tremor manifests the rare
the quickening across these settlements disturbs what wind

bleed echoing apparatus to the empty
for relish weed earths territories breeds
of knives thats how the unhinged in its course all night

source surely each within the diamond of the throat
dark and declared for bread abyssal within the marble
across an empty could buzz thrones behind their staggering

grows to each there to recount spilling down
in measured orchard matter waters for cold
and dominations the nodding weakness leaves sky

the exaltation to take in by breaking through stars and through
broth though scarcely in the air and is it that this simply is words
devastation fell attending headbone the high

bounds the watching snatches of the source
there is nothing either finished or not yet begun
blind frosts as joints and impersonal

courses ghosts disclose from high
there is nothing either finished or not yet begun
creak what soft amends rage but even these lost their

stars from elsewhere the system of stone traffic
perhaps truly savage already and to follow garrisons fishing
grip throughout may be attended to and strike the clock

shock until the fixed the disintegrating through the empty
the empty brief zones any more intelligence and not begun
outside the foundries the clumsy the deadlocked disintegrates

squares mesh of close actions
griefs are grounds the twig of bone of time and
the sun sun where they sleep centuries as new

abstracts attention of clocks so that eventually stay
empty still tamed rage is heavy influence
leaves howling as wood does not rise

you attend and to the distracted mum unerringly
elements turn the tempting until there come reduced
broke sometimes fierce the dream on the grass

hearing each hour and the child to the infinities
metals in parks only perhaps along the words over
and weary the shadow is mistaken disordered

will answer even what it must it sounds of numbers with all its clamouring
now quite forgotten of the air do not the furthest bounds in their
pulse one will sprawl from old stock of the vaulting

brood a history not know which shattering
sleep whats the air may be some dirt they fly and last
white and rest of sand is voices

of all the ordinary you realize the shriek jerking
of all bright a little ghost and these are even uncertain ever when the sun leans
its harsh roaring were joining beyond the bounds

cannot but end in aches routinely that is the change
down and lifts the asterisms the filling as we speak contained in
obliterates throat on your arm no silence no in a round

we suffer an exposure to the tune of several millions
when the thieving sea will fit in three quart jugs
and then there is this sound the red noise of bones

NOTE TO SYZYGY:

In the mediaeval musical form known as cancrizans, one or more parts proceed normally, while the imitating voice or voices give out the melody backwards. The name derives from *cancer*, the Latin term for a river-crab or sea-crab, though, as one authority observes, crabs tend to move sideways rather than backwards. This palindromic form came into use in the fourteenth century, and surfaced again in the serial music of our own time.

David Munrow notes, of Guillaume de Machaut's *Ma fin est dans ma commencement*, that "the words of the popular mediaeval aphorism provide less of a text than instructions for performance" and, remarking that in such a canon "the words inevitably obscure the overall symmetry", he elected to go for a purely instrumental performance. In addition to the antecedent voice and the reversed consequent, Machaut had added a third voice which is itself compactly palindromic, moving from its opening to a point, exactly midway in the piece, from which it meticulously undoes itself, note by note, until it rearrives at its commencement.

In the present instance, the drift having been established, the identical voices are intermeshed to weave the palindromic net. This is roughly analogous to Machaut's canon, with the first four voices combining to produce the first line of each composite verse, the second four making the middle lines, and the final four contributing the last line of each verse. Here too, words obscure the symmetry, which was implemented using an industry-standard computer spreadsheet.

You already know a diamond is forever, and that gold is a noble and perfect metal. I can't now recall where to find the clearest account of how ideas of order, of exact cyclical repetition, were first derived from the periodicity of the stars.

According to a citation in the Opies' *Dictionary of Superstitions*, "on the East coast [of Scotland] the salmon is the red fish, the liberty fish, the foul fish, or simply the fish". Sometimes, 'salmon' being a taboo word, it was called 'The Beast'. The weather-cock on the top of St. Anne's Church in Shandon, Cork, is a giant salmon, indicating the importance of the fishing industry of the River Lee to the citizenry of two centuries ago. The tower on which it sits summarises the neighbouring geology in its two faces of silver limestone, two of red sandstone. The turret-clock within is known locally as 'the four-faced liar' as each of its faces renders its own version of the time. In his paper on The Fish of Life and the Salmon of Life, the Swedish folklorist Bo Almqvist documents "the belief that the soul or principle of life manifests itself in the shape of a fish".

The first Emperor of China standardized measures in the subjugated lands, and his successors enclosed exotic game within 'intelligence parks' for hunting and amazement. Sir William Petty in his seventeenth-century Survey imposed a new taxonomic order on the territories of Ireland, completing their reduction. In the final chapter of her Purity and Danger, Mary Douglas describes how "the attitude to rejected bits and pieces goes through two stages. First they are recognizably out of place, a threat to good order, and so are regarded as objectionable and vigorously brushed away... This is the stage at which they are dangerous; their half-identity still clings to them and the clarity of the scene in which they obtrude is impaired by their presence. But a long process of pulverising, dissolving and rotting awaits any physical things that have been recognized as dirt. In the end, all identity is gone... So long as identity is absent, rubbish is not dangerous. It does not even create ambiguous perceptions...."

The line "and then there is this sound the red noise of bones" is from the poem Agua Sexual in the second volume of Neruda's *Residencia en la Tierra*. Sean Ó Boyle records, when discussing The Irish Song Tradition, the curse of an old woman, having finished a song on the wreck of a fishing-boat on its way to the off-shore grounds: "the thieving sea, the thieving sea. They say it will go into three quart jugs on the day of Judgement". The fear that we may suffer a severe exposure was expressed in the financial pages of some paper I've long forgotten.

BHANU KAPIL

PHOTO: AUTHOR'S ARCHIVE

BHANU KAPIL was born in England but now lives in the US, where she teaches at Naropa University and for Goddard College. She is the author of five books of poetry: *The Vertical Interrogation of Strangers* (Kelsey Street Press, 2001), *Incubation: a space for monsters* (León Worls, 2006, reprinted in a new edition by Kelsey Street Press, 2017), *humanimal [a project for future children]* (Kelsey Street Press, 2009), *Schizophrene* (Nightboat Books, 2013), and *Ban en Banlieue* (Nightboat Books, 2016). She can be found on Twitter at @thisbhanu and maintains a widely read blog: www.thesparklyblogofbhanukapil.blogspot.com.

from **BAN EN BANLIEUE**

Where is the group? I hate the group. Where's the group?

"The day of the riot dawned bright and lazy with a giant silky cloud sloughing off above the rooves."

 "The mouth of the riot was a stretch of road."

It is so excruciating to write about these subjects that I take years, months: to write a sentence or two.

The many earth and sea layers make me sick.

In a scene for Ban, pink lightning fills the borough like a graph. All day, I graph the bandages, race passion and chunks of dirt to Ban – plant-like, she's stretching then contracting on the ground.

Three streets over, a mixed group nears a house. Their faces are pressed to the blood-flecked window, banging their forehead on the glass. Inside the house, a woman arranges the meat on a tarp. She tucks and pins the shroud behind its ears with quick-moving hands, looking up from time to time at the crowd that's gathered to watch.

That night, I dream of exiting the subway at the interface a car would make with the M25. The commuters are processing around a semi-rural roundabout, their hands on imaginary steering wheels, their wing-backed loafers shuffling on the tarmac, the black road, like wheels. *Evening Standard*s tucked sharply beneath their arms.

The dream requires something of me.

It requires me to acknowledge that my creature (Ban) is over-written by a psychic history that is lucid, astringent, witty. No longer purely mine.

NOTES FOR BAN:

Ban fulfills the first criterium of monstrosity simply by degrading: by emitting bars of light from her teeth and nails, when the rain sweeps over her then back again.

I like how the rain is indigo, like a tint that reveals the disease process in its inception.

Above her, the pink lightning is branched – forked – in five places.

A brown ankle sparkles on the forest bed.

Genital life gives way to bubbles, the notebook of a body's two eyes. Are you sick and tired of running away? I pull myself up from my knees to clean.

I clean the street until all that's left is a ring of oily foam, the formal barrier of a bad snow.

It snows that April for a few minutes, early in the day. Children walking on the Southall Broadway open their mouths to receive the aluminium snowflakes. In their bright pink and chocolate brown dresses, tucked beneath the heavy navy blue coats, these immigrant children are dazzled by the snow, even though they were born here, a train-ride from a city tilted to receive the light, its sprig bending over in the window of a bank.

Many years later, I return. To place a daffodil on the Uxbridge Road.

Is zinc an element? It's a sheen. Spread it on the ankle of Ban.

Is there a copper wire? Is there a groin? Make a mask for Ban.

Cobra Notes for Ban

I want a literature that is not made from literature. A girl walks home in the first minutes of a race riot, before it might even be called that – the sound of breaking glass as equidistant, as happening / coming from the street and from her home.

What loops the ivy-asphalt / glass-girl combinations? Abraded as it goes? (Friction.) (Concordance.) I think, too, of the curved, passing sound that has no fixed source. In a literature, what would happen to the girl? I write, instead, the tiniest increment of her failure to orient, to take another step. And understand. She is collapsing to her knees then to her side in a sovereign position.

Notes for Ban, 2012: a year of sacrifice and rupture, murderous roses blossoming in the gardens of immigrant families with money problems, citizens with a stash: and so on. Eat a petal and die. Die if you have to. See: end-date, serpent-gate. Hole. I myself swivel around and crouch at the slightest unexpected sound.

When she turned her face to the ivy, I saw a bunch or cube of foil propped between the vines. Posture made a circuit from the ivy to her face. The London street a tiny jungle: dark blue, slick and shimmering a bit, from the gold / brown tights she was wearing beneath her skirt. A girl stops walking and lies down on a street in the opening scene of a riot. Why? The fact of the riot decays around her prone form and at points it rains. In a novel that no one writes or thinks of writing, the rain falls in lines and dots upon her. In the loose genetics of what makes this street real, the freezing cold, vibrating weather sweeping through South-east England at 4 pm on an April afternoon is very painful. Sometimes there is a day and sometimes there is a day reduced to its symbolic elements: a cup of broken glass; the Queen's portrait on a thin bronze coin; dosage; rain.

This is why a raindrop indents the concrete with atomic intensity. This is why the dark green, glossy leaves of the ivy are so green: multiple kinds of green: as night falls on the "skirt." The outskirts of London: *les banlieues*.

SOME NOTES: I WANTED TO RE-IMAGINE THE BOUNDARY.

Perhaps I should say that I grew up partly in Ruislip. The Park Woods that bounded it were rimmed, themselves, with land forms that kept in the boar. I used to go directly to those masses and lie down on them, subtly above a city but beneath the plate of leaves, in another world.

One morning I went there though it was raining.

To soften this scene would require time travel, which I am not prepared to do. I am not prepared to take off my clothes. I am not prepared to charter or re-organize the cosmic symbols of Sikhism, Anglican Christianity and the Hindu faith. One night, I went home, and my hands were caked in dirt and dew. My skirt was up around my ears. My legs were cold. The insides of my eyes were cold. The bath I took, I couldn't get it hot enough. That night, my eyes turned blue.

*

More recently, I've been obsessed with the image of a dark-skinned girl walking home from school.

*

I think about a monster to think about an immigrant, but Ban is neither of these things.

*

Imagine your fingertips are animals that still carry the imprint of a plant memory.

*

And the veins of the nearby plants flood with sugar. The sugar and the ivy and the sky orient to the body of a black woman. Pinned there, scrawled, like a name.

In this scene without depth, she is supine, lifting her arms very carefully then setting them down; an image that is never exhausted, though I write it, and read it, again and again. *Don't hit a black woman.*

With a careful hand.

The slab of pavement tilts; the rain and blood slide off. A dress slides off. A black long hair is carried to Yeading High Street on the sole of a shoe. And it's there, behind *The White Stag*, a skinhead pub on the border with Hayes, that the mouth of the riot opens and begins to sing.

*

It's time to go home. As we coast up the estuary, veering left and north towards Heathrow, I can see the Southall water tower and the golden, balloon-shaped minaret of the Sikh temple. I look down as we fly over and there, close enough to touch, is the setting of *Ban*. I describe the creamy clouds in my notebook, how they emit dark silver beams of light. I analyze my glimpse of the asphalt.

*

Many hours later, I open the window and below me, inches away, is Greenland. I see white mountains slashed with black vertical marks. I try to connect with Greenland. I place one hand on my chest and one hand of the chest of Greenland, ignoring the plastic barrier between us, the sky.

*

In this way, I made the ivy go faster like a carpet or rug I could pull.

Ban turns her head, at some points in that last night, to the wall.

Imagine a cloud of milk as it dissipates, spilled on a London street in an act of protest.

Imagine mica glinting in the oily curd of the pavement.

Imagine that the rough, pink tip of her tongue slips out, extending to the ivy's salt.

What did Ban do that outweighed art? What kind of art did she produce?

*

Returning home, I dig a rectangle of mud and lie down in that, re-moving my clothes and exposing my body with its waist and hips and suitcase of limbs. Above me, in a bush of late summer flowers – white pom-poms with deep green leaves – migrating finches make a choral sound.

*

Radical modernity requires something of me.

An aesthetics of violence.

To write the larger scene.

    *

From one angle, she is slick, like the emerald or indigo tint of ring feathers.

Volatile, starving, the girl's body emits a solar heat, absorbed in the course of a lifetime but now discharging, pushing off. Ban.

    *

What is Ban?

Ban is a mixture of dog shit and bitumen (ash) scraped off the soles of running shoes: Puma, Reebok, Adidas.

Looping the city, Ban is a warp of smoke.

To summarize, she is the parts of something re-mixed as air: integral, rigid air, circa 1972-1979. She's a girl. A black girl in an era when, in solidarity, Caribbean and Asian Brits self-defined as black. A black (brown) girl encountered in the earliest hour of a race riot, or what will become one by nightfall.

April 23rd, 1979: by morning, anti-Nazi campaigner, Blair Peach, will be dead.

It is, in this sense, a real day: though Ban is unreal. She's both dead and never living: the part, that is, of life that is never given: an existence. What, for example, is born in England, but is never, not even on a cloudy day, English?

Under what conditions is a birth not recognized as a birth?

Answer: Ban.

And from Ban: "banlieues."

(The former hunting grounds of King Henry VIII. Earth-mounds. Oaks split into several parts by a late-century lightning storm.) These suburbs are, in places, leafy and industrial; the Nestle factory spools a milky, lilac effluent into the Grand Union canal that runs between

Hayes and Southall. Ban is nine. Ban is seven. Ban is ten. Ban is a girl walking home from school just as a protest starts to escalate. Pausing at the corner of the Uxbridge Road, she hears something: the far-off sound of breaking glass. Is it coming from her home or is it coming from the street's distant clamor? Faced with these two sources of a sound she instinctively links to violence, the potential of violent acts, Ban lies down. She folds to the ground. This is syntax.

Psychotic, fecal, neural, wild: the auto-sacrifice begins, endures the night: never stops: goes on.

As even more time passes, as the image or instinct to form this image desiccates, I prop a mirror, then another, on the ground for Ban.

A cyclical and artificial light falls upon her in turn: pink, gold, amber then pink again. Do the mirrors deflect evil? Perhaps they protect her from a horde of boys with shaved heads or perhaps they illuminate – in strings of weak light – the part of the scene when these boys, finally, arrive.

The left hand covered in a light blue ash. The ash is analgesic, data, soot, though when it rains, Ban becomes leucine, a bulk, a network of dirty lines that channel starlight, presence, boots. Someone walks towards her, for example, then around her, then away.

I want to lie down in the place I am from: on the street I am from.

In the rain. Next to the ivy. As I did, on the border of Pakistan and India: the two Punjabs. Nobody sees someone do this. I want to feel it in my body – the root cause.

POETICS

What is a text? What is the body of the text? Is it too boring to even say that, as if Hélène Cixous never peeled an orange on a balcony then wrote it? That juice. Those pips. I am increasingly thinking of a text as performance instructions for my own: body. Between the first drafts and the last, I want to figure something out. I take the posture, for example, of the bodily life I am trying to describe. For four years, recently paused – with the publication of the manuscript by Nightboat Books in New York – I wrote the story of *Ban*: a girl who lay down in the first minutes of a race riot. A race riot, that is, that unfolded [happened] in my neighborhood – on the border of Southall and Hayes in west or greater: London – London as "shit-hole" – immigrant, industrial London, that is – *les banlieues* – on April 23, 1979. That day, Blair Peach, a teacher from New Zealand and an anti-racism protester – died – protesting the decision of the National Front to hold their annual meeting in a non-white community. In 2010, the inquest – resolved – and the Metropolitan Police – publicly acknowledged that Blair Peach had died as the result of police brutality that day. He died in Ealing Hospital, later that night or the next morning. In this way, writing *Ban* – I wanted to write into the – space? – created by this event but somehow, also, beneath it, running next to it: at the same time. I wanted to work on the body in the riot, but in ways that would allow me to process: the riot: in other ways. What is this other body: deflected, erased before it appears in the document of place? What is a girl – never born – or apparent – in the society she is "born" in: never acknowledged – as a member of that society – thus never, perhaps, completely: born? This is perhaps something – that resolves – as well – upon the question of Englishness. I am not saying this well. "What are the somatic effects of oppression?" This is a research question that a colleague of mine at Naropa University – Christine Caldwell – a pioneer in the field of Somatic Psychotherapy – is working on. Like her, I want to work out the intersection of narrative and non-verbal factors. How the girl's body registers so many different kinds of violence at once, a register I wanted to work out through the contractile-extensive tissues – but also the rough, overlapping and acoustic arcs of the violence to come. The violence, that is, that had already happened. This is logic. Ban lies down because she is, to use and also mis-use Agamben's language of sacrifice in *Homo Sacer*: "already dead." Is the sound of breaking glass coming from Ban's home, or the street? How can writing be the place where you get to work on the inside and outside at the same time? How can I do all of this and still honor the body of the protester who died that day? How can a work that is about trauma, but also the neighborhood, also be the occasion of this – trauma – moving through? At the same time that it preserves a cultural memory of a part of London that is already over-written by more contemporary arrivals and other immigrant histories?

From somatic approaches to trauma – derived from Babette Rothschild, Peter Levine and Pat Ogden – I understood that both the image and the narrative sustain the vortex or loop of traumatic memory. How to de-loop? How to build a counter-vortex? How to stay, longer than narrative or even poetry might [could] demand, with sensation itself? To "complete something that was never completed" in the time it was written [happened] – to paraphrase my friend Laura Vickers, trained through Levine's model of discharge – is something I am very interested in. That is why I want a sentence that shakes. A sentence that takes up the cadence of the nervous system as it discharges a fact. To map this sentence, in other words, to the gesture-posture events.

That is why writing has become the place where I lie down too. In London, and in the mud rectangle in my back garden, a diasporic garden, I have been lying down – to take the pose of "Ban." I want to feel it in my body – the root cause. On a butcher's table in Los Angeles, I got into a meat sack and rotated and glitched: nude, bulky – disgusting – to work on the compound scene. How it feels inside the sack. And to be witnessed: the audience on the grass outside, on the slope beneath Schindler's studio in West Hollywood. This was as part of an event curated upon the theme of voyeurism; I have never forgotten the invitation to embody the things I was [am] attempting to write about.

What kind of book can come from these activities? When my book was accepted, I was frustrated. I wanted to strike a blow. I wanted to strike a blow to the manuscript, something resembling but not repeating the social violence or impacts that obliterate lived form. And so, with a "click, click, delete," I deleted, in the space of three minutes, the end section of the work, thirty-five pages of autobiographical stories.

And how a blow of this kind has its own history and on-going effects. This is why it has to be prose. I want to write an anti-colonial prose: a prose of the body that is destroyed, yes, killed off, yes, but also – revolutionary, with a capacity to become: again: re-figured from its gametes: the colors of the body on the floor. Earth memory, and its unguents. Incarnate form becomes an interest here. I am interested in the residual and concave surfaces and materials produced, as detritus, as imprint, as portal, following: the cardinal act or activity: of writing: something: that resists: its position in a public space: which: is: to be observed, carried forward, or seen.

*

The problem with my accompanying statement, the statement I have just made, is that everyone I am looking to, to derive a framing argument, is white. Part of this is my desire to keep certain conversations, alliances and loves: in turn: unseen. Part of this is extreme habit. I need to re-train.

NATHANIEL MACKEY

PHOTO: AUTHOR'S ARCHIVE

NATHANIEL MACKEY is the author of six books of poetry, the most recent of which is *Blue Fasa* (New Directions, 2015); an ongoing prose work, *From a Broken Bottle Traces of Perfume Still Emanate*, whose fifth volume, *Late Arcade*, is forthcoming from New Directions in 2017; and two books of criticism, the most recent of which is *Paracritical Hinge: Essays, Talks, Notes, Interviews* (University of Wisconsin Press, 2005). *Strick: Song of the Andoumboulou 16-25*, a compact disc recording of poems read with musical accompaniment (Royal Hartigan, percussion; Hafez Modirzadeh, reeds and flutes), was released in 1995 by Spoken Engine Company. He is the editor of the literary magazine *Hambone* and co-editor, with Art Lange, of the anthology *Moment's Notice: Jazz in Poetry and Prose* (Coffee House Press, 1993). His awards and honors include the National Book Award for poetry, the Stephen Henderson Award from the African American Literature and Culture Society, a Guggenheim Fellowship, the Ruth Lilly Poetry Prize from the Poetry Foundation and the Bollingen Prize for American Poetry. He is the Reynolds Price Professor of English at Duke University.

SONG OF THE ANDOUMBOULOU: 40

Asked his name, he said,
"Stra, short for Stranger."
Sang it. Semisaid, semisung.
"Stronjer?" I asked, semisang,
half in jest. "Stronger,"
he
whatsaid back. Knotted
highness, loquat highness,
rope turned inward, tugged.
Told he'd someday ascend,
he ascended, weather known as
Whatsaid Rung... Climb was
all anyone was, he went
on,
want rode our limbs like
soul, he insisted, Nut's
unremitting lift...
Pocketed
rock's millenarian pillow...
Low
throne we lay seated on,
acceded to of late, song of
setting out rescinded, *to
the bone* was what measure
there was. *To the bone* meant
birdlike, hollow. Emptiness
kept us
afloat. What we read said
there'd been a shipwreck. We
survived it, adrift at sea...
An awkward spin it all got,
odd
aggregate. Occupied. Some
said possessed... Buoyed
by lack, we floated boatlike,
birdlike, bones emptied out
inside.
We whose bodies, we read, would be
sounded, *We lay on our backs'*
low-toned insinuance tapped,
siphoned into what of what aroused

us arrested us,   tested us
                    more
than we could bear...
              Loquat
highness's goat-headed look's
  unlikely lure... Lore made of
less-than, more than he'd admit,
                muse
made of wished-it-so... Ubiquitous
  whiff had hold of our noses,
    nostrils flared wide as the
sky. Gibbering yes, that must have
  been how it was, what there
              was
at all a bit of glimpsed inwardness,
  buffeted cloth, bones in black
             light
  underneath... *To the bone* meant
                to the
  limit, at a loss even so,   eyes,
    ears, nostrils, mouths   holes in
our heads a stray breeze made flutes
               of,
  rungs what before had been water,
bamboo atop Abakwa drum... An acerbic
    wine dried my tongue, my top lip
    quivered. "Perdido...," I sang,
               offkey.
So to lament beforehand what would
  happen... Rope what would before have
                been

breath

   *

Whatsaid sip they lit Eleusis
with it seemed. Barley mold
  made them wince... Heartrending
sky, held breath held high
              as a cloud,
  Hoof-to-the-Head knocked hard,
  no bolt from on high but their
  lips' convergence came close,
              Maria

ruing the movement of ships...
   The sunken ship they at times
took it they were on   no sooner
                      sank
   than sailed again. Failed or
   soon-to-fail form, sisyphean
                      rock,
    rough, andoumboulouous roll.
                      Serpent
   wave, serpent wing, hoisted rag
   snapped at by wind. Flag she
   saw he lay bound up in, insisting
     they'd meet again. Lag anthem
   suffused every corner, music
                  more
  the he she saw,   we the escaping
   they, calling out names no where
                   we'd
   arrive would answer to, nowhere the
                  louder
we'd shout

   Dark wintry room they lay shivering
in...
    Late would-be beach they lay
under the sun on...
     Sarod strings dispatching the fog
   from Lone Coast, fallaway shore
   they lay washed up on...
                Their
  lank bodies' proffered sancta
               begun to
    be let go, Steal-Away Ridge
   loomed larger than life. Extended
   or extinguished it,   no one
  could say which,   the soon-to-be
               saints
    arrayed in rows at cliff's edge, our
    motley band uncomfortably among
    them. A school of sorrow seeking

                                        sorrow's
      emollient, albeit seeking may've meant
          something more, older than seeking, re-
          mote coming-to, barely known, of a piece,
                                              beginning
          they broke taking
      hold

BEGINNING "WE THE MIGRATING THEY"

—ANDOUMBOULOUOUS ÉTUDE—

      We the migrating they we
      instigated, those in whose
      name we went. To get where
          they were going and lie
                                  down
      was all we wanted, love's
          choric voices convening,
      caroling home, home ex-
          ploded long since... It was
              up and be gone again,
                                  crab
          shell taken for sun where
      there was no sun, without
          or about hope no one could
                                  say...
      We the migrating they we
      stared out at, prodigal wish to
      burn elsewhere intransigent,
          Stella's high skylight were
                              Stella
          suddenly one of us, she the
      one who said move on...
          They were not the dead
                              but
      dolls of the dead, a dream of
          coming back as we were going.
      Eyes wide but eyes nothing
                              looked

out from, effigies adrift in the
dark...
A parsed pomp and circumstance
it was, not being there but the
   image of being there what they
were caught in, lagleg retreat,
emic
  advance... Inside the bubble
the house became we saw each
   awake one, puffed-up
ascendance all there was of
com-
  ing back, an effigy of each if
not
each its own effigy, each an unlikely remit... Everyone someone
we
  knew, resemblance mocked us,
faces doll hard, clavicles crossed.
Each with a big mouth, telling on
  everyone, what so-and-so did,
what
  so-and-so thought... Who they
   otherwise were we fell away from,
equate their going with our going
  though we did... Who they were
they
  otherwise were, the away what there
was
of it still

—ANDOUMBOULOUOUS ÉTUDE 2—

  We the migrating they they
said come see, lean though
we did and look, sort of see,
  night sky no less remote.
They
were the stars, we the stars'
  understudies, night's
love love's lit recompense,
  night's far fetch a black
well

dipped into, horns' bells
   burrowing in... Would-
be recompense. Ythmic
largesse... Far fling as if all
  touched other, we their

          press
   outward unimpelled...
              They
  the open sea and we the raft
I clung to, left leg scissored
   by hers, we lay ensconced,

            we
  within the we they elicited,
   ours newly raveling out...
Not to be attached we told ourselves, ratchetless advance

         we'd
  come abreast of lip to inquis-
   itive lip, tongue to ingenuous
  tongue... Lift it otherwise was

           no
matter, we drew back, we's rum-
   maging they let go. An exercise
in touch it turned out to be, we
   their would-be stand-in, pre-,

           post-,
  pan-pronominal consort, to see
ourselves we set ourselves adrift...
  Curve and declivity. Protuberant

         hip...
  Immanent ether. Astral dispatch...
  They light's arrival's delay, we
their someday stand-in, ages we

         took
  to reach them, we the migrating
         they...
  That they were roots in the sky
  moving's muse insisted... Star flux...
         Far

star... Far fix

—ANDOUMBOULOUOUS ÉTUDE 3—

We the migrating they their
studies in touch. Stand to
their step, a studied pass, we
stood... Studies inasmuch

            as
we were steps, we stood.
Studies, we ran in place...
Stood what they'd have called

                pat,
we called ready, poised on a
brink we saw fall back...
Stood, we wanted to say,

              what
chance there was were chance
in doubt, step stand's re-
condite flicker, step stand's

               tonic
duress... "Blue Bossa" came
in from a distance, a version no
one had yet heard. Step some
indigenous drift it turned
out, led to export stay, Stella's

             man-
date notwithstanding, end wanting
what would not be there... It
wasn't music but a stepped ab-
scondity, a music before music's

             com-
promise. Stand resisted step, step
stand, moot martyrdom, stride's
true marriage's bossa, Itamar

           and
Stella's vow... A stepped incon-
sequence it might've been,
automatic étude, step's new
nonchalance. They the migrating they the step we took, step

            the
stand we took... Step, we wanted

           to
say, stood in stay's way. It was
the old and new school we were

enrolled in, syllabic devotion
recalling Baul, Bengali, qawwal...

Scat

academy grads though we were, we
bit our tongues, beat back say's excess. They the migrating we were
automatic, step's expected star

so

imminent a winding stairway it was
we were on... School of tangency,
glancing contact... Blasé stasis...

Pre-

tend impasse... Never not to've gone
but be going, a stepped incumbency...
Step's evacuated finality. Finality's

evac-

uated fit

—ANDOUMBOULOUOUS ÉTUDE 4—

We the migrating they translated. Draft meant drift meant
scheme meant sketch. We

the

migrating they were back
in school... Step's incline
toward stride, we stood instructed, theirs the advance

we

were learning, rote's auto-
mata, rail we were bound by
scraped as we verged outward,

we

the magnetic they they turned
out to be... Step fell away
the longer we lasted, collapsed or
contrived itself anew. There

was

a rail one stood at, stuck where
one stood, caught by Stella's
backsides the way she went
forward, celestial mechanics,

cos-

mic rump... Itamar called it
astral, heavenly. Chant the names
  of God we were told... Itamar. Stella. Scrape, caress,

                    ca-
  reen... Crab, sun, bell ad
infinitum... A worked incerti-
  tude it seemed albeit abounding,
insist, "I do believe," though

                    we
  did. Scrape, caress, careen,
    crab, sun were all names.
  Bell another name, they went
on and on... Stride, bubble,

                    rum-
  mage a rut we were caught
in, ran only running in place.
  Rotating stations we worked

                    our
  way loose from, effigy, skylight,

                        scat...
Ran as though pedaling, knees at
  one's chin. Curve, doll, declivity.
  Lip, leg, star. Name after name
sang change, rang changes, God's

                    need
  not to be still... String the names
  as one we were told, one without need of us though they were,

                    we
  the migrating they again going,
    raft, root, tangency, touch... A
studied sputter, spin, step taken

                    up...
Ratcheted, not yet ratchetless. Fix,

                        dip,
  flicker. Brink, stair-
way, step

from **SOUND AND SENTIMENT, SOUND AND SYMBOL**

Senses of music in a number of texts is what I'd like to address – ways of regarding and responding to music in a few instances of writings which bear on the subject. This essay owes its title to two such texts, Steven Feld's *Sound and Sentiment: Birds, Weeping, Poetics and Song in Kaluli Expression* and Victor Zuckerkandl's *Sound and Symbol: Music and the External World*. These two contribute to the paradigm I bring to my reading of the reading of music in the literary works I wish to address.

Steven Feld is a musician as well as an anthropologist and he dedicates *Sound and Sentiment* to the memory of Charlie Parker, John Coltrane, and Charles Mingus. His book, as the subtitle tells us, discusses the way in which the Kaluli of Papua New Guinea conceptualize music and poetic language. These the Kaluli associate with birds and weeping. They arise from a breach in human solidarity, a violation of kinship, community, connection. *Gisalo*, the quintessential Kaluli song form (the only one of the five varieties they sing that they claim to have invented rather than borrowed from a neighboring people), provokes and crosses over into weeping – weeping which has to do with some such breach, usually death. *Gisalo* songs are sung at funerals and during spirit-medium seances and have the melodic contour of the cry of a kind of fruitdove, the *muni* bird.[1] This reflects and is founded on the myth regarding the origin of music, the myth of the boy who became a *muni* bird. The myth tells of a boy who goes to catch crayfish with his older sister. He catches none and repeatedly begs for those caught by his sister, who again and again refuses his request. Finally he catches a shrimp and puts it over his nose, causing it to turn a bright purple red, the color of a *muni* bird's beak. His hands turn into wings and when he opens his mouth to speak the falsetto cry of a *muni* bird comes out. As he flies away his sister begs him to come back and have some of the crayfish but his cries continue and become a song, semiwept, semisung: "Your crayfish you didn't give me. I have no sister. I'm hungry … For the Kaluli, then, the quintessential source of music is the orphan's ordeal – an orphan being anyone denied kinship, social sustenance, anyone who suffers, to use Orlando Patterson's phrase, "social death,"[2] the prototype for which is the boy who becomes a *muni* bird. Song is both a complaint and a consolation dialectically tied to that ordeal, where in back of "orphan" one hears echoes of "orphic," a music which turns on abandonment, absence, loss. Think of the black spiritual "Motherless Child." Music is wounded kinship's last resort.

In *Sound and Symbol*, whose title Feld alludes to and echoes, Victor

Zuckerkandl offers "a musical concept of the external world," something he also calls "a critique of our concept of reality from the point
of view of music." He goes to great lengths to assert that music
bears witness to what's left out of that concept of reality, or, if not
exactly what, to the fact that something *is* left out. The world, music
reminds us, inhabits while extending beyond what meets the eye,
resides in but rises above what's apprehensible to the senses. This
coinherence of immanence and transcendence the Kaluli attribute
to and symbolize through birds, which for them are both the spirits
of the dead and the major source of the everyday sounds they listen
to as indicators of time, location and distance in their physical environment. In Zuckerkandl's analysis, immanence and transcendence
meet in what he terms "the dynamic quality of tones," the relational
valence or vectorial give and take bestowed on tones by their musical context. He takes great pains to show that "no material process
can be co-ordinated with it," which allows him to conclude:

> Certainly, music transcends the physical; but it does not therefore
> transcend tones. Music rather helps the thing "tone" to transcend
> its own physical constituent, to break through into a nonphysical
> mode of being, and there to develop in a life of unexpected full-
> ness. Nothing but tones! As if tone were not the point where the
> world that our senses encounter becomes transparent to the action
> of nonphysical forces, where we as perceivers find ourselves eye to
> eye, as it were, with a purely dynamic reality – the point where
> the external world gives up its secret and manifests itself, immedi-
> ately, as *symbol*. To be sure, tones say, signify, point to – what? Not
> to something lying "beyond tones." Nor would it suffice to say that
> tones point to other tones – as if we had first tones, and then point-
> ing as their attribute. No – in musical tones, being, existence, is in-
> distinguishable from, is, pointing-beyond-itself, meaning, saying.[3]

One easily sees the compatibility of this musical concept of the
world, this assertion of the intrinsic symbolicity of the world, with
poetry. Yeats's view that the artist "belongs to the invisible life" or
Rilke's notion of poets as "bees of the invisible" sits agreeably beside Zuckerkandl's assertion that "because music exists, the tangible
and visible cannot be the whole of the given world. The intangible
and invisible is itself a part of this world, something we encounter, something to which we respond". His analysis lends itself to
more recent formulations as well. His explanation of dynamic tonal
events in terms of a "field concept," to give an example, isn't far
from Charles Olson's "composition by field." And one commenta-
tor, to give another, has brought Sound and Symbol to bear on Jack
Spicer's work.[4]

The analogy between tone-pointing and word-pointing isn't
lost on Zuckerkandl, who, having observed that "in musical tones,

being, existence, is indistinguishable from, *is*, pointing-beyond-itself, meaning, saying," immediately adds: "Certainly, the being of words could be characterized the same way." He goes on to distinguish tone-pointing from word-pointing on the basis of the conventionally agreed-upon referentiality of the latter, a referentiality writers have repeatedly called into question, frequently doing so by way of "aspiring to the condition of music." "Thus poetry," Louis Zukofsky notes, "may be defined as an order of words that as movement and tone (rhythm and pitch) approaches in varying degrees the wordless art of music as a kind of mathematical limit."[5] Music encourages us to see that the symbolic is the orphic, that the symbolic realm is the realm of the orphan. Music is prod and precedent for a recognition that the linguistic realm is also the realm of the orphan, as in Octavio Paz's characterization of language as an orphan severed from the presence to which it refers and which presumably gave it birth. This recognition troubles, complicates and contends with the unequivocal referentiality taken for granted in ordinary language:

> Each time we are served by words, we mutilate them. But the poet is not served by words. He is their servant. In serving them, he returns them to the plenitude of their nature, makes them recover their being. Thanks to poetry, language reconquers its original state. First, its plastic and sonorous values, generally disdained by thought; next, the affective values; and, finally, the expressive ones. To purify language, the poet's task, means to give it back its original nature. And here we come to one of the central themes of this reflection. The word, in itself, is a plurality of meanings.[6]

Paz is only one of many who have noted the ascendancy of musicality and multivocal meaning in poetic language. (Julia Kristeva: "The poet... wants to turn rhythm into a dominant element... wants to make language perceive what it doesn't want to say, provide it with its matter independently of the sign, and free it from denotation."[7])

Poetic language is language owning up to being an orphan, to its tenuous kinship with the things it ostensibly refers to. This is why in the Kaluli myth the origin of music is also the origin of poetic language. The words of the song the boy who becomes a *muni* bird resorts to are different from those of ordinary speech. Song language "amplifies, multiplies, or intensifies the relationship of the word to its referent," as Feld explains:

> In song, text is not primarily a proxy for a denoted subject but self-consciously multiplies the intent of the word.
> ... Song poetry goes beyond pragmatic referential communication because it is explicitly organized by canons of reflexiveness and

self-consciousness that are not found in ordinary talk.

The uniqueness of poetic language is unveiled in the story of "the boy who became a *muni* bird." Once the boy has exhausted the speech codes for begging, he must resort to another communication frame. Conversational talk, what the Kaluli call *to halaido*, "hard words," is useless once the boy has become a bird; now he resorts to talk from a bird's point of view... Poetic language is bird language.[8]

It bears emphasizing that this break with conventional language is brought about by a breach of expected behavior. In saying no to her brother's request for food the older sister violates kinship etiquette.

What I wish to do is work *Sound and Sentiment* together with *Sound and Symbol* in such a way that the latter's metaphysical accent aids and is in turn abetted by the former's emphasis on the social meaning of sound. What I'm after is a range of implication which will stretch, to quote Stanley Crouch, "from the cottonfields to the cosmos." You notice again that it's black music I'm talking about, a music whose "critique of our concept of reality" is notoriously a critique of social reality, a critique of social arrangements in which, because of racism, one finds oneself deprived of community and kinship, cut off. The two modes of this critique which I'll be emphasizing Robert Farris Thompson notes among the "ancient African organizing principles of song and dance":

> *suspended accentuation patterning* (offbeat phrasing of melodic and choreographic accents); and, at a slightly different but equally re-current level of exposition, *songs and dances of social allusion* (music which, however danceable and "swinging," remorselessly contrasts social imperfections against implied criteria for perfect living).[9]

Still, the social isn't all of it. One needs to hear, alongside Amiri Baraka listening to Jay McNeely, that "the horn spat enraged soci-ologies,"[10] but not without noting a simultaneous mystic thrust. Im-manence and transcendence meet, making the music social as well as cosmic, political and metaphysical as well. The composer of "Fa-bles of Faubus" asks Fats Navarro, "What's *outside* the universe?"[11]

This meeting of transcendence and immanence I evoke, in my own work, through the figure of the phantom limb. In the letter which opens *From A Broken Bottle Traces of Perfume Still Emanate* N. begins:

> You should've heard me in the dream last night. I found myself walking down a sidewalk and came upon an open manhole off to the right out of which came (or strewn around which lay) the dis-assembled parts of a bass clarinet. Only the funny thing was that, except for the bell of the horn, all the parts looked more like plumb-ing fixtures than like parts of a bass clarinet. Anyway, I picked up a particularly long piece of "pipe" and proceeded to play. I don't recall seeing anyone around but somehow I knew the "crowd"

wanted to hear "Naima." I decided I'd give it a try. In any event, I blew into heaven knows what but instead of "Naima" what came out was Shepp's solo on his version of "Cousin Mary" on the *Four for Trane* album – only infinitely more gruffly resonant and varied and warm. (I even threw in a few licks of my own.) The last thing I remember is coming to the realization that what I was playing already existed on a record. I could hear scratches coming from somewhere in back and to the left of me. This realization turned out, of course, to be what woke me up.

Perhaps Wilson Harris is right. There are musics which haunt us like a phantom limb. Thus the abrupt breaking off. Therefore the "of course." No more than the ache of some such would-be extension.[12]

I'll say more about Wilson Harris later. For now, let me simply say that the phantom limb is a felt recovery, a felt advance beyond severance and limitation which contends with and questions conventional reality, that it's a feeling for what's not there which reaches beyond as it calls into question what is. Music as phantom limb arises from a capacity for feeling which holds itself apart from numb contingency. The phantom limb haunts or critiques a condition in which feeling, consciousness itself, would seem to have been cut off. It's this condition, the non-objective character of reality, to which Michael Taussig applies the expression "phantom objectivity," by which he means the veil by way of which a social order renders its role in the construction of reality invisible: "a commodity-based society produces such phantom objectivity, and in so doing it obscures its roots-the relations between people. This amounts to a socially instituted paradox with bewildering manifestations, the chief of which is the denial by the society's members of the social construction of reality.[13] "Phantom," then, is a relative, relativizing term which cuts both ways, occasioning a shift in perspective between real and unreal, an exchange of attributes between the two. So the narrator in Josef Skvorecky's *The Bass Saxophone* says of the band he's inducted into: "They were no longer a vision, a fantasy, it was rather the sticky-sweet panorama of the town square that was unreal."[14] The phantom limb reveals the illusory rule of the world it haunts.

NOTES

[1] Examples of gisalo and other varieties of Kaluli song can be heard on the album *The Kaluli of Papua Niugini: Weeping and Song* (Musicaphon BM 30 SL 2702).

[2] *Slavery and Social Death: A Comparative Study* (Cambridge: Harvard UP, 1982).

[3] *Sound and Symbol: Music and the External World* (Princeton: Bollingen Foundation / Princeton UP, 1956), p. 371. Subsequent citations are incorporated into the text.

[4] Stephanie A. Judy. "'The Grand Concord of What': Preliminary Thoughts on Musical Composition and Poetry," *Boundary 2*, VI. 1 (Fall 1977) pp. 267-85.

[5] *Prepositions* (Berkeley: University of California Press, 1981) p. 19.

[6] *The Bow and the Lyre* (New York: McGraw-Hill, 1973) p. 37.

[7] *Desire in Language: A Semiotic Approach to Literature and Art* (New York: Columbia University Press, 1980) p. 31.

[8] *Sound and Sentiment: Birds, Weeping, Poetics and Song in Kaluli Expression* (Philadelphia: University of Pennsylvania Press, 1982), p. 34.

[9] *Flash of the Spirit: African and Afro-American Art and Philosophy* (New York: Vintage Books, 1984) p. xiii.

[10] *Tales* (New York: Grove Press, 1967) p. 77.

[11] Mingus, Charles. *Beneath the Underdog* (New York: Penguin Books, 1980) p. 262.

[12] Bedouin Hornbook (Charlottesville: Callaloo Fiction Series / University Press of Virginia, 1986) p. 1

[13] *The Devil and Commodity Fetishism in South America* (Chapel Hill: University of North Carolina Press 1980) p. 4.

[14] *The Bass Saxophone* (London: Picador, 1980) p. 109

D. S. MARRIOTT

PHOTO: AUTHOR'S ARCHIVE

D. S. MARRIOTT is a poet and critic born and educated in England. He received his PhD in literature from the University of Sussex. His most recent collections of poetry include *In Neuter* (Equipage, 2013) and *The Bloods* (Shearsman Books, 2011). A new critical book, *Whither Fanon?* is forthcoming from Stanford University Press. He is also currently completing a new book of poetry, titled *The Nothing*. His present project, *The Two Freedoms*, is a critical study of C. L. R. James and Jules Marcel Monnerot. He lives in California and teaches at the University of California, Santa Cruz.

LOREM IPSUM Means "Pain itself"

Looking at signs these days
      is all I can manage,
  the world adrift in glances
    as if so much flotsam & jetsam
is where it begins
  and what disturbs the eye is the line
    where boredom subsides
        beneath paneled ceilings.
             It is the ground
pwned because of a lifetime,
    when projects burn
      in thrall to new flames,
  and heads roll as if by magic,
      and the revolution feels cheap
because no longer immaculate (especially in summer),
    maybe because the intervals
           are now much longer, and the signs
  not so easy to read because, like most of us,
they sweat too. The red ones wink at me as I go past.
        Objects are not things.
Among the poplars
      the lynched body does not resemble
an image. Only the other can save us,
      even though he wears funny peasant shoes
and walks like a German. In the cellar,
  a smell of mold and excrement,
and, in the obscure darkness,
the blackened and burnt stumps
of existence. Hard to forget the relief
    of not taking a bath,
  having just gotten reacquainted
    with the swarm inside my crotch.
Things are not objects.
    I lie down in the rain,
        decked out in my tiredness,
  bound to what must be remembered,
what is absent.
    I reach out my hands but see nothing…
In a poem, silence sounds like a gunshot.
To the flame darkness is an offering,
          in the moment
    just before something happens…

[Handwritten annotations:]
- The poem is full of illusions
- Bleakness to the poem.
- A seriousness to the poem
- Outsider tone within the poem
- Lyric violence
- Humanity's effect on the world – polluting the world
- Pain is expressed throughout
- Narrative poem
- Statement of Poetics

RHAPSODE

In a damp crawlspace, he said, no one can hear you,
the poets and translators are of no help. They
have grown bored of the jet-lagged soliloquies,
the irredentist theft. Words burrow like phantoms,
like clever remarks at a 3-star hotel. O croutons!
The dry heave as wastelands burst asunder
and the Lilliputian temples crack,
and somebody whispers: chaos
sleeps on your golden tongue.
Besides, the real terror is here,
the names dropped no longer
fall into the ears of princes,
as everyone knows save the modest Japanese.
The libations duly said I count
my money in my sleep. To whom
do I speak without giving answers,
to whom do I give in without pleas or demands?
I no longer scat-sing. I've tried being laden,
but my lederhosen caught on fire, and train rides
with the masses did not see them
beat their bloodied heads in grief.
          Married to words, divorced from posterity,
I pander ok?: but please don't tell the big guns
with their elegant *néant*. Luckily, there is no refuge
for my nerves, nowhere to be entombed.
I am the exquisite throwback. I will not be
shot in the head, like Lorca, and my little red notebook
will not cause libraries to burn. Property is theft
only for the loyal servant. The blacklists exist
only for those teetering on the brink of fate.
I know all this because of fiction
but can't seem to stop playing the Vaudeville dame.

The next morning as you disembark,
finally home after the vast continents & snow-covered territories,
women turn their heads, men burn
signs at the cemeteries, a one-legged man
runs behind you saying something strange and incomprehensible,
and children shout 'pedo pedo'
at you from across the tracks.
You know that there will be no triumph,

And no rendition of 'Parnassus, my Hokum'.
Just dirty laundry, and the invalid,
who has to move backwards through the gates.

A SEQUEL

1

The world with no evil is evil itself
I burn like a dying sun

The world with no evil is lost to love.
When you look into my past

You see
only

a poor man the worse for drink...
a man who did not want to be loved.

2

Why on this morning
Is every thing hurled against the glass?
Why at this moment
do you sit there
with your hands on your mouth?
A word,
a sorrow mourned for,
is evil, but when it goes unexpressed
does it thirst for love?
Why on this morning
do you look for sights
unleaving, struck brutally dumb?
The birds are corpses, yes,
look at the window
is this not the substance of love?

3

I walk
down a path dark as pitch
I go down the path and hear a girl sing
Fine and Mellow
along the path of emptiness and recollection
along the path of reflection and reminiscence

I touch her bruised flesh
I penetrate her with my tongue
I caress her, but not with love or kindness
Thorns for the awaited journey. Vinegar for the uncommon dust

4

Oh
the glory and the malice
the bodies kept alive by the sacred places
and the leafmeal cleaved
next to burnt out skulls

5

The world is evil, but it is not evil
What it has are fragments and expectation
What it has are genesis and death
I burn, words burn,
a bonfire of leaves in a wood

I will not go back to the shack
I will drink glass after glass
as if it were holy, I will wipe my face with ashes
I will close my eyes, and see my wife and child again
I will bury the corpses with love

ELSE, IN LIMBO

What's happening to me I deserve it
as the pitiful emptiness descends
                              once more
owing for the rent, sucking like a lost boy
            on the melancholy of funfares –

A series of meaningless errands
              the whole place gone quiet
    as penguins perform Shakespeare in a barn,
                        a shooting gallery
to layer the stillness, nobody hurt this time round,
                          and you,
          you're just enjoying the improbable dignity
of the word 'politics'
              (everyone waits for permission to enter
                        the streets of the mind... We
Marxists).

              Whatever today promises I deserve it
as the pitiful emptiness descends
once more
                    I choose my moment
to find a carcass in the woods
                          the smell pungent
          the name an unexpected gift
in days handed over
            to the loud
    creaking of a directionless tiredness,
or the usual hope of a world worlding... but
              instead I drive slowly
              careful not to upset the sirens & the ghosts –
                    the wound is language.

RESPONSE TO RACE AND THE POETIC AVANT-GARDE

What is "avant-garde poetry"? is a question long on answers, if short on consensus. On the one hand, the notion of the avant-garde is invariably seen as a historical category. The history of modernism and the authority of certain authors converge here in a kind of hermeneutic presumption, as if the meanings and values of both constituted readymades. The avant-garde poet emerges as a figure (invariably male, invariably white) that history and culture no longer need to put in question. But on the other hand, those European and American avant-gardes posed a question about the relation between the reading and practice of poetry that goes beyond the category of the avant-garde itself. If certain forms of poetry can now be so easily decoded or read as avant-garde, then clearly the culture industry and the historical avant-garde are now analogous. But somehow if a discrepancy between poetry and the culture industry in part defines what it means to write experimental poetry, then perhaps the very notion of the 'avant-garde' is no longer relevant. It is as if the category of the 'avant-garde' now inheres in such an anachronistic sense of form and value that it escapes reflection, and so is no longer adequate to the very notion. How can this gap be overcome?

When one turns to black avant-garde writers and poets, these impasses (at the level of definition) are inadequate. In the history of black avant-garde poetics, the aestheticization of the term avant-garde was invariably seen as a shibboleth: that is, a refusal to think what the alienation of human being in the modern era was made of. Aimé Césaire was very aware of the dangers of conflating poetic form with hermeneutic readymades – as, for example, in modernist racist discourse, which both historicized and aestheticized race as sentiment and meaning (traces of which can be seen in all white modernist authors). But the double sense of form on which Césaire insists indicates that avant-garde poetry and radical politics are not the same, and that we must explore the productivity of their relation without reducing either to presupposed concepts or categories. The problem is that in the scholarship of modernism and the reading practices which have now become commonplace, black experimental form has itself become a readymade in the marketplace of modernist content, which is precisely why contemporary black avant-garde poetry is only read (often very badly) insofar as it resembles the old modernist boudoir, or imitates the avant-garde's wishful resembling of its own lost discrepancy.

Amiri Baraka, theorist of black musical and political form, revolutionized how we should understand their relation by suggesting

– after years of close study of black music – that chiasmus rather than dialectic was the exact form of black avant-garde poetry. This was avant-garde criticism with a capital A, but only in an existential and analogical sense. In fact, Césaire was much more radical and expressed his insights into revolutionary black poetry via a language of the unconscious in which syntax rather than lexis, nonsense rather than sense takes precedent. His belief was that in order to be modern (and in a way which is never simply, or historically, avant-garde) the black poet had to become a scientist of the marvelous in which radical unintelligibility is not so much the exception as the rule. Césaire's immense productivity consists in creating a poetry of events that does not have form or content as its end, but is rather the pursuit of their irremedial alienation. Instead of claiming, as the various European avant-gardes did while reading Marx, say, or Freud, that he was producing a new dialectics (of culture, or meaning), Césaire claimed that poetic production was productive because it consumed knowledge. Or rather–that it was the 'poetic' itself that was productive, often against the express conscious and political wishes of the poet. As Césaire explains in his famous letter to Maurice Thorez:

> I'm not going to confine myself to some narrow particularism. But I don't intend either to become lost in a disembodied universalism.... I have a different idea of a universal. It is a universal rich with all that is particular, rich with all the particulars there are, the deepening of each particular, the coexistence of them all.

I can think of no better statement of why black avant-garde poetry should not be reduced to the usual modernist dilemma of aesthetics versus politics, or why its attentiveness to richly diverse modes of being should not be seen for what it is, i.e., a politics of the word defined by an incessant fidelity to creative negation. If this is a fidelity which can too easily be appropriated by the forces of cultural industrial control, that is because the value of its creation coincides with the terrible universal insecurity that is both its origin and truth, but one that also defines how each particular gives on to the world a newly embodied universal which provides for and bears along its own richness of meaning. As a result, Césaire remains for me the incomparable world-historical producer of black poetic form and one who continues to haunt.

CHRIS McCABE

PHOTO: JACK GOFFE

CHRIS McCABE's poetry collections are *The Hutton Inquiry, Zeppelins, THE RESTRUCTURE* (all Salt Publishing) and, most recently, *Speculatrix* (Penned in the Margins, 2014). He has recorded a CD with the Poetry Archive, and was shortlisted for The Ted Hughes Award in 2013 for his collaborative book with Maria Vlotides, *Pharmapoetica*. His plays *Shad Thames, Broken Wharf* and *Mudflats* have been performed in London and Liverpool and he has read his work at venues including Southbank Centre, the British Library, the BFI, the Whitechapel Gallery and the Wellcome as well as performing at festivals such as Latitude and Ledbury. He is writing a series of creative non-fiction books that aim to discover a great lost poet in one of London's Magnificent Seven cemeteries. This began in 2014 with *In the Catacombs: a Summer Among the Dead Poets of West Norwood Cemetery* (which was selected as an LRB Bookshop book of the year) and was followed in 2016 with *Cenotaph South: Mapping the Lost Poets of Nunhead Cemetery*. He is also the author of *Real South Bank* (Seren, 2016) and his short story *Mud* has been published in the Galley Beggary Digital Singles series. With Victoria Bean he is the co-editor of *The New Concrete: Visual Poetry in the 21st Century* (Hayward Publishing, 2015).

 # 555: GEORGE W. BUSH

hacking memes   okay
gave up the ruddyred liquor
couldn't control the leaside road
gave up too slavering 60s' pipedreams
follow : boots to shins shirts three quarter
the texan way   what's under as important
as what's on top
follow me up from toe to tonguetip
camerastop to describe
each pitstop to armpits
easier than leaders' names
lioncourage of my face can't be aped
the rest is all in the mind.
him   crawfished stiff
stiffing the world
I won't make do with symbolic
brains homes hearts
balloondrifting & shoeclicking
believe me folks   when I get to oz
I'm going to look inside that smoked machine
'til I find the real thing

AXIS IS

7 July 2005

faceless threat of terrorism
with still enough lips to eat
I ran to find your messages
(mobile networks jammed)
it was eating my carrier bags

a monster that can't be staked
soft accent of evil, but those
were real human hands
that touched the bus

five sticky fingers tack tack tack
and a sucker of sweat

I went to buy a remote control

in one hand she held a mobile
phone, the other was in
a bargain bin: 'James is okay
but he can't get home'.

I realised we hadn't spoken.

a monster without a face
eating my bags as I ran
asking me as I walked :
axis is as axis does.

52 people who left for work
names on credit cards
of no identity –

at the hub of news & content
page 110 said
Blasts Won't Shake UK Economy

A 98p VOICEMAIL MESSAGE TO BLAISE CENDRARS

Dear Blaise,

They still shout outside my door : get your Nokias out for the
lards. Take this take on progress : last night I watched *The
Greatest Hits of R.E.M.* & Stipe's hair grew back song-by-song. A
culture of bacon & beans over here : I dropped a rasher on the
dresser & wiped it clean on my jeans. She said her brain had
turned to mush, I must soak my peas. How does the brain
work (excuse me, a white van just pulled up). Mine not so
much pulp as wild knitted plaque. We tried to do a Sunday
escape to Paris 1913 on the Trans-Siberian Rail but the icecream
man did his jingled route & broke the dream. It was
like Dagenham was a trinket box & the lid, lifted. Blaise,

you're breaking up. Are we very far from Montmartre, she
asked. Yes Ness I said, this is still Becontree Heath. Take this
take on democracy: they strut a fetish around the doors of
the gig because they won *free* tickets. How I was always
Nature Boy, she knows that Blaise. It makes such sense that
French tag for toad: *crapaud*. In September we're going to
ensnare one – a toad that is – & drop its dolloped hop on the
grave of Apollinaire. We'll tie coloured balloons to Beckett's
tomb. I hope you can be there. Take this take on desire : he
fell in love at just sixteen but she married the local undertaker
at a turn. I seem to get more confused as the week ties
up, like an actor's wife turned on by the roles he plays. And
those poems you gave to us – thanks for those. Blaise you're
breaking – Blaise you're gone

JACK STRAW

John Whittaker Straw, Labour politician, would not pardon
the Pendle witches, not in 1998, or any time after.
John Whittaker Straw, one of the Blair Witches,
who changed his name to that of Watt Tyler's
sidekick, or pseudonymous fiction, Jack Straw.
A name like Black Kat or John Bull, a crack in folklore.
John Whittaker Straw may have stood With Gordon Brown
as John Rakestraw, or Rackstraw, as Jack was known,
and address the House to say 'duplicitous' to weapons
of mass destruction. He did not do that under the name
of the Jack he aped, who was a preacher, or a priest, inciting
a crowd to rise like revenants from an Essex churchyard.
John Whittaker who changed his name to one who confessed
his plans to kill 'all landowners, bishops, monks, canons & rectors
of churches'. His plan to burn down London.
Had Jack watched his daughter violated by a tax collector
and in his anger seethe to see metropolis burned black?
'He Jakke Strawe & his meinee', Chaucer wrote,
'wooden any Fleminge kill'. From Jack's Straw Castle,
a hay wagon on Hampstead Heath, the rebel preached.
John Whittaker Straw took that Jack then served like milk
for thirteen years the Labour cabinet.

A NEW WAY TO PAY OLD DEBTS

> Spoken by Alworth in rage against
> Overreach, an aspiring landowner whose
> daughter Margaret he has fallen in love
> with. Overreach is determined for his
> daughter to marry the noble Lord Lovell.
> We are here, Drury Lane, 1621.

Toenails blàck in the petty càsh   burnt pennies
    You cormorant   You catspaw   You cruel
extórtioner   beer & debt gnaw my endórphins
    You brach   You dogbolt   You hellhound
    beats & kicks him   ThIS IS THe ANNiversArY
of SELlINg YoUR SoUL TO H+t INsURAncE ApR
549%   This credit card you don't want has your name
on it   it can be couriered by Three Creditors
    You lean skull   You privy creature   You sláve
to meat   Fill this glass with whíte froth & watch me
knock it off   You   buyer   You drudge
      You ditch to what's inside   Enter "human skulls in
the Thames"   ERROR 404   You hedge-funders to our
best Players   You bond-slave   You cur

    You son of incest   You cherrylipped mannequin of
blàck plots   After The George & the youth you saw
in my face   outside the Barclays where I signed my
name like a hair in whítebroth   *buttermilk cheeks*
      where I knew, at the Strand, there was no money in
poetry   but heard   in the truth of gráves   *after*
drinkings, when you lodg'd upon the Bankside   there
is   NEVER   any   poetry   in   càsh

CHANGING ALL THAT IS METAL IN THY HOUSE TO GOLD:
THE POLITICAL AS PERSONAL

I'm returning to Russell Square, except I was never there. At least not on the day I wrote my poem 'Axis Is', on the 7th July 2005. I wrote it five hours after the three bombs were detonated on the underground, skimming the surface swamp of confused media which I'd followed closely since being refused access to London's rail network that morning.

The poem's final line was its ignition, a response to a squib of cold resistance in a Teletext news headline, published in Pac-Man-sized pixels in the fizzle-out of adrenalin. It's at moments like this that you see the media as it really is, reality beyond its comprehension, railing with cryptic resilience like Poor Tom on the heath. This was the kind of pseudo-intellectual reporting which was the opposite, and sister to, *The Sun*'s later account that a man had been seen to 'explode' on the bus at Tavistock Square. At both ends of the spectrum reportage dehumanises, turns the individual to a stock market point or a half-processed Pokémon.

In that moment of writing the poem, at around 3.30 pm, I'd just found out that my wife, Sarah, who was working at Canary Wharf that day, was safe. I realised then that the urgent facts of information – who and how many had died, where relatives should to go to find out details of what was happening etc – were already being replaced with interpretative commentary. With banking at the top end of concerns. 'Blasts won't effect UK economy' the headline ran, with a slight typo that I retained in my poem.

At that moment of the headline being published on television screens across the UK the numbers of known dead was still in the forties, with the final number of fifty-two yet to be known. The actuaries were exploring the economic repercussions of the explosions before the bodies had not only cooled but been counted. 'James is okay', I'd heard a mother speak into her phone earlier that day, 'but he can't get home.'

I'm returning to Russell Square even though the Piccadilly Line train – the third to be blown up that day – never made it there. The explosion went off about a minute after it left King's Cross (it takes one minute and fifty-four seconds for the tube to travel between those stations, I've timed it). The Piccadilly Line is a deep-level tube, the effect of its depth being to compact the repercussions of the detonated bomb. The most visible, and obvious place to commemorate those who died that day would be a few minutes walk away at Tavistock Square, where the bus explosion took place an hour after the tube attacks, killing sixteen of the fifty-two people.

I walk past the first site of the Faber and Faber offices, its residence before the business moved to Queen Square and then to its current location at Great Russell Street. When Faber offered to publish the work of the Beat-inspired, deeply troubled poet Harry Fainlight, Fainlight's response was to light his manuscript and push it through the publisher's post box. Xerox in a jumpsuit of flame and shadow. An inversion of the known conundrum of the rejected poet. Fainlight was made the offer, sucked up the detail and spat it out like an owl pellet. The tiny skull of poetic possibility squirming in the torn rags. He rejected the publisher: not many can say that.

'Axis Is' is one of maybe ten poems I've written that I can perform from memory. A reclamation of personal language against Bush and Blair's morality drama. The title of the poem was drawn from Bush's axiom that he was waging war on the 'axis of evil'. I'd mined this material at length for my first collection, *The Hutton Inquiry*. There had been a weird tension building since the decision to go to war on Iraq was made, arguments combining the registers of post-atomic conflict, *The Wizard of Oz* and the English medieval epic. This was Blair's version in any case: we fall asleep in a field one day and wake up transformed, finding danger closing in. Beowulf. Plowman. Pearl. 'A monster without a face' I described it in the poem. This monster could be anything, whatever was needed to confirm Blair in his role of knight errant. 'Axis Is' was one of the few poems in my second collection *Zeppelins* to be written completely in lower case: a riposte to those buccaneering news headlines.

'Axis Is' is a poem of the fringes. It could only have been written in Dagenham, in personal crisis, using the automated neurosis of quick media as its source. It's easy for me to feel the rhythm of this poem in the pacing I did that day, up and down the tiny sunlit hall, waiting for the networks to clear so I could be sure that Sarah was okay. That tiny terrace, locked like a living cell in the network of cells that make Dagenham's empire of terraces was where we lived, all in all, for nearly a decade. The house we first brought Pavel home to, laying down the car seat he was in (though we didn't drive) like a basket of fruit. I had no trouble writing poems there. Dagenham was a project in modern living which had been mostly farmland until as late as the 1930s. It had the right kind of balance between human life and industrial and natural landscape to provide the material for the kind of projective, place-responsive poems I was set on writing. The pubs were without pretension, and cheap. You could sit all afternoon and listen. Iain Sinclair wrote to me years later saying that the poems I'd put together for *Zeppelins* confirmed what he'd predicted years before, that the poets of the future would come from Dagenham. A long way from afternoons dappled by the oaks of Russell Square, languorous agenda papers stippled with biscuit crumbs and reams of submitted poems to consider, verses aligned like suburban tennis courts and enough tea to keep you seated until the bladder spasms.

Three years later Russell Square became a retreat from a personal crisis. My son, Pavel, was born with one functioning kidney and his health returned us repeatedly for surgery at Great Ormond Street. Sleepless nights laid out flat on a pullout bed in a Victorian ward. Nurses hovering like orbs on the fringe of consciousness, dosing out liquids and scratching numbers onto charts. Uncertainty and claustrophobia. One morning before Pavel's surgery, I recognised the surgeon who was going to operate on him later that day. Relaxed, he walked through the doors of the hospital in casual clothes, coffee in hand. It was like we were condensing our whole world for handover, giving it to this man we didn't know. It was a rare moment of possibility: maybe after this I could be of *use*, retrain as a doctor, help people. Then four hours later I'm cutting and refining the experience into the cubist logic of a poem. The only positive use I've ever been able to make of experiences I'd rather forget.

Throughout those years of visiting the hospital, Russell Square was the *other*, separated by Southampton Row from the Victorian ghosts of the hospital which was embedded like a cheese in the sniffy rind of Bloomsbury. Southampton Row served a similar function to the Thames: a crossing place symbolising pilgrimage and arrival. On an hour's release from the hospital I'd stride through the British Museum with Pavel on my shoulders, slipping into a single stream of time with Aztecs and Incas. A sanity-saving tactic which allowed us to see ourselves at distance, atoms in time, passing through on our way to a happier place. The poems written during the years of living in and out of Great Ormond Street went into my third collection THE RESTRUCTURE. Mental illness was an outcrop of the experience. As was the financial recession. But set against both was the energy and linguistic inventiveness of my growing son.

2

When I was putting THE RESTRUCTURE together it started to make sense to think of my first three collections as a trilogy. What begins in *The Hutton Inquiry* with poems about the war in Iraq moves forward in *Zeppelins* to include poems about the inevitable backlash to the war, the July Bombings and the tortures of Abu Ghraib. THE RESTRUCTURE addresses the financial collapse that turned Blair's

summer of love into a winter of depleted serotonin. Not unrelatedly,
I hit a crisis of depression, which the poems also document. The political is always personal in my poetry, it's the only way I've found
to make global politics bear my fingerprint. The experiences in the
hospital in Bloomsbury and listening to people on public transport
created the textures for 'THE RESTRUCTURE' sequence itself:

> it's important to listen for once
> THE RESTRUCTURE wants to think its world in you

A large number of the poems I've found myself able to produce
couldn't have been written without the weight of external politics pressing down on me, but the poems resist global messaging
through being written from the perspective of the personal moment,
through a personal style. There are other places to go for chants,
soundbites and collective leftist ripostes. I think of these poems as if
structured through a double helix with one spine documenting political events, twisting across another spine of simple captured experience. Poems that turn background white noise into foreground,
then return it to background. At that point in my writing life how
could I know whether what was happening in the world, or happening to me in Bloomsbury, was the cause of my serotonin drop?
My poems found lyric in it all, without distinction.

3

Writing *Speculatrix* introduced a new strand to my poetics.
Where the earlier poems had listened-in to the distortion of media
and conversations broken by tannoy announcements on the tube, I
now found a new source of minable language in Jacobean drama.
I hadn't considered at such length before how contemporary poetic language can be sharpened through proximity to early modern
English and the poetic work of long dead poets. These poets had
informed my work but I hadn't had the awareness, or perhaps confidence, to bed-trick them. The affect was like the luminance contrast on a visual display, whereby the image is sharpened through
increasing the difference between values: the bilious black palette
of Jacobean registers sharpened contemporary language. The displaced and virtual realm of early modern pleasure-seeking was
forced to meet the quick displacement of the web. Globe culture
flattened to a handheld screen. Meet me on the bank of the Thames,
meet me there and be ready. No: just Tweet me.
Writing these poems involved carrying a copy of an original play
around the city in readiness for the moments of lyric flight that trav-

elling through London has always excited in me. The early modern text was disposable beyond the completion of my poem. At the moment of writing, the language of the play would reveal itself as if through a synced-in channel and became an adaptable parable to the hysterical drive of human life in the current capital. When London elicited its sonatas in me – as it always does – the text of the play was there, like a slab of white flesh ready to be transplanted into the poem taking shape on my phone. Somehow the right phrase or word was always there in the text of the play, waiting to be found, which I then italicised in my poem for ease of reference and also for effect. Italics are quicker on the eye, have the jaggedness of a rapier cut. Working in this way removed the narrative completely from the original play, which was fine, as that wasn't what I was interested in: I was seeking the taut music of the lyric.

Part of my poetic consciousness is embedded in the reality of the poetic self as other to functioning society. The poet as the last custodian of language, on the fringes of capital landfill, and somehow free of it. Watching with a hysterical nerve in the jowl. The poet as the only sane one in the theatre of poseurs, sidelined to the wings. But I'm part of that slovenly mass too, the unhealthy pace of London, a slippery aspirant in next year's Burberry, ferrying labour like cattle, prompted by a Google alert. And there was also, perhaps, something in the poems I was writing that took a barbaric approach to the thing I care about most in my writing: literature itself. After all, to make the poems work I had to disembody Jacobean drama with a scalpel. This was very strange to experience: the disgust I held for capital greed became embedded into the speed and tone of my own practice as a poet. I was the one – the poet – getting what was needed, ruthlessly, through any means possible, cutting apart Webster and Jonson. Mind the fucking gap.

Each of the poems in the *Speculatrix* sequence was written from the perspective of a character from one of the plays; Vindice; Duke of Brachiano; Alsemero; Alworth; Lovewit; Jasper; the Duchess of Malfi; Leantio and Duke Altofront. But these are no dramatic monologues in the sense of seeking character distinction, each of the speakers are reduced by bigger factors, reduced to bits by a superstructure that bewilders them – which prevents them from reaching their most intimate desires. The political as personal. All human yearning for touch, texture, ingestion, is stalled by invisible skies: capital, class, gender. I had this vision of the characters I spoke in – the real character of the actor, that is – suddenly being thrown from the stage and onto the streets of London. I enacted this by setting each of the poems in the location of its first performance. There is a doubling of the metaworld here: the invented play is taken over by the real people who acted in them, now turfed out of time and place, and into the gutters of London. They still try to speak as their character, wearing the character's clothes, but also curse the playwright who has allowed for this situation to unfold ('John Marston how could you do this to us?'). The prosperous must experience London as the poor do: as voyeurs of consumption, rags in a wind of digits, the most eloquent voices of the city, beyond the encoding of any device.

These poems forced me to address the issue of form head-on. I've always made up my own forms, led by the ear and the internal structural possibilities of a poem. I can often see the poem's form before I write it, like a shadow behind the eye, before the text is laid. The crosswise placement of cadences which will knit it together. As much as I love the free, open lines of Apollinaire, the mulch of my poetic accent is always with the Anglo Saxon. In the *Speculatrix* poems I was drawn towards creating a tension between the music of the lines and their physical shape on the page. I found the solution in contrast; through the technique of using rising and falling accents over words to emphasise the music within the lines, and presenting the poems in what might appear to be chunks of prose but are actually prose sonnets. I used a dividing line at the end of any poem that ended on a fifteenth line to separate it from the sonnet structure. This form allowed me to bring the many disparate strands of the poem into cohesion, to give some order to the wandering players out on the streets of London and the floating shreds of language registers. What appears to be blocks of data is linked through music to the tightness of the early modern sonnet. Form can synthesise chaos.

This felt like a new approach in my work, distinct from the trilogy of the first three books. A different approach in form, tone and subject. A new way to pay old debts. But it wasn't completely new, not quite, and I've come to see the poems differently since their publication. Feedback from reviewers and readers has forced me to reassess what I thought I was doing in these poems, and where they sit within the context of my earlier work. There is the theme of money, for example, the lance of capital, which has been there since *The Hutton Inquiry*, the first word of which is the subtitle: 'PAYDAY'. 'This night I'll change all that is metal in thy house to gold' Jonson writes in *The Alchemist*. My poetry has always been written from the sidelines of the aspiring classes in that sense, an attempt to foist my DNA, and experience, into the ink of the page.

4

Jack Straw was easy to miss back at the time of the decision to go to war on Iraq. A stretched and sedated Moomin, talking to camera as if the world had been muted. Sixteen years later I discovered by chance that he'd actually named himself after Peasant's Revolt insurgent Jack Rakestraw, or Rackstraw as he was known. The force of the youthful leftist had dispersed into cold water like air from a lilo. Robin Cook, House of Commons leader and one of the highest profile figures in the Labour party at the time, resigned over the incident. Cook died a year later, his family deciding on his own words for his epitaph: *I may not have succeeded in halting the war, but I did secure the right of parliament to decide on war.* The kind of un-ironed openness we've not seen until Corbyn, who would, I've always thought, make a decent librarian.

At the time of writing 'Jack Straw' is a new poem, written five years after the *Speculatrix* poems and over a decade after those in *The Hutton Inquiry.* 'Jack Straw' surprised me by fusing together the themes of *The Hutton Inquiry* with this new approach of using the language of previous literature. The poem brings together my interest in the early modern with my writing about the Iraq War. I never thought that would happen. These politicians who excuse themselves from the Darwinian clearance house, their prostatic secretions beginning with a walnut-sized arousal and ending with nerve gas in a stranger's face. The Labour cabinet's nuzzling of Bush prefigures Theresa May's coveting of a special relationship with Trump. Men in suits, nurturing a metastasis in their drying balls, flashing for the President, exposing far-off victims to their fantasies. Justifying apocalypse under the false pagoda of the prospective greatest good for all. Pleased with the flight paths of their career but confused by the vapourtrails. Greased hearts racing like apoplectic peasants.

GERALDINE MONK

PHOTO: ALAN HALSEY

GERALDINE MONK has been writing poetry since the mid-seventies. Her major collections include *Interregnum* (Creation Books), *Escafeld Hangings* (West House Books) and *Ghost & Other Sonnets* (Salt Publishing). *The Salt Companion to Geraldine Monk*, edited by Scott Thurston, appeared in 2007 and in 2012 she edited the collective autobiography *Cusp: Recollections of Poetry in Transition* (Shearsman Books). Her latest collection *They Who Saw the Deep* was published by Parlor Press / Free Verse Editions.

Monk has been the recipient of many awards and her most notable commissions are *Hidden Cites* for The Ruskin School of Art, Oxford University, *Reworking the Title*, Museums Sheffield and *The Three Stepping Stones of Dawn* for the BBC's *Dawn Chorus Celebration*.

She is an affiliated poet at the Centre for Poetry and Poetics, Sheffield University.

PENDLE

(brooding dislocation)
limits
push
over
iced Pendle water   warm English beer
sipspeed
under
grazing
headlights
catch
odd eye
startles
hearts
odd creatures
sometimes missed

sometimes hit
warm runny things
cold unmoving tarmac
(lascivious sprawl   conscious and livid)

THE GREAT ASSEMBLY & FEAST

Loped & strungalong the calmquake forests of astonished branches.
Crissed rivers teeming spring. Much upona. Clambered hummock
and dung and sleeping animal-hill. Ganged Malkin Tower to fest and
murder plot. Grow semtex – a likely. Banged up L/caster (via forbid
Trough). Run proof. Bolt-stare of stone. S'easy. Blow away – fuft.

Tread flesh & flagstone. Skip cobble nicks. Go dizzy hand-linked
rounds. Jitter. Belly knot. Brewst hysterical terror. Turn mindlimbs
out their course. Spasmics. Consort then with demons. Drift deep.
On rafts of fish skins.

They glamour. They bleed. Deceive. Imperfect animal. Barely
once removed from. Come. Snake woman. Wolf woman. Whore
woman. Witch. Deformed and depraved mother woman. Worry-
to-death woman. Howl all night under reeds. Girlgrace. Blood
to nothing. Love seed. Nether smell. Pro terra. Contra mundum.

More than meat or drink.   Better than stars and water.
Words birthed.   Made flesh.   Took wing.   Horrids and
enormities.   Chantcasters.   Daubing lunarscapes.
Stench polluting skies.   Broadcasting vile tales.   The
abortus embalmed.   Babyface on the chopping block.

Death of Our Perpetual Succourpap.   Swingalong with
Satan.   Donkey cock.   Hot crosses.   Jack Nazarene and
the Five Bleeding Wounds of Passion sing in a-boo.
Sad-Jack-J in a Waa-Waa.   Twisted tales.   Tired.
Abominations and filthiest excess.   Words took flesh took
flesh.   Winged backwards.   Shock of hind sight.   Foreflight.
Special-speech.   Litanies.

Tower room turned.   Video shift.   Zoom clausto.   Hanging
rafters.   Meat hooks.   Unread omens.   Mills about.   Satanic.
Dark.   Heaving parox.   Over come in waves.   Passion nudge.
Crushed smiles.   Lips slip around stigmatas.   Witchmarks.
Wild web.   Slip on woman's slippers.   Man-made.   Thinly
spun man's skin.   Lurex.   Spindle pricks.   Weavers.   Spider
rites.

Hare spit fire.   Green glass gob.   Trine.   Sextile.   Convergence
of Time.   Mother winders out your moons.   Mashing tea.
Sucklers.   Crating hurtables.   Webbing exquisites.   Gagging
jeers.   Flouting magnificence.   Slobbering warmth and familiars.
Tib.   Dandie.   Fancy.   Ball.   Mock transfixions.   Giving up the.
Ghost.

ALICE NUTTER REPLIES

[handwritten: It's a reply]

Alice through the centuries
of unrecorded silence. *[handwritten: We know what's at stake]*
That is my story: *[handwritten: Pushing back - bold poem]*

[handwritten left margin: Reminds us of children]

Your bedtime night-night *[handwritten: The poem changes in tone]*
fairy tales fill
cells *[handwritten: Sarcasm and mortality]*
with injury
hurt the heart and *[handwritten: Using language of violence and confinement]*

[handwritten: very angry]

bleed the kick from
words
hanging limp from my
lips
those perfectly wrought
curlicues of sentences
dripped to my feet.

[handwritten: Harsh consonants; can feel the anger within the sound]

[handwritten: we need to bring our own meaning to the Poem]

Sound spirited away. Unwrit
forever
my inconvenient reasoning
my one stab at life
cut....

GHOST SONNET 29

[handwritten: The uncertainty]

A second glance and then another
[handwritten: Unnatural line breaks]
Swift. Was it me or? Were my
Eyes in the back of my beyond-head
Reeling a bird-riff? I can't rightly
[handwritten: The mumbling sound created by the 'r']
Remember never having called
Quits with beak. It did a flambé
[handwritten: Soft like a ghost]
Shim. Joy within the saucer flipped its
Own volition over. A rare day. So
This was spirit. Dunk away! Tasty
[handwritten: Rhyme within the line]
Dregs leave me wanting.
Tell me it's true what I saw in the
[handwritten: Ghostly language]
Doodle behind the drab.

[handwritten on left margin: something no one can express quite ghostly]

Burnt toast. Spectaculars undreamt at
Breakfast. Blinds I drew. Ruffle-down riot.

GHOST SONNET 32

Onto my frozen fingers came
Unsolicited words. Laying a ghost

The design of our silent eyes we never –
Even our dreams being sheer snow
Shadows keep piling up surfaces to a
Higher level of appearance on the
Timepiece taxidermal. Ticker. Heart
Skips. Trapeze. Motion tracking
Sound. On light. Partly stone.
Partly the absence of stone. Trickery.
Surge of swirling limb defines the bandage.
Partly the absence of limb.

[handwritten left margin: Shadows, ghostliness *]*

[handwritten right margin: Panicky feel to the poem *]*

[handwritten right margin: Ghosts and the trickery of the brain *]*

Who sent this terrifying beast
To hold my eyes absurdly stiffened with arc.

BISCAY. TRAFALGAR. FITZROY.

Cyclonic. Occasionally severe gale 9.
Rough or very rough.

Who sails here? Fisher folk. Finisterre a word
haunting itself with end of the earth
all our yesterdays on a loop-tape in the
Wild Bay of the Departed.

What's going down on the event horizon?
A motley crew comes into view with
clinker constructs & papal banners.
Gilded figurehead crafts a bawling infant
blowing poisonous bubbles out its ivory
trumpet spout.

Marauding Normans. Coming for uz
butter-stinkers crouched in ditches
umbles pounding louder than a force
eleven gale awaiting our genocide.
Praying for a storm surge to save our
dark-night soul-sob bacon.

A storm surge did arrive but in 1099 not
1066 the last two digits belly-up and bedevilled.

We were all long gone by then. Dead or
interbred. Women tuk brunt ut latter.

>*After six leagues the darkness was*
>*thick and there was no*
>*light. You could see nothing*
>*ahead and nothing*
>*behind.*

Fine words butter no fish. Parsnips.

Heron cuts a slash across the dusk.
Rheumy-eyed. Bedraggled. A right sorry sight.
Set upon and proper upset. Come home pet. Come home.

FAEROES. SOUTHEAST ICELAND.

Westerly 3 or 4, backing northerly 6 to
gale 8. Very rough or high. Snow showers.
Good, occasionally poor.

Colossal displacements of cloud clusters.
The fearful & forsook set sail on death
ships. Nightly ebb and flow of nascent
diasporas listing in the wake of good ship
Tye the Triton from Iceland patrolling this *'pig of a sea'*.

It's very low key this World War III.
Not declared just accumulated conflicts.
Pathological structural remodelling of hearts
traverse the Mare Nostrum from Syria. Afghanistan.
Libya. Bangladesh. Nigeria. Mali. Somali. Eritrea. Et…

Many arrive in new shoes. If they arrive. Survive
abandonment. Junk freights. Animal folds.
Scuttlings. Two-faced faceless crews. Masked
amputations. Dehydration. Desponds. Exposure.
Hungry waves. Requiem sharks.

*After ten leagues the darkness was
thick and there was no
light. You could see nothing
ahead and nothing
behind.*

Seabed sunken cities tenderly catch the daily
fall of new inhabitants. Lampedusa awaits its
loggerhead turtles. Deeply meandering jet
stream. An inconsolable fog of steam rises
from the almost-ready Sunday lunch.

Old Saharan air. A Spanish Plume rents
asunder. Severe atmospheric underbellies.
Doves have had enough. They perform a no show.
That's it. Dishing up.

ARTEMIS COMES TO TEA

The lacuna of the afternoon
tempts apparitions
in stop-gaps of space.
Vinegar flies or motes or
floaters in my eyes
construct the middle
distance show –
atomic baubles of
lo-salt spray-on no-fat.

With a sigh I excavate my spectacles.

Food must be prepared for rare visitations.
Artemis of Ephesus will beam through
my inner kitchen door her unblinking
orbs fierce with unseeing.

Here she comes!

Rivers of goats and griffins preening
        breasts

bee eggs
        leopard breath
horny things
        electric claws
lion wings all creatures great &
small gully down her teeming
pleats and plaits.

I examine the fare – would she prefer
pomegranates
            blue cheese
              green
       tea
time assorted biscuits – bull's testicles?

I close the door gently and
pray like a mantis.

from **INSUBSTANTIAL THOUGHTS ON THE TRANSUBSTANTIATION OF THE TEXT**

Vocalised (private)

> *More than meat or drink. Better than stars and water.*
> *Words birthed. Made flesh. Took wing. Horrids*
> *and enormities. Chantcasters. Daubing lunarscapes.*

Cabinet readings " ".
       Cabal. Acronym variable.
Amongst friends only. *gsts.*
Givens already known.
Inner sanctums. []
Domestic inanimates hovering.
The quiet page ruffled ~~
words up like sap. Exit with frou-frou ~~
vibrations shimmy the anatomy of skull~~
the architecture of viscera ~~
carnal sweetbreads.

Words birthed. Made flesh.

Curved enunciation. *Shussh. Giraffe shway*s.
Naked face expressions. **O**
Un-demon-strative gestures.
Off guard quirks . Gaffs. (A misplaced laugh is not
swotted. Swigged. Wiped on cuff).
Unworried **l o v e s** *Soft Wanderings.*
Conversations punctuate.
Body reclining.
Internal organs curled.
Limbs laxed.
The off-shoot flicker. Psyches. Light on
intimate. Stocking
feet. Foot cramp_. (Un*cool* dance may come later.
Low-glow performance. Conserve with energy.
Shared murmurs in the wilderness.
Can tumble suddenly to perilous.
Stark doubt of mutterance:
Letric
is a (j)eeled live wire?
Made flesh.
Is it within a hair's breadth or a hare's breath?

Vocalised (public)

> More than meat or drink. Better than stars and water.
> Words birthed. Made flesh. Took wing. Horrids
> and enormities. Chantcasters. Daubing lunarscapes.

Public and *pubic* are too close for typographical comfort.
Spoken so pointed it should be spiked with a double 'k'.
Out in the big wide w. be bold.

The bodied poet
broke on the back of phonemes
and puns within heart-reach
or slightings.
Placed rudely in
temporary cradles of
burnt out kirks. Bright
college rooms. Upon-
a-time shops. Portuguese
secret gardens. Dreary
halls of 'is this all there is'
weariness. Any *shrug* or *wow* aspace
to hold
and be
have. (have.)

The show goes on....

                              Poet as an Exhibition.
Body limited in overdrive:
          upright / uptaut / double-bent / kathakalic.
Voice exitings:
          inc(h)ants / warbles / sprechgesang / gutturals.
Nerves:
          edgling up arterials of interior weather maps.
Humours:
          four and growing. Corporeal compass points.
Text-gesturals:
          Rhythm. Ythmm. Timing. Timbre.
The Happening-stance:
          The preposterously loud death-thud of the fledgling
          against the bedroom window.

Max somatic dynamics.
Rod-ram.

Downy.

Took wing.

Poet as an Exhibition
reveals the contours of origin:
gender-age race species height
weight dentistry speech defluct
stam 'r twitch.
Fashioning of image:
          from Armami to Market.
Tracery of accent:
          from Sink to Estuary to Estados Unidos.
It's a matter to hoaxers:
          Is the red panda really
          a real bear and well-red?
Mean-time exposure.
Revelation.
          O alpha in extremis.
Personas decamp.

Body mass is conduit.
Words birthed.
Made flesh.
Stiffening conceits into concretes:
A happy maddening.

Adrenaline rush-hour.
Spinal column working overtime.
Neural overload.
Backache in an occupational hazard.
Bony hangovers.
Invertebrates may not perform.
Performers may slither.

Horrids and enormities

VALZHYNA MORT

PHOTO: PIETER VANDERMEER.

VALZHYNA MORT was born in 1981 in Minsk, Belarus and now lives in Ithaca, New York where she teaches at Cornell University. Her English-language books, published by Copper Canyon Press, are *Factory of Tears* (2008) and *Collected Body* (2011). She is the editor of two poetry anthologies, *Something Indecent: Poems Recommended by Eastern European Poets*, and *Gossip and Metaphysics: Prose and Poetry of Russian Modernist Poets* (with Ilya Kaminsky and Katie Farris). Mort has received the Lannan Foundation Fellowship, the Burda Prize for Eastern European authors, the Bess Hokins Prize from Poetry, the Amy Clampitt Fellowship, as well as fellowships from Sylt-Quelle and Internationales Haus der Autoren Graz.

JEAN-PAUL BELMONDO

it begins with your face of a stone
where lips repose like two seals
in a coastal mist of cigarette smoke
you move through the streets –
listing them
is as useless as naming waves.

(that city is so handsome for a reason –
it was made out of your rib)

it continues with my
skidmarked by a dress
body. i stand on the border
on heels like my sixth toes
and show you
where to park.

that very night
lying together
in the dogs yard
– flowers are biting my back! –
you whisper:
        the longer i look on the coins of your nipples
        the clearer i see the Queen's profile.

for you, body and money are the same
as the chicken and the egg.
the metaphor of "a woman's purse"
escapes you.
stealing, you like to mumble:
a purse is a purse is a purse is a purse.
also:
a real purse in your hand is worth
two metaphorical purses over your mouth.

they tell me
you are a body
anchored to the shore by its rusting blood.
your wound darkens on your chest like a crow.
i tell them – as agreed – that you are my youth.
an apple that bit into me to forget its own knowledge.

death hands you every new day like a golden coin.
as the bribe grows
it gets harder to turn it down.
your heart of gold gets heavier to carry.

your hands know that a car has a waist
and a gun – a lobe.
you take me where the river once lifted its skirts
and God, abashed with that view,
ordered to cover that shame with a city.

its dance square
shrank by the darkness to the size
of a sleeping infant's slightly open mouth.
i cannot tell between beggars' stretched hands
and dogs' dripping tongues.
you cannot tell between legs –
mine – tables' – chairs' – others'.

that dance square is a cage
where accordions grin at dismembered violin torsos.
beggars lick thin air off their lips.
women whirling in salsa slash you
across the chest with the blades
of their skirts soiled with peonies.

SYLT I

Lie still, he says.

Like a dog on the beach
he starts digging
until the hole fills up with water.
He has already dug out two thighs of sand
when she finally asks, what's there,
convinced there's nothing.

There's nowhere he can kiss her where she hasn't already been
    kissed by the sun.

Every evening she goes to the ocean with her three sisters and
    their old father.
They strip in a row,
their bodies identical as in a paper garland.
Bodies that make you think of women constantly chopping vegetables
        – it is like living by the train station,
their father swears –
and always putting the last slice into their mouths.

For her, there is not even a knife left in the whole house.
The sound of a cuckoo limps across the dunes.
She takes a beam of sunlight sharpened side by side with stones
and cuts with it
and you can tell her vegetables from the others'
by how they burn.

By now they already stand wrapped in cocoons of white towels,
her teeth, crossed out by a blue line of lips, chatter,
scratching the grains of salt. Her bitten tongue
bleeds out into the mouth a red oyster,
which she gulps, breathless.

Their father turns away to dry his cock,
but the girls rub their breasts and crotches openly,
their hands skilled at wiping tables,
their heads as big as the shadow of the early moon,
their nipples as big as the shadows of their heads,
and black so that their milk might look even whiter.

She, too, is rough and indifferent towards her full breasts,
as if she were brushing a cat off the chair
for her old father to sit down.
They drink beer in the northern light that illuminates nothing but itself.
Sailboats slip off their white sarafans
baring their scrawny necks and shoulders,
and line up holding on to the pier as if it were a dance bar.

It bothers her, what did he find there after all?
So she touches herself under the towel.
It is easy to find where he has been digging –
the dug-up spot is still soft.

The water is flat like fur licked down by a clean animal.
A bird, big even from afar,

believes the ocean is its egg.
So the bird sits on the ocean patiently
and feels it kick slightly now and then.

MARIA

Maria does her washing by the wall
so bare that you'd think she shaved it.

The window's open, any one can see.
Soap hisses. Air-raid warning rings
like a telephone from the future.
Her dress is nailed onto the laundry line.

From this gray garment, that is either guarding
or attacking the house, three yards of darkness
fall across the floorboards. She stands inside,
like on the bottom of a river, her heart an octopus.

Her hands so big, next to them,
her head is a small o,
          (the neighbors squint)

stuffed hungrily with stubborn hair.

PSALM 18

I pray to the trees and language migrates down my legs like mute cattle.
I pray to the wooden meat that never left its roots.

I, too, am meat braided into a string of thought.
I pray to the trees:

luminescent in the dark garden
is the square star

of a window frame, my old bedroom.
Ghosts, my teachers!

In the branches of lindens – breathe, my ghosts,
(blood to my ears!),

in the lindens – cheekbones, elbows
of my dead – in these green mirrors.

    *

How could it be that I'm from this Earth,
yet trees are also from this Earth?

A laundry line sagged under bedding among weightless trees,
yarrow and burdock, Bach's fugue, Bach's silence on our
clean wet sheets.

Fugue's Bach turns in the keyhole of the Earth.
Behind glass – portraits of the dead.

Close the curtains – motionless, they watch.
Open the curtains – they tremble.

Close the curtains – speechless, they watch.
Open the curtains – they whisper.

Trees, curtains – tremble.
On them
the dead wipe this prayer off their tongues.

    *

At dusk, like eyesight, mint and dill
tense their smell. On a light curtain

wind polishes its bones.
Two beds along one wall,
where, head to head, we sleep.

The grave of memory, grave
upon grave of memory: a train of coffin-wagons,
head-first, rushes, head-first

rushes, rushes, train upon train
arrive into the earth.

At the next stop: my ghosts, come out, take a breath,
I would be waiting there. I would bring
fresh dogrose tea in our Chinese thermos.

LISTENING BY THE WESTERN GATE

When I read a poem, my body takes the shape of this poem. When I write a poem, my body takes the shape of that poem. In the beginning of every poem is composition. Composition – a poet's sense of the whole – comes as a vision: a poet sees a ghost of an unwritten poem. This vision allows and affects rhythm, line, image. Rhythm is the breath, in and out, materialized by a word. Rhythm affects the poem's sound structure. The sound structure and the semantic structure are two magnets. When the two magnets click, they send a flash through the reader's body – truth! Poetic truth originates in the illusion of the effortless magnetic coincidence of form and subject. The subject – any subject – is worthy, interesting, engaging, brilliant – because it has found its perfect form.

The opening line of E. A. Robinson's poem 'Luke Havergal' allows for the stress of every non-auxiliary word on its first syllable until the very last word with its stress on the final syllable closing the line and the message: "GO to the WEstern GATE, LUKE Haver-GAL." The urgency of this order is not only emphasized by language but is predestined by it: HaverGAL has to GO to the GATE. In fact, Luke Havergal's own name is a kind of gate on the hinges of the opening and closing "L"s with two unstressed syllables in between. The poem continues: "There, where vines cling crimson to the wall…" We should expect that the gates where the unknown voice is sending somebody named HaVergal would be covered in Vines. And when we read that these vines cling crimson, we hear exactly that very clicking of poetic magnets: the language doesn't just communicate this image but embodies it. Cling does cling to crimson by tightly following a stressed syllable with another stressed syllable: "cli" jerks into "cri" like a hand of a mountain climber. There is no place – not even half a breath – to add or subtract a sound.

Poetic form demands clear-cut conclusiveness, absolutism. The poems I love are absolute completion, a single gesture. "I see no difference between a poem and a handshake" (Paul Celan). Replace one word with another, move words around, and it should signal a wrong note, a mistake. When words are exchangeable, when syntax is interchangeable, the poem hasn't yet reached its tension, its own music and form: it hasn't worked up enough strength to firmly squeeze the invisible hand of its reader.

A poem doesn't necessarily want to be a song, but it does want to be sung, the way a prayer is sung. I see poetic shapes almost exclusively as musical shapes, prosodic patterns – in the light of melodic patterns. The art of arranging such patterns is, truly, the art of diversifying. Take a four-part instrumental work, such as a sonata, a string quartet or a symphony: fast-slow-dance-fast. Several separate themes are worked out, developed, varied, transformed, until they are separate no more (metaphor is poetic composition in miniature). Perhaps there is no better way of learning poetry writing than through understanding that fast should be followed by slow. When we follow a melody, ignorant of its future movements, surprised by the turns it takes (or not) in the next measure, surprised by the melody that disappears and suddenly reappears, we learn the art of poetic composition. Take fugue and learn the ancient art of repetition. Take a chorale: a melody is sung by soprano along with three lower voices. This is a recipe for a poem: the key image (soprano) is accompanied by three more independent images (three lower voices) according to the laws of compositional harmony. In a poem, the three lower voices would be introduced with one of the main compositional devices: a leap, a rapture, a break, a turn.

A turn is essential since, signifying the original meaning of verse, it allows for lines and stanzas, images and metaphors to be connected not logically, but reflecting the movements of the poet's musical self. What we get then is the juxtaposition of images without smooth transitions, a collage of metaphors that reach out in all directions. This is why a poem is never interested in "What?" Instead, what matters to a poem is "What After What?" and "What Before What?"

Squeezed into the tight poetic line, bound to the demands of its rhythm, a poetic word is deformed. This mutation opens a possibility for a word to mean if not something different, then at least to mean differently than in prose. In this manner, a personal 'I' deforms into a lyrical 'I,' and this lyrical 'I' speaks with words that have become musical words in the unbearable circumstances of the line. In a poem everything is raptured: continuously stretching meanings of words, enjambments, the argument of sentences and lines, unbefitting objects slovenly glued together into grotesque metaphors, severed limbs of stanza breaks. All these elements find themselves in the clean hospital of form where medicine is given on the o'clock, temperatures are taken, where the nurses' heels tap-tap-tap along the corridors to the soft sound of a fugue.

And so Luke Havergal cannot help but go to the western gate. Perhaps the unknown voice calling him is the voice of his own name. Contextual closeness of alliterations creates a connection that might have never been there genealogically, yet is newly established, refreshing and stretching the semantics. Every day our language finds itself in the process of constant de-etymologization. Poetic image, through rapture, stretching, tightening, and deformation, offers language both its ancient and non-genealogical – musical – etymology. Semantic possibilities of a poetic word, read both horizontally and vertically and isolated inside a poetic line, are endless.

ERÍN MOURE

PHOTO: KARIS SHEARER

ERÍN MOURE has published 16 books of poetry in English and Galician / English, a book of essays, and has translated 15 volumes of poetry from French, Spanish, Galician and Portuguese, by poets such as Nicole Brossard (with Robert Majzels), Andrés Ajens, Louise Dupré, Rosalía de Castro, Chus Pato and Fernando Pessoa. Her work has received the Governor General's Award, Pat Lowther Memorial Award, A. M. Klein Prize twice, and has been a three-time finalist for the Griffin Prize. Her latest works include *Planetary Noise: Selected Poetry of Erín Moure*, ed. Shannon Maguire (Wesleyan University Press, 2017), *Insecession*, a biopoetics published with Chus Pato's *Secession* (BookThug 2014) and *Kapusta* (Anansi, 2015). Her latest translations are François Turcot's *My Dinosaur* (BookThug, 2016), Chus Pato's *Flesh of Leviathan* (Omnidawn, 2016, Rosalía de Castro's *New Leaves* (Small Stations, 2016), Antón Lopo's *Distance of the Wolf: A Life of Uxío Novoneyra* (Fondación Uxío Novoneyra, 2017), and Wilson Bueno's *Paraguayan Sea* (Nightboat, 2017).

from **THE FALL**

Lisbon is sleeping;
the spaces under the staircase breathe like
a lung.
The loneliness inside horse-drawn vehicles
was transferred to us on their demise.
Rain falls into the Tejo.
Reverence waits in the streets
and on the roof tiles.

The city of Lisbon is asleep.
The Phoenician city is asleep and the Roman city is asleep
It is Sunday and the city of Lisbon
breathes like a lung
breathes like a lung
asleep on its side

a dog asleep on its side in a house in the Lapa
a chandelier on its side in the Bairro Alto.

25 Janeiro 2004

Some hands are slicing potatoes in the kitchen.
I am alone in the streets of Lisbon.
The cobbles are kicked up
fractured, the hands keep cutting potatoes.

The player falls dead on the field;
for a moment, pain's syncope, then nothing!
The hands in the kitchen cut potatoes.
Potatoes come from the earth!
Far earth. Earth below Lisbon.
Pain like that is surprising
but doesn't last long.

Sea.

Pessoa: The sea (*scribbled*.)... How haughty of the lung!

The mouth of the sea?
A lungs' mouth too common in an aching world
So many ancestors wore their molecules differently
coats
meals, sweaters
as the wind comes up. Will you be there?

When you're hungry you move
so fast you bear snow in you.

50 years since it's

snowed in Lisbon.

The wind in the street at dawn
The street winds and dawn dawns
Pieces of alegria
When I see her, she's haloed in light
I dream, I dream
she pulls the dawn with her

and with the dawn, daylight
and with daylight, absence
which is mine.

Or the hill could wash dream from my very clothing?
You were with me, did the wind pull my shirt loose?
And tore the light so darkness foundered.
And tore the darkness so dawn came!

Alba, dawn. I cherish your spring, your water.

[534] #569 O Rei Dom Dinis

I can t sleep for grief.
I can t sleep for longing.
I can t sleep for wanting happiness!
Mother, how will I live.
Who will sing a canticle?
The word bower?

(I can t sleep, I don t believe now in service
to the king! The king s a traitor.
He s going to kill what I most love!)

[776] #833   [777] #834
Pero da Ponte

A heart in a corner.
A pocket-sized heart?
An electric register: cephaloid.
A heart like a pine cone you can see into.
Into!
"When I walked *out* the door,...

What would you do to capture green?
I have gone in another direction.
Someone gave me their sail too
I am unfolding it, hesitant
There s a cataract in my lung
I could sail on
for I can t sail on a sea!

(I wanted to talk and didn t dare.
I wanted just to look at your shoulder!)

I wanted a new lung, and a comb.
Or a new lung, and snow!

Ehrn Çihrij
wherein Senhor is world and my vassalhage is love of world

from **O CADOIRO: POSTFACE**

O cadoiro is, literally, *the place where falling is made*. In Galician, *ca-doiro* is one word for waterfall. *Cataract*, perhaps. Thus, *the fall*. This to me is the place of poetry. For whoever writes poetry must be prepared, ever, to fall down.

And I did fall. Having already fallen into Galician and thus Portuguese, I had barely stood up again when I fell – or leapt – into one of the founts of lyric in Western Europe, the troubadour poetry of the medieval Galician-Portuguese songbooks, the *cancioneiros*. These songbooks hold what remains to us of the 200 years of medieval Iberian poetry, all written in Galician-Portuguese, predecessor of both modern Portuguese and modern Galician. Influenced by Provençal verse of courtly love, the Iberian peninsular cantigas also bent and amplified that lineage, incorporating indigenous elements, such as evocations of the sea, or the tradition of women's song.

The troubadour verse speaks to us in the first person singular, in a breach with the epic narrative mode and with ecclesiastical modes of praise. Gregorian chant, and Arab love poetry, preceded and infiltrated it, just as Provençal poetry was concurrent with it. Richard Zenith, attentive translator of these Iberian cantigas into English,[2] in his *An Unsung Literature* (July 2004), wrote: "The troubadour poetry that began in Provence and spread in all directions – northern France, Germany, Italy and Iberia – was one of the first expressions of the unrelenting individuality that was to shake the Church's foundations via heterodox reform movements and eventually lead to the Renaissance." In this verse, the speaker's own subjectivity, own feelings, are the poetic "substance," yet these are quite consciously *constructed* by the poet, never "unmediated," always social, intended, and profane: directed toward another human, not to God. This human "turn" is at the very root of lyric, and the act of turning is a movement of incredible fragility and febrility – a turning away from God's love and its purported sufficiency toward a secular love which never purports sufficiency.

[...]

The most extensive of these three songbooks, the *Cancioneiro da Biblioteca Nacional*, holds over 1600 cantigas of all types. It was copied, or created, in the sixteenth century, 350 years after the cantigas were first written and, curiously, not in Portugal or Galicia but in Italy, from an earlier copy or perhaps two copies on *rótulos*, rolls, disintegrating at the time of transcription, which may have been contemporary with the troubadours. At the time of this copying, the first grammars of Portuguese were only just appearing; the written language was not yet as settled as our English is now.[3] As such, the cancioneiro's script follows the pace and expression of the troubadours' voices. In these songbooks poetry works against itself as mythic quantity, as transcendence, as voice; here, writing itself scratches the lyric.

By closely studying the poems in a lithographed reproduction of a photographic facsimile (the original too fragile) of the sixteenth-century manuscript, itself copied from an "original" and vanished apograph, and studying later transcriptions as well – critical / diplomatic but also modern anthologized versions – I hoped to respond with my own corporeal presence to questions that burned, and burn, for me:

What is a work of art?
What is an archive?
What does it mean to "trobar" today?

[...]

The *cantigas de amor* especially and perversely drew me. They are the poems most influenced by Provençal verse, that is, by the conventions of courtly love, and express a kind of sexless longing where bodies never touched and names were never named: a sexual tension and withholding. These cantigas are so repetitive, predictable, yet within a few set phrases and conceits, schemes of very regular rhyme and metre, they induce such *saudade*, longing, *soidade*, loneliness. Their sonority is their beauty; their repetition is their glamour. They embrace banality on banality's terrain and then exit it on some other field entirely. What emerges is an expression of great peace and longing and breath and orphic variability. Variability, yes, for mastery was often shown by deviations, by a simple twist, a break, by a line that didn't rhyme. These disruptions of expectation, these disjuncts, marked delight, excellence.

The *cantigas de amigo* are much closer to what we today "know" of lyric – on the surface. Beneath it, there's a sexual mixage and usurpation – men writing in the voices of women, borrowing a long-standing local tradition of women's song that may predate Roman occupation and is still present in Galicia today. These poems are not "courtly" but "common" and, in them, concrete images emerge for the first time. In response, I wrote plaints of my own, enacting, mixing and echoing, translating but two or three poems and enclosing them among those that are sheer invention, and attributing my own poems impulsively to whichever troubadour's name was most proximate in my notebooks.

[...]

The forms and plaints of the cantigas thus seeped into my work, unseating forms, compelling variegated sounds and capacities, irregularities. So that, I hope, the cantigas, rife with ambiguities and errors, can resonate for us, too, in Canada, in English. With the *cancioneiros* as *fond* from which to draw sounds and layerings of interpretation, transcription, my sole aim was to transpose a tone and delicacy, a splendour, a visual pleasure. A wandering and turn.

[...]

NOTES

[1] The attribution of number and author appears utterly speculative. On other authority, we know María Pérez or Balteira or A Balteira as *soldadeira,* a dancer and singer salaried to amuse men of court and soldiers, her name used in the satirical *cantigas* to scorn those whose wood she milled. Yet the 40 missing cantigas... if she be *trovadora* too? The Vatican, where the intact copy of the songbook had been placed, is silent on the matter 350 years later.

[2] Richard Zenith's *115 Galician-Portuguese Troubadour Poems* (Manchester: Carcanet, 1995) is, alas, out of print. It holds the most extensive selection in English of the 1163 poems.... I'm hoping Zenith will be able to bring it back into print again.

[3] The first Portuguese grammar, by Fernão de Oliveira, dates from 1536. The first Galician grammar in Galician, *Grámatica do idioma galego*, by Manuel Lugrís Freire, appeared in 1922.

M. NOURBESE PHILIP

PHOTO: GAIL NYOKA

M. NOURBESE PHILIP is a poet, essayist, novelist and playwright who was born in Tobago and now lives in Toronto. She practised law in Toronto for seven years before deciding to write full-time. Philip has published four books of poetry, one novel, and three collections of essays. She was awarded a Pushcart Prize (1981), the Casa de las Americas Prize (Cuba, 1988), the Tradewinds Collective Prize (1988), and was made a Guggenheim Fellow in Poetry (1990). Her most recent book of poetry is *Zong!* (Wesleyan, 2008). *She Tries her Tongue, Her Silence Softly Breaks* was re-published by Wesleyan in 2014 with an with a foreword by Evie Shockley.

from **ZONG!**

#2

                                the throw in circumstance

          the weight in want

                    in sustenance

     for underwriters

                    the loss

     the order in destroy

                    the that fact
                    the it was
                    the were

negroes

                    the after rains

from **'SAL'**

too

din din

dong

aide moi i   ration the truth   the she negro

ruth   drives me mad

and the facts

whore they laid her

to rest she died

lave the slave   invest in

tin   in

rum   in

slaves   in

negroes serve   the preserve

the jam   and jamaica

rum i   remain god s jest

rimed

with sin rest   master rest we

have the ram   is it

just or just

us i *rêve* of   aster s

éclair s

and ruth   such a good

dog pat   pat nig

            nig nig

                        nog

                        nag the man

            ran the slave   ran ma

    ma *mma ma*   *mai* bard sing

stir my thirst   for song a ruse

            run ruth run

TESTIMONY STOOPS TO MOTHER TONGUE

> 'Tis a figure, a symbol, say;
> A thing's sign: now for the thing signified.
> ROBERT BROWNING, *The Ring and the Book*

I

Stone mourns
            haunted
into shape and form
by its loss
        upon
            loss

honed keen
as the feel of some days
at the very centre of every word,
the as-if of yesterday it happened;
mind and body concentrate
                        history—
the confusion of centuries that passes
as the word

        kinks hair
        flattens noses
        thickens lips
        designs prognathous jaws
        shrinks the brain
to unleash the promise
                in ugly
the absent in image.

    II

those who would
                inhabit
the beyond of pale
where the sacrilege of zero
                disputes
the mathematic of heart,
erect shrines of stone to the common
                      in us

      —anathema—
touch tongue to tongue
                release
the strange sandwiched between
tongue and cheek and lip

    III

the somewhere of another mother's tongue
                    tongues
                      licks
into nothing
the prison of these walled tongues
—speaks
      this /
      fuck-mother motherfuckin-
      this /
      holy-white-father-in-heaven-
      this /
  ai! ai!
  tongue
that wraps
    squeezes

the mind round
            and around

   IV

this tongue that roots
            deep
in
  yank
  pull
  tear
  root
out
that I would
         chop
            in
pieces
     a snake
each to grow
         a head
(Gorgon—
to turn my tongue to stone)
         a tail
and haunt the absence
         that mourns
/ haunted into shape and form….

   V

Oh, but shall I?
         I shall
tame them—
         these snakes
feed them
      milk
from black breasts

  (stroke and caress into
lactate)
         to hush
the slithered silk of tongues
            split

—sliver and silver into forty pieces—
words ride again
                        across
mared nights

let me—
            I shall
lie
    with them
    bed them with silence
these snakes
                wisdomed
with the evil
                of words
to breed the again and
again
        in breed
—a new breed
—a race
—a warrior race
                    Of words
—a nest-egg
                that waits
to hatch the ever
                    in wait

        VI

shall I
        strike
under tongue and foot
them
            —these words
hold in aloft
                up
in either hand
                harmless
the word
            that claims
and maims
            and claims
again
or

in my mother's mouth
shall I
      use
the father's tongue
cohabit in strange
mother
      incestuous words
      to revenge the self
              broken
upon
      the word

from **THE ABSENCE OF WRITING OR HOW I ALMOST BECAME A SPY**

Some people are born writing, some achieve writing and some have writing thrust upon them. My belonging is to the last group, coming slowly to accept the blessing and yoke that is writing, and with so doing I have come upon an understanding of language – good-english-bad-english english, Queenglish and Kinglish – the anguish that is english in colonial societies. The remembering – the revolutionary language of 'massa day done' – change fomenting not in the language of rulers but in the language of the people.

Only when we understand language and its role in a colonial society can we understand the role of writing and the writer in such a society; only then, perhaps, can we understand why writing was not and still, to a large degree, is not recognized as a career, profession, or way of being in the Caribbean and even among Caribbean people resident in Canada.

What follows is my attempt to analyse and understand the role of language and the word from the perspective of a writer resident in a society which is still very much colonial – Canada; a writer whose recent history is colonial and which continues to cast very long shadows.

Fundamental to any art form is the image, whether it be the physical image as created by the dancer and choreographer, the musical image of the composer and musician, the visual image of the plastic artist or the verbal image, often metaphorical, of the writer and poet. (For the purposes of this essay I will be confining myself for the most part to the concept of image as it relates to the writer.) While, however, it may be quite easy to see the role of image as it relates to the visual artist, it may be less easy to do so with respect to the writer. The word 'image' is being used here to convey what can only be described as the irreducible essence – the i-mage – of creative writing; it can be likened to the DNA molecules at the heart of all life. The process of giving tangible form to this i-mage may be called i-maging, or the i-magination. Use of unconventional orthography, 'i-mage' in this instance, does not only represent the increasingly conventional deconstruction of certain words, but draws on the Rastafarian practice of privileging the 'I' in many words.[1] 'I-mage' rather than 'image' is, in fact, a closer approximation of the concept under discussion in this essay. In her attempt to translate the i-mage into meaning and non-meaning, the writer has access to a variety of verbal techniques and methods – comparison, simile, metaphor, metonymy, symbol, rhyme, allegory, fable, myth – all of which aid her in this process. Whatever the name given to the technique or form, the function remains the same – that of enabling the artist to translate the i-mage into meaningful language for her audience.

The power and threat of the artist, poet or writer lies in this ability to create new i-mages, i-mages that speak to the essential being of the people among whom and for whom the artist creates. If allowed free expression, these i-mages succeed in altering the way a society perceives itself and, eventually, its collective consciousness. For this process to happen, however, a society needs the autonomous i-mage-maker for whom the i-mage and the language of any art form become what they should be – a well-balanced equation.

When, in the early 1900s, Picasso and his fellow artists entered their so-called 'primitive stage' they employed what had traditionally been an African aesthetic of art and sculpture and succeeded in permanently altering the sensibilities of the West toward this aesthetic. In the wake of European colonial penetration of Africa and Oceania the entire art world was, in fact, revolutionized and the modernist art movement was born. These changes did not necessarily increase the understanding or tolerance of the West for Africans and Africa, but people began to perceive differently.

I-mages that comprised the African aesthetic had previously been thought to be primitive, naive, and ugly, and consequently had been dismissed not only by white Westerners, but by the Africans themselves living outside of Africa – so far were Africans themselves removed from their power to create, control and even understand their own i-mages. The societies in which these New World Africans lived – North and South America, England, the Caribbean – lacked that needed matrix in which the autonomous i-mage-maker could flourish. The only exception to this is to be found in musical traditions, where despite the hostility of these predominantly white societies, the African i-mage-maker in musical art forms was successful in producing authentic art which has also permanently influenced Western music.

Caribbean society has been a colonial society for a much longer time than not, and the role of the i-mage, i-mage-making, and i-mage control are significant. The societies that comprise the Caribbean identity may be identified by:

(a) significant lack of autonomy in the creation and dissemination of i-mages;

(b) opposition by the ruling classes both at home and abroad to the creation of i-mages that challenge their i-mage making powers and the status quo;

(c) restricting of indigenously created i-mages to marginal groups, e.g. reggae and calypso.

While changes like independence have improved some of these circumstances both within the Caribbean and within Caribbean societies in the large metropolitan centres overseas, these factors continue to affect the artist and particularly the writer. The tradition of writing for the Caribbean and Caribbean people is a brief one, and briefer still is the Afro-centric tradition in that writing.

I argued above that at the heart of all creative writing is the i-mage; the tangible presentation of this is the word, or word symbol as I prefer to describe it. The success of the execution of this i-mage, be it poetical or in the extended metaphor of the novel, depends to a large degree on the essential tension between the i-mage and word or words giving voice to the i-mage. Tension is created by the interplay of i-mage and word – i-mage creating word, word giving rise to further i-mage and so on. This process is founded upon familiarity with word and i-mage, 'familiarity' being used here in the sense of being kin to, a part of, related to. What is assumed here, but probably should not be, is also a growing familiarity with be-ing and how it relates to the outer world.

If this process is as it should be, then the autonomous i-mage-maker serves the function of continually enriching the language by enlarging the source of i-mages – in particular, metaphorical i-mage. If we accept that living language continually encapsulates, reflects and refines the entire experiential life and world view of the tribe, the race and consequently of society at large; and if we accept that the poet, the story-teller, the singer or balladeer (through their words), express this process in their work, then we must accept that this process becomes one way in which a society continually accepts, integrates and transcends its experiences, positive or negative. For it is through those activities – poetry, story-telling and writing – that the tribe's experiences are converted and transformed to i-mage and to word almost simultaneously, and from word back to i-mage again. So metaphorical life takes place, so the language becomes richer, the store of metaphor, myth and fable enlarged, and the experience transcended not by exclusion and alienation, but by inclusion in the linguistic psyche, the racial and generic memory of the group.

The progenitors of Caribbean society as it exists today created a situation such that the equation between i-mage and word was destroyed for the African. The African could still think and i-mage, she could still conceive of what was happening to her. But in stripping her of her language, in denying the voice power to make and, simultaneously, to express the i-mage – in denying the voice expression, in fact – the ability and power to use the voice was effectively stymied. We could go further and argue that with the withering of the word in the New World, not only did the i-mage die, but also the capacity to create in one's own i-mage. The bridge that language creates, the crossover from i-mage to expression was destroyed, if only temporarily. Furthermore, alien and negative European languages would replace those African languages recently removed and, irony of all ironies, when the word / i-mage equation was attempted again, this process would take place through a language that was not only experientially foreign, but also etymologically hostile and expressive of the non-being of the African. To speak another language is to enter another consciousness. Africans in the New World were compelled to enter another consciousness, that of their masters, while simultaneously being excluded from their own. While similar prohibitions extended to music at various times, language was one of the most important sites of struggle between the Old World and the New World. The outcome of this struggle was the almost absolute destruction and obliteration of African languages. Together with the accompanying act of renaming by the European, this was one of the most devastating and successful acts of aggression carried out by one people against another. African musical art forms probably owe their survival and persistence to the fact that they were essentially non-verbal.

Once the i-mage making power of the African had been removed or damaged by denial of language and speech, the African was then forced back upon the raw experience without the linguistic resources to integrate and eventually transcend it. The resulting situation became one in which the African was decontextualised, except in so far as her actions generated profits for the owners. The language within which that decontextualisation flourished was in itself and *at best* a decontextualised one for the African. At worst the language would serve to destroy. Language, therefore, succeeded in pushing the African further away from the expression of her experience and, consequently, the meaning of it.

The African in the Caribbean could move away from the experience of slavery in time; she could even acquire some perspective upon it, but the experience, having never been reclaimed and integrated metaphorically through the language and so within the psyche, could never be transcended. To reclaim and integrate the experience required autonomous i-mage makers and therefore a language with the emotional, linguistic, and historical resources capable of giving voice to the particular i-mages arising out of the experience. In summing up his efforts to augment the English language in the sixteenth century, Sir Thomas Elyot wrote, "I intended to augment our Englyshe tonge, whereby men should as well expresse more abundantly the thynge that they conceyved in theyr harts (wherefore language was ordeyned) hauynge wordes apte for the pourpose." That the African needed to express "more abundantly the thynge... they conceyved in theyr harts" is undisputed; that the English language lacked "wordes apte for the pourpose" cannot be denied. Over and above her primary function as a chattel and unit of production, the English language merely served to articulate the non-being of the African. The purpose for which language was ordained would remain unfulfilled. I would argue further that it is impossible for any language that inherently denies the essential humanity of any group or people to be truly capable of giving voice to the i-mages of experiences of that group without tremendous and fundamental changes within the language itself. In the instant case, however, since there was no possible expression of the New World experience within any African language, the i-maging could only be expressed through the English language.

Essentially, therefore, what the African would do is use a foreign language expressive of an alien experiential life – a language comprised of word symbols that even then had affirmed negative i-mages about her, and one which was but a reflection of the experience of the European ethnocentric world view. This would, eventually, become her only language, her only tool to create and express i-mages about herself, and her life experiences, past, present and future. The paradox at the heart of the acquisition of this language is that the African learned both to speak and to be dumb at the same time, to give voice to the experience and i-mage, yet remain silent. That silence has had a profound effect upon the English-speaking African Caribbean artist working in the medium of words.

Speech, voice, language, and word – all are ways of being in the world, and the artist working with the i-mage and giving voice to it is being in the world. The only way the African artist could be in this world, that is the New World, was to give voice to this split i-mage of voiced silence. Ways to transcend that contradiction had to and still have to be developed, for that silence continues to shroud the experience, the i-mage and so the word. As the poet, Cecilia Bustamente, writes in *The Poet and Her Text*:

> ... within this radius (of language) she discovers that having adapted herself as a vehicle of communication for historical and cultural moments between a dominant culture and a dominated one, language is becoming one more tool of subordination, replacement, pressure and distortion. Its potential is unexpressed, a proof that it suffers from margination of the dominated, or rather – the threat of being unable to internalize her own culture which has been violated. In order to express this reality, the social function of language fosters either its communicative values or *silence* [my emphasis]. Reflecting a similar stress it detects the multiple structures of violence,

its authenticity is tested in the confusion of recognition in the tense structures of violation and domination that, whether paradoxical or contrary, are always obstructive....This is the dilemma of the dominated: to disappear or change at the prices of their lives.

Concerning literature and the Caribbean, C. L. R. James has written that "language for us is not a distillation of our past."[2] If by 'language' is meant Queen's or King's English as we know it, this statement is true, because that language, for all the reasons given above, can never be a distillation of our past. But what the ordinary African, the African on the Papine bus, or the Port-of-Spain route taxi, or the Toronto subway, produced from the only linguistic behaviour allowed her – that is, functionality (at its barest level) in the English language – is truly and surely a distillation of her past. It may not be the clearest distillation, but it remains a distillation all the same.

In the vortex of New World slavery, the African forged new and different words, developed strategies to impress her experience on the language. The formal standard language was subverted, turned upside down, inside out, and even sometimes erased. Nouns became strangers to verbs and vice versa; tonal accentuation took the place of several words at a time; rhythms held sway. Many of these 'techniques' are rooted in African languages; their collective impact on the English language would result in the latter being, at times, unrecognizable as English. Bad English. Broken English. Patois. Dialect. These words are for the most part negative descriptions of the linguistic result of the African attempting to leave her impress on the language. That language now bears the living linguistic legacy of a people trying and succeeding in giving voice to their experience in the best and sometimes the only way possible. The havoc that the African wreaked upon the English language is, in fact, the metaphorical equivalent of the havoc that coming to the New World represented for the African. Language then becomes more than a distillation, it is the truest representation, the mirror i-mage of the experience.

Language of the people. Language for the people. Language by the people, honed and fashioned through a particular history of empire and savagery. A language also nurtured and cherished on the streets of Port-of-Spain, San Fernando, Boissiere Village and Sangre Grande in the look she dey and leh we go, in the mouths of the calypsonians, Jean and Dinah, Rosita and Clementina, Mama look a boo boo, the cuss buds, the limers, the hos (whores), the jackabats, and the market women. These are the custodians and lovers of this strange wonderful you tink it easy jive ass kickass massa day done Chagaramus is we own ole mass pretty mass pansweet language. A more accurate description of this language would be to call it a demotic variant of English. The Caribbean demotic. The excitement for me as a writer comes in the confrontation between the formal and the demotic within the text itself.

NOTES

[1] Readers interested in exploring Rastafarian language further are referred to the works of the Jamaican writer, Valma Pollard.
[2] James, C. L. R. "The Artist in the Caribbean," in *The Future in the Present* (Westport: Lawrence & Co., 1977) p. 184

CLAUDIA RANKINE

PHOTO: JOHN LUCAS

CLAUDIA RANKINE is a poet, playwright, essayist and editor. She has published five collections of poetry, including *Don't Let Me Be Lonely: An American Lyric* (reissued by Penguin Books in 2017) and *Citizen: An American Lyric* (Graywolf Press / Penguin Books, 2014) which won both the PEN Open Book Award and the PEN Literary Award, the NAACP Award, and the National Book Critics Circle Award for Poetry and was a finalist for the National Book Award. *Citizen* also holds the distinction of being the only poetry book to be a *New York Times* bestseller in the nonfiction category. Rankine has edited several anthologies, most recently: *The Racial Imaginary: Writers on Race in the Life of the Mind* (Fence Books, 2015). She is the recipient of the Poets & Writers' Jackson Poetry Prize and fellowships from the Lannan Foundation and the National Endowment of the Arts. In 2013 she was elected a chancellor of the Academy of American Poets and she is a recent recipient of the MacArthur Award. Currently, she lives in California and teaches at Yale University as the Frederick Iseman Professor of Poetry.

from **CITIZEN** (part V)

Words work as release—well-oiled doors opening and closing between intention, gesture. A pulse in a neck, the shiftiness of the hands, an unconscious blink, the conversations you have with your eyes translate everything and nothing. What will be needed, what goes unfelt, unsaid—what has been duplicated, redacted here, redacted there, altered to hide or disguise—words encoding the bodies they cover. And despite everything the body remains.

Occasionally it is interesting to think about the outburst if you would just cry out—

To know what you'll sound like is worth noting—

*

In the darkened moment a body given blue light, a flashlight, enters with levity, with or without assumptions, doubts, with desire, the beating heart, disappointment, with desires—

Stand where you are.

You begin to move around in search of the steps it will take before you are thrown back into your own body, back into your own need to be found.

The destination is illusory. You raise your lids. No one else is seeking.

You exhaust yourself looking into the blue light. All day blue burrows the atmosphere. What doesn't belong with you won't be seen.

You could build a world out of need or you could hold everything black and see. You give back the lack.

You hold everything black. You give yourself back until nothing's left but the dissolving blues of metaphor.

*

Sometimes "I" is supposed to hold what is not there until it is. Then what is comes apart the closer you are to it.

This makes the first person a symbol for something.

The pronoun barely holding the person together.

Someone claimed we should use our skin as wallpaper knowing we couldn't win.

You said "I" has so much power; it's insane.

And you would look past me, all gloved up, in a big coat, with fancy fur around the collar, and record a self saying, you should be scared, the first person can't pull you together.

Shit, you are reading minds, but did you try?

Tried rhyme, tried truth, tried epistolary untruth, tried and tried.

You really did. Everyone understood you to be suffering and still everyone thought you thought you were the sun—never mind our unlikeness, you too have heard the noise in your voice.

Anyway, sit down. Sit here alongside.

     *

Exactly why we survive and can look back with furrowed brow is beyond me.

It is not something to know.

Your ill-spirited, cooked, hell on Main Street, nobody's here, broken-down, first person could be one of many definitions of being to pass on.

The past is a life sentence, a blunt instrument aimed at tomorrow.

Drag that first person out of the social death of history, then we're kin.

Kin calling out the past like a foreigner with a newly minted "fuck you."

Maybe you don't agree.

Maybe you don't think so.

Maybe you are right, you don't really have anything to confess.

Why are you standing?

*

Listen, you, I was creating a life study of a monumental first person, a Brahmin first person.

If you need to feel that way—still you are in here and here is nowhere.

Join me down here in nowhere.

Don't lean against the wallpaper; sit down and pull together.

Yours is a strange dream, a strange reverie.

No, it's a strange beach; each body is a strange beach, and if you let in the excess emotion you will recall the Atlantic Ocean breaking on our heads.

from **CITIZEN** (part VII)

Some years there exists a wanting to escape—

you, floating above your certain ache—

still the ache coexists.

Call that the immanent you—

You are you even before you

grow into understanding you

are not anyone, worthless,

not worth you.

Even as your own weight insists
you are here, fighting off
the weight of nonexistence.

And still this life parts your lids, you see
you seeing your extending hand

as a falling wave—

I they he she we you turn
only to discover
the encounter

to be alien to this place.

Wait.

The patience is in the living. Time opens out to you.

The opening, between you and you, occupied,
zoned for an encounter,

given the histories of you and you—

And always, who is this you?

The start of you, each day,
a presence already—

Hey you—

Slipping down burying the you buried within. You are everywhere and you are nowhere in the day.

The outside comes in—

Then you, hey you—

Overheard in the moonlight.

Overcome in the moonlight.

Soon you are sitting around, publicly listening, when you hear this—what happens to you doesn't belong to you, only half concerns you. He is speaking of the legionnaires in Claire Denis's film *Beau Travail* and you are pulled back into the body of you receiving the nothing gaze—

The world out there insisting on this only half concerns you. What happens to you doesn't belong to you, only half concerns you. It's not yours. Not yours only.

And still a world begins its furious erasure—

Who do you think you are, saying I to me?

You nothing.

You nobody.

You.

A body in the world drowns in it—

Hey you—

All our fevered history won't instill insight,
won't turn a body conscious,
won't make that look
in the eyes say yes, though there is nothing

to solve

even as each moment is an answer.

Don't say I if it means so little,
holds the little forming no one.

You are not sick, you are injured—

you ache for the rest of life.

How to care for the injured body,

the kind of body that can't hold
the content it is living?

And where is the safest place when that place
must be someplace other than in the body?

Even now your voice entangles this mouth
whose words are here as pulse, strumming
shut out, shut in, shut up—

You cannot say—

A body translates its you—
you there, hey you

even as it loses the location of its mouth.

When you lay your body in the body
entered as if skin and bone were public places,

when you lay your body in the body
entered as if you're the ground you walk on,

you know no memory should live
in these memories

becoming the body of you.

You slow all existence down with your call
detectable only as sky. The night's yawn
absorbs you as you lie down at the wrong angle

to the sun ready already to let go of your hand.

Wait with me
though the waiting, wait up,
might take until nothing whatsoever was done.

To be left, not alone, the only wish—

to call you out, to call out you.

Who shouted, you? You

shouted you, you the murmur in the air, you sometimes
sounding like you, you sometimes saying you,

go nowhere,

be no one but you first—

Nobody notices, only you've known,

you're not sick, not crazy,
not angry, not sad—

It's just this, you're injured.

Everything shaded everything darkened everything
shadowed

is the stripped is the struck—

is the trace
is the aftertaste.

I they he she we you were too concluded yesterday to know whatever
was done could also be done, was also done, was never done—

The worst injury is feeling you don't belong so much

to you—

JEROME ROTHENBERG

PHOTO: AUTHOR'S ARCHIVE

JEROME ROTHENBERG was born in 1931 and has published over seventy books and pamphlets of poetry. He has published widely on poetics since the 1950 and is credited as being the first translator to bring Paul Celan into the English language. In 1968 he edited *Technicians of the Sacred*, a book of poetry from across the world, founding what he calls 'ethnopoetics' at this time. Rothenberg's books include *Poland / 1931* (published by New Directions in 1974) and a Selected Poems: *Poems for the Game of Silence* (2000). His books have been translated into multiple languages; two of them have been turned into stage plays and performed in several states of the US. He lives in San Diego, California.

from **THE JIGOKU ZOSHI HELLS: A BOOK OF VARIATIONS**

Variations on the Hell of Measures

> *How can any of you know what it feels like*
> *to count coins in Hell?*

Hell has windows as the skin has numbers, & the sun flashing on the sidewalk blinds the little customers who bathe in it.

In my head as on my flesh the poems appear, responding to my call.

My palms turn violet & blue, smoother than Chinese silk.

My room is filled with rain, as Hell with fire, while an eyebrow slightly raised signals deceit.

The other Hells are kept in store.

A Hell of numbers follows one with rhymings.

Ribs grow heavy.

The night is meant for grief no lotions over legs or fingers can assuage.

Lost in the smoke we wait for day to come, for coins to burn the swindlers who demand them – like a brand.

Crates pile up.

Windows break.

Death makes the mind turn white.

Hands open Hell for others.

Let its fires trap the birds who fly through them.

Let disaster make them all turn black.

Let them cry out with pain, the counters filling up with cloth in boxes, broken open in the night, unmeasured, boxes smelling of the sea, the intellect imprisoned in their darkness, knowing the right questions but afraid to ask.

Make it pliable like wax & let it drip over the outlaw's cashbox.

Words have their birth in it, & metals drawn out of the earth & melted give us coins.

The years ahead are green.

The bedposts where we rest are iron.

Our eyes are iron too & blind us.

Call it Hell.

VARIATIONS ON THE HELL OF THIEVES

The thieves, the thieves, the lovely thieves are no more.

When a wind blows
in from the sea, a door
swings open & light
white as Hell
nearly blinds us.
Night begins later,
the skin on my fingers
flakes off. A rank wind
shakes the ladders
we climb on,
the earth more distant,
for which we still
hunger, the sea
filling up with our tears,
our voices lost
in the wind.
Thieves who scour
our shores at evening,
whose voices sound under
our windows, whose tears
hide our pain,
cry out with one voice,
past shadows & windows.
One voice for
earth & one voice
for water,
& thieves dressed
like thieves,
a Hell like
no other, a house
overlooking the sea,
on a night
when coins
ring & death
has a voice,
like a thief's voice,
earth returning
to earth,
then to water,
a voice

thieves dissemble
in dreams.
Thieves & a sea
& a chimney
down which thieves
clamber. More
thieves in the snow,
skin & hair
growing white.
A shadow that thieves
spill like blood,
like the voice
from a stone,
the voice
of the dying.
Thieves & voices,
shore, wind, & sea,
tears & eyes,
fingers spinning
a thread,
in fear of the sky
& the earth,
of thieves
lost at sea,
a grave
& a stone
left for thieves
where thieves
vanish.

VARIATIONS ON THE HELL OF EXCREMENT

Do you see them
Do you see the pederasts in that yellow wetness

1

Urine defiles us & voices are distorted, broken, perjured, while remaining voices. Hands are what we claw with when we claw or horns are & are either maimed or twisted. Hell is never far away, to which we cling as managers may cling to satchels, jealous of whatever's crammed inside them. There the songs that priests sing rattle through its empty halls. Faces take strange shapes, more visible at dawn, & straws through which we suck are only a delusion. In that nether kingdom, all creatures seem deformed.

2

Sun draws mud out of the earth & leaves it there to dry. A river flushes sand out & goes on its way. Men watching from above know only turmoil. They are patting themselves dry with towels. I am hiding vases where no one can find them. Something dreamy on a phonograph drifts in & out around us. What I take between my teeth will likely choke me. Everyone we know's afraid of bats. The river teems with reeds like eyes beneath the water. There is neither love nor kindness where you lurk. There are only worms.

3

A whirlpool miles from shore. Hands raised to block it until it's lost from sight. Something also about pederasts. A city long forgotten where we used to live. Should we turn our backs on it? Or linger in their rooms? Or look for migrant birds through broken glasses? *Fall down on your knees, we're told, & pray. When it's morning paddle out with oars & watch the sun rise. See the sunlight mask the earth.* There's a kind of love beyond your knowing. A kind of country you can never reach.

4

A wetness over everything, the moon awash with colors, boys who wade through marshes, night that leaves no quarter when it's full. Always on call the bellhops come with whips & perfumes. Those who throw off cassocks stand with bellies like fat frogs. The boys slip into broken boats & soon draw nigh. The kingdom straight ahead is Hell; the one behind them is a different kingdom.

5

To speak of pederasts no longer. To speak of lights as well as shadows, shining on your lips, reflected on your sheets. In hotels guests are moving back & forth. They dust themselves with powders, sleep between moist sheets, clutch at their testicles while racing down the stairs. *Open the windows and you'll see the rushes floating by. You'll hear the voices calling as they fade away. Your elbows ache the more you try to free them.* It is too sad to name a kingdom & to call it Hell. The fatal difference between love & love.

VARIATIONS ON THE HELL OF CRUELTY

They wait forever at those windows
watching me

1

time breaks apart for them
& Hell does too
stuck in their mouths
who run from here to broadway
skin drawn tight around them
& in the darkened doorways
colors rise & fade
spin cockeyed on its sidewalks
tissues sucking it all up
from here to herald square
until the light becomes so strong
it flares like anger
Hell is nowhere different
once the fire dies away
& with it pity
& the keys to all you love
all murdered by that light

2

if god is nowhere
he is also now here
where he displays his many faces
& with his thousand golden hands
he feels the flesh of others
burning in his fires
their voices calling out to him
with cheeks aglow
& sockets that no one can heal
the wounds forever festering
whatever covenant was theirs

annulled, whatever sky
between them torn apart
their bellies split open, written on
with tiny letters no one there
can read   there is a cock
that cries out in the wind

a harbinger from Hell
god's cruelty alive inside them
nowhere to hide

3

out of those empty lots who follows?
who beneath his lids is watching
with what beaks is tearing loose
all that escapes the fire?
looking from their windows
where his hands grow hot & wet
the sweat exuding from them
strings of men who drop down
from on high who turn to pulp
before him   where the sun
turns black, the faces
vanish, & the cry of sex
is only felt as pain
a flower never more than that
the key to what he gives them
dead & hidden in his shadow

4

beaks are only beaks
& night is only night
the streets run into other streets
on which boys fight with boys
their life the only life they know
flesh beating against flesh
the mind forgetting what the mind has lost
links leading them to other links
to pain they seek for pain's sake
eyes wide open or eyes blind
from acid & what acid leaves behind
they stumble running past from curb to curb

where 23rd street is still 23rd street
backs stripped bare are backs stripped bare
& bred as gamecocks they are gamecocks
shirtsleeves torn & shirtsleeves red with blood
& stepping over eggshells crack them
shatter them like eggshells

5

disfiguration first
in words
then faces,
frenzied with hatred,
fair enough & yet
no point to it,
the cock crows where it rises,
and the ones with knives
at ready, stare at you
from windows high above,
on times square
or wherever else
they wait   their teeth
leave scars behind them
like a hungry pack
decked out in furs,
then drop down raging,
in a Hell where time
is absent
& is only Hell

VARIATIONS ON THE HELL OF GRIEVING WOMEN

Because she breathed too wildly in the sun
Because the sun had risen for her because it fell into her lap
Because she held a bird between her legs, eyeless, but the face still
                warm, still tender
They have left her

Mornings are never the same.
Some bring wounds while others bring love.
The rose in her hair is alarming.

Her shadow is too.
Under a lingering star the wind drives a boat.
It is dawn.
Dawn is never as tender as night is.
And if somebody cries when it's morning,
forgive her.
She lives near the center,
away from the hills & the beaches.
Her gut is heavy with water.
It throbs.
Magnetos start fires,
& houses & bridges burn down.
Her face is the face of a bird,
leaves no traces
when caught in your wheels.
Between cities & suburbs eyes stare,
milk runs dry.
She knows sorrow.
A road runs down to the sea.
We change places.
In her womb a chimera waits to be born.
It is time to leave town,
the moon halfway risen to guide her.
She has sores on her lips,
shadows falling like rain.
The sea has turned into Ocean.
With death on her hands
she sleeps in a room without doors.
The wind drops seeds on her lap.
Soon death will lodge in a convent;
a highway will vanish in rain,
its autos in darkness.
Casinos & ferries will crumble.
A river as green as a salamander
sleeps in her spine.
Her voice flows over her teeth
like the blood on her window.
Like comets & echoes.
Like shadows.
A flower drops from her fingers.
Her shawl soaked with rain,
she ties it back with a hairpin.
The rain doesn't stop.
It reaches down to the roots.

Is the road to Hell strewn with bandages?
A virgin is praying in silence.
Locked in their offices who counts the rain?
Dawn brings hunger.
A birth takes place in a graveyard,
a wake in a spa.
A submarine sun can't be seen.
A second sun over the factories
lights up the tiles.
Fibers wrap around stones
& stones shine like glass.
Eyelids burn.
Throats go dry.
Rain traps horses in stalls & spiders in sand.
Outside her room a trolley runs by.
Night beginning, a sundial goes dark.
Her veins fill with lymph,
her mind with blue shadows.
Blind as a lion, now dead,
she knows sorrow.
Shadows cover the shore.
Flowers die.
Even the sunlight won't heal them.
Fear everywhere.
Desperation.
Nothing to say.

VARIATIONS ON THE HELL OF SMOKE

> *The houses of men are on fire*
> *Pity the dead in their graves*
> *& the bones of the living*

1

First he saw graves and after that saw ashes strewn around & molten metal. The man was standing at his door, his mind so steeped in blood, he seemed adrift in darkness. Children spun around him, changing places, scooping sand that burned like glass. So hot, he thought, will it not scorch the bird atop that pine tree? I'll call them fire-raisers & I'll watch them running through the smoke & how the smoke drains color from their skin, the man thought.

2

Dead waters like the sweat that issues from his skin, like thunder that assaults him, that the man feels in his marrow, that his eyes search in the darkness. Spaces open in his blood & fire from the sun invades his darkest places. Shadows in the morning, long & thin & hot, fall on his skin, his arms, & sear his mind.

3

And from the roofbeams fire rises skyward. Bones in the desert sands, so small & frail, are all he sees. The images of cities disappear. The places where the man walks even now are hot & glowing through the smoke. On the man's skin little teeth are biting, leaving traces, red & green. The smoke is harbinger of death, & where the smoke is thickest, he will raise a torch & set the bones on fire. When he sees them flaming, he will rest.

4

A man is what he is, not what he seems. For those we call the living clouds turn golden in the sun, black in the rain. All that is hidden from his eye still issues from his voice but leaves his eyes in darkness. With a stick he hobbles between places, feels the veins inside his right eye throbbing & his left eye blinded by the smoke. Will the fire-raisers flee on metal wings, those whom the man calls fire-raisers, & will the fires they have wrought remain? Will he then have an eye to look not one to see?

5

Houses no longer homes, how hot the clouds are that enclose them. Between his teeth a cry shakes down the clouds, the rain breaks on the house in which the man, bereft & lonely, hones his sight. More bones, more sand, & still more bones. A hot night follows and his house sinks slowly in the earth. Why do the children spin around us? They are the ones the fire sweeps away. The fire frozen in the Hell of smoke.

A Note on the Preceding

In the 1990s I composed a series of thirty-three 'Lorca variations,' drawing vocabulary, principally nouns, from my previously
published translation of Federico García Lorca's early gathering of
poems, *The Suites*. I later made use of this method of composition
for homages to Jackson Mac Low, Octavio Paz, & others as a step
beyond translation but with an idea of translation – or what Har-
oldo de Campos called "transcreation" & I called "othering" – as
one of the defining characteristics of poetry as a whole. The obvious
difference in the variations presented here is that I apply the same
procedure to an earlier work of my own, *The Seven Hells of the Jigoku
Zoshi*, a series of *eight* poems (not *seven*) drawing themes but not
specific images from ancient Japanese painted scrolls of that name
& their accompanying verbal descriptions. The first publication of
that work goes back to 1962, & it has remained in print for many
years now as part of the first gathering of my selected poetry, *Poems
for the Game of Silence* (New Directions, 1971). As with other variations – other translations for that matter – the procedure, if it works,
doesn't so much annihilate the original version as bring it into a
new dimension, where both versions can lead an independent if in-
terlinked existence. The fifty-year gap between them adds its own
strangeness to the mix.

ZOË SKOULDING

PHOTO: ROBERT EDGE

Zoë SKOULDING is director of Creative Writing at Bangor University; her main interests lie in sound and performance, ecopoetics and urban space, and translation as a creative practice. Much of her work has centred on how place shapes and is shaped by language. The poetry collection *The Museum of Disappearing Sounds* (Seren, 2013) is concerned with what it means to listen to the world around us in its human and non-human aspects, as it explores the poem as a space of tension between music and noise. Skoulding is collaborating with the visual artist Ben Stammers on rAdda, a poetry, photography and performance project on the Adda, Bangor's little-known culverted river. Translation is another important area of Skoulding's practice-based research, with translations of the work of Luxembourgish poet Jean Portante into English. She also co-translated the American poet Jerome Rothenberg into French. She has been nominated and received many awards and her most recent work can be found in *Teint: For the Bièvre* (Hafan Books, 2016).

from **TEINT**

for the Bièvre

I

Not a river but its
                    shadow harmonics hidden
level in the glass note
                    glissando between a
movement and a sound
                    half in the performance
where I ran to you I
                    ran as tainted water

while tarmac shines in rain
                    the channels you don't touch
well up on tomorrow's
                    tongue to flower there don't
leave or was it this way
                    that now I'll run from you

III

Not a beginning but
                    backwash hidden upstream
industrial blood scrubbed
                    clean away chopped offal
the skins you didn't see
                    stitched into the polis
rinsed into leather boots
                    for wars fought in footsteps

if blood hangs in sight lines
                    reddening the mirrors
look away as water
                    swallows every story
the city's vibrating
                    skin behind it more skins

VI

Not a torrent but furred
                              mud silks through time stopped up
to flood a future where
                              beavers have vanished with
only *bièvre* to bite
                    its way into the tongue
castoreum musky
                    your sillage at arm's length

dog-river bares its teeth
                              at the devil's dye-house
this quality of water
                              mordant how do you like
my scarlet what will this
                              will it never be clean

X

Not black ribbon but white
                              silences deserted
streets a bleached dust under
                                   August moon cool ermine
traced with silver thread
                              shivers under scraped skins
say snow of leather or
                    city drowned in feathers

you can't get far enough away
                                   to see the glacial picturesque
without the ripped hide
                              stench and bloodstains
seeping into utterance
                    between the river and itself

XII

Not a thread but a gut
                              strung along arrondissements
where the feeling is
                    microbial love that passes

understanding in our
                              blue gentian candida
streptococcus waterlily
                              phage from everywhere at once

why this is Paris in the
                              weather repeating itself
nor are we out of it
                              nor am I out of you
from secret to secretion
                              as water undoes us

    XIII

Not a stream but a laundry
                              where the washergirls are
wringing and beating and
                              thumping the linen
rain running down their necks
                              to the arch of the back
no longer smelling of
                              amber and benzoin says Huysmans

the air that chokes them is
                              fecal bass notes overture
of soap to animalic
                              accord a memory
in the dry-down of moss
                              earth harsh on the skin

    XVII

Not memory but moire
                              in the silkstream's marbled
lines wet layers pressed on
                              cloth shifted like ray trace
or a photograph of
                              television before
it existed before
                              the river changed to this

bee hanging in breeze sus-
                           pended water's version
of itself held in a
                     breath doubling up as speech
behind Paris seething
                       its lava of events

        XVIII

Not water now but ink
                       the river's leaking black
staining my hand in this
                           blotting out of image
its refusal to be
                   anything but body
touching its own absence
                           blind in concrete channels

curved and folded a
                     skin tattooed with its own
mottled pulse a tremor
                        sloughed off running in the
hollows all its water
                       pure evaporation

        XIX

Not flooded marsh but ice
                           with skaters engraving
continuous serifs
                   on the halted water
hacked white slabs a buried
                             meaning held till summer
cold in the mouth as speech
                             or the memory of it

what I'm selling you is
                         sepia standstill print
unlike the slow creak
                       of water vanishing
under its name a score
                        of the city's movement

xx

Not channel but wave form
                    in this arrangement still
looping from the mouth and back
                         streaming all ears balance
tipped in its own labyrinth
                    how do you even say that
when voice accumulates
                    every river's accent

children yelling in a
                    cul de sac you can't go
back to where you came from
                         it already floods you
echoes over high walls
                         rain pooling on tarmac

UNDERGROUND RIVERS: NOTES TOWARDS A ZOEPOETICS

The first word I remember writing was, unsurprisingly, my own name: Zoë. The Greek term *zoe*, as the widest definition of life itself, has always interested me, and I grew up knowing its Biblical interpretations, 'eternal life', or 'life in all its fullness' thanks to my clergyman father, who also tried to teach me when I was far too young to write it in Greek, ζωή, the strange forms of the letters escaping into unfathomable loops and scrawls of crayon across the page. I'm not claiming any kind of poetic destiny here, since my father also had a small sailing dinghy called Felicity, and our names were very nearly the other way around. It was much later that I came to Georgio Agamben's account, particularly relevant to the current state of exception, of the unstable distinction between the *bios*, the politically qualified life of the citizen and *zoe* as the state of 'bare life', a non-human status excluded from the body politic. *Zoe*, in his account, is life in its most vulnerable form, subject to the sovereign's power over the embodied subject. More recently, Rosi Braidotti has contested Agamben's emphasis on death, following Spinoza and Deleuze in arguing for an understanding of *zoe* / life as a generative force, and for a '*zoe*-egalitarian' politics. In her view, *zoe* is a productive means of thinking beyond the exclusions that have defined humanism:

> 'Life', far from being codified as the exclusive property or the unalienable right of one species, the human, over all the others [...] is posited as a process, interactive and open-ended. This vitalist approach to living matter displaces the boundary between the portion of life – both organic and discursive – that has traditionally been reserved for *anthropos*, that is to say *bios*, and the wider scope of animal and non-human life, also known as *zoe*. *Zoe* as the dynamic, self-organising structure of life itself stands for generative vitality. It is the transversal force that cuts across and reconnects previously segregated species, categories and domains (p. 81).

The issue at stake in Braidotti's argument is that our response to the scale of difficulties facing humans in the present moment should not be allowed to reinforce the structural inequalities that have persisted within humanism. She sees this as a continuation of feminist concerns, writing: 'my sex fell on the side of "Otherness", understood as a pejorative difference.' Building on the understanding that the human organism is not completely human, and is continuous with all living beings, she offers a restructuring of ideas about the body and subjectivity, presenting them as wholly interconnected.

I began this piece autobiographically, that is, with *bios*, a story of a singular person being made in writing, through her own name. But what does authorship have to do with *zoe*? What I hope will allay your suspicion of narcissism in this line of enquiry is that *zoe* breaks the boundaries of the personal. It can't be owned, just as writing a single line of a poem activates memory of speech, tone, other texts, and etymologies that encode the viral travelling of language from the beginning of human communication. I can't think of language's travail without its travel from your mouth to mine; my name is simply one more connective coincidence of the kind that language makes all the time, and which poetry puts under closer examination. A more literal response to Braidotti's concerns might be Christian Bök's well-known *Xenotext* project of enciphering a poem in a bacterium, but all poetic forms offer possibilities for generative life. Recent reframings of lyric acknowledge it to be intrinsically social; a voice crowded with others is what 'I' am, while you could be anyone – or anything. The poem is a collaborative space, open, as Denise Riley writes, to 'the live, the dead who worked through me' ('Wherever you are, be somewhere else', p. 47). Knowledge of the human microbiome suggests that I'm just a host, or a crowd of guests, which I have to understand as being the same thing, and both hostile and hospitable. It's in the poem, with its multiplication of meaning, that these structures can be explored, along with their potential for other shapes of living.

To think in terms of *zoe*, which is borderless, is not to ignore citizenship or its borders, but to enter a contact zone where everything is translation. When etymologies open up, what will be carried across? The simplest thing I want to say involves a mesh of interconnected meanings, echoes and distortions: there is the suggestion of thickening in poetry in German as 'Dichtung', leading to Ezra Pound's well-known connection: 'Dichten = condensare' (p. 36). Translation reveals the tendency of language to carry over, adapt and entangle. As I'm listening in that space, time slows down. This is an antidote to the rush of greased memes on social media, which call for split-second identification rather than thinking. Reaching the other side is not the point: it's only here I can keep moving. The notion of 'nomadic poetics' proposed by Pierre Joris is not about romantic individualism in the sense of freedom to travel, but an insistence on poetry's displacing of boundaries and categories as: 'a poetry that takes into account not only the manifold of languages & locations but also of selves each one of us is constantly becoming' (pp. 43-44). If translation suggests a movement between human cultures and an opening into the unknown, the current ecological crisis requires that this unknown also encompasses the non-human.

Language is tangled up with things and other beings: poetry is the act of attending to that tangle, a form of attention all the more urgent at this point when the impact of humans and their language on the planet has reached a geological scale. As a response to this Anthropocene era, Donna Haraway proposes the term 'Chthulucene', which is a compound of *kainos*, 'a time of beginnings', and *khthôn*, the chthonic (p. 2). It marks an identification with the underground and the unseen materialities entwined with human existence, as a means of 'staying with the trouble'. A zoepoetics might therefore be connected with another of Haraway's terms, a sympoesis, or a making-with. I want to work towards this possibility, but what follows is conjectural rather than a justification of a method.

Imagine a river as a transverse section, cutting through urban and rural spaces, connecting different times and cultures that are themselves in flux. A border circles a national identity; a river cuts through it. Every river is joined to every other river; it can't be owned, even though forms of belonging might gather around its course. My interest in a forgotten French river, the Bièvre began with a different river altogether, the Afon Adda in Bangor, north Wales, close to where I live and work. When the construction of new retail space ran into problems with flooding in 2005, this was the first I'd known about Bangor having a river at all. An accidental trickle into a valley too big for it, it's what used to be known as a 'misfit river', a term that suits its sulky darkness tucked away in the city's underground. Discovering it made sense of the gap I sensed in the town, the absence of a centre and a strange dislocation between communities and locales. I thought that writing to the river or about it might help to fill that void and make possible different ways of imagining the city. I started trying to find out about it but there is very little context to go on, just rumour, hearsay and the functional information held by the agencies responsible for taking care of it. Some of the Adda was culverted when the railway came to Bangor in the mid nineteenth century, and a major part of the culverting took place after a typhoid epidemic in 1881. A river that left its traces in street names along its route – Glan Adda, The Three Salmons – has disappeared from view. The Adda, alias Afon Cachu, Shit River, filthy secret, semi-sewage, resists lyric eloquence but drew me in to a set of conversations, some of them with other citizens of Bangor as we walked the river together, and with the sound of the river itself, half-heard under the metal plates of the observation chambers along its route. This work, still ongoing as I write, is part of an effort to follow, perhaps too literally, Gary Snyder's injunction to 'find your place on the planet, dig in'. Here, *zoe* is inchoate subtext, risk of infection, the structure of everything that can't be named as *bios*.

When in 2014 I had the chance to spend time in Paris on a residency at Les Récollets, I took the Adda with me and started looking underground. I knew Paris had vast networks of tunnels that could only be entered illegally, as well as sewers, abandoned railway tunnels, catacombs, canals and a metro system, but it was only after I told a friend about my plans that she suggested the Bièvre, which ran near where she lived. An internet search revealed sepia photos of nineteenth-century back streets, and I discovered that it had disappeared just a few years after the Bangor river, for much the same reasons. J. K. Huysmans had written about it as an innocent country girl who comes to town, only to be cruelly exploited by the various industries, from leather working to dyeing cloth, that take place along her banks. In his depiction she ends up as a stinking old woman, good for nothing but burial. The injustice is reinforced in French by the feminine gender of the word *rivière*, a river that flows into another river, rather than the masculine *fleuve*, which flows into the sea. I became fascinated by the idea of the river as an ageing woman who must be buried in concrete to get rid of her, but then sentimentally evoked as soon as she's safely out of the way. This abject little stream has provoked complex reactions, from the revulsion that caused it to be culverted and then re-routed to, nowadays, an impassioned lobby for its liberation to the air. I started to think about other kinds of burial and suppression via the troubling myth of the *Parisienne*, sometimes a term used for the river but also a marketing concept particularly aimed at my own white, middle-aged, female demographic; the presence of refugee bodies; the scale of homelessness, and all the sharp juxtapositions of wealth and poverty that make Paris the city it is.

I wanted to think into and under the city, to learn how I was connected with its movements and everyday surfaces. However, the privileged situation of a residency is, by definition, not at all like everyday life, and walking the river's route was a conscious performance in the footsteps of Walter Benjamin, Michel de Certeau, Guy Debord, Alice Notley and others. As I became aware of my habits because they were all broken, Georges Perec became my guide to Paris. We live in predictive texts that are always completing the next sentence, the next day's work, the next government – before we've caught up with ourselves. The founders of Oulipo understood that there is no escape from these algorithms except by creating one's own; as Raymond Queneau explained, an over-identification with control is the only way to reveal the rat's labyrinth we all inhabit (p. 201). Perec's obsessively banal notations of the everyday in *Tentative d'épuisement d'un lieu parisien* (Attempt to Exhaust a Parisian Place) reveal not banality but the distinctiveness of what it means to be in a particular place at a particular time, for example alongside the pigeons and buses of the Place Saint Sulpice. Perec reveals our radical interconnectedness by enabling us to stand critically outside the constraints of unthinking habit; with scientific detachment he shows the human as organism, shifting beyond individual life to look at patterns and movements, *zoe* as algorithm. At a time when the algorithms of big data are being used secretly by the powerful to measure, predict and influence the behaviour of individuals, work like Perec's remains relevant because the complacency that has allowed data to turn into a form of religion came from a mistaken trust in the objectivity of mathematics. Mathematical procedures may be objective, but the use to which they are put is not; the playful arbitrariness of Oulipian constraint reveals the importance of the questions we ask.

I turned the river into a question by following its line across the city – a line that cuts through every kind of life – and walking it repeatedly, while its name became a search term drawing a different kind of line through French literary history. If the route of the river gave me a constraint, it also suggested a form, and a way of breaking it. Translating the Luxembourgish poet Jean Portante's 'earthquaked' sonnets from French had made me think about how a landscape might exert pressure on a form. I had also translated some poems from *Prononcé second* by the French poet Marie-louise Chapelle, where split lines introduce a doubtful pause, an absence like the undertow of speech. Walking the Bièvre, I discovered its two parallel routes marked on the pavement as 'live arm' and 'dead arm', from where it was split to create hydraulic pressure for industrial purposes. Accordingly, I approached the river via the sonnet, with a syllabic line broken in two, as a means of listening to its undercurrents, and of thinking about the poem as a space intersecting with the city.

Relations between cities and bodies are only partly metaphorical: in Paris, I felt the subtle changes in my own body from being in a different place – a great energy from walking, sometimes a sore throat from pollution, disturbances of microflora. In learning my habitat, I became aware of my body as a moving habitat continuous with it; a zoepoetics extends this habitat to the poem. However, the metaphor of the river is inescapable: against a backdrop of rising fascism in France and the UK, with its rhetoric of 'floods' of immigrants, rivers both affirm local identity and insist on movement, change and in-fluence, because every river comes from somewhere else, and is on its way out to sea. That said, metaphors also need testing rigorously. Money is often figured as water, from cash-flow and liquidity to draining of resources, but drawing a parallel between ecological and economic systems makes capitalism seem natural and inevitable, masking important differences: water runs to the lowest point but money, as in the myth of 'trickledown', doesn't.

The Bièvre has multiple sources, so it's fitting that its trace in literature is also multiple. Going to the library was my day's work, my *dérive* often a textual one, most often in the Bibliotheque historique de la Ville de Paris. The shape of the poem began to coalesce around a cluster of references that revealed patterns of connection between human and non-human histories. The French and archaic English word *Teint*, the name of the sequence, came from the association of the river with the dye works or *teinturie* at the famous Gobelins tapestry factory, the tinting of the water, and its uncleanness. It's also complexion, most often seen in *fond de teint*, foundation, a covering for the face. The story of the river unravels as one of paradoxical celebration and exclusion, in parallel with historical presentations of women, who are positioned in the same way as 'other' to the city and all it represents. Rabelais tells an origin story for the Bièvre in which the frustrated Panurge sends dogs (with the help of a special potion) to urinate on the woman he couldn't seduce: their urine becomes the river. The river defined in this way by an act of symbolic rape points to the problem of personification that is also presented by Huysmans' text; it naturalises violence, presenting it as an inevitable feature of the landscape. I include both of them in my text since they are part of the Bièvre's literary history and the reason for its disappearance, so I wanted to expose the cruelty of these particular narratives. However, the work of writing poetry is searching (if not always successfully) for a new and better language to think in. In this case I'm trying to connect 'segregated species, categories and domains' by imagining the river and the human body less as representing each other, although they sometimes do, than as intertwined, drawn into intimate connection by material forces and microbial life.

A chthulucene perspective recognises the kinship that comes from co-existence rather than birth: lives depend on each other, on multitudinous others, and it's this fact that the disappearance of the river elides. Just after the book came out there were catastrophic floods in Paris for which I claim no responsibility (the Bièvre is largely rerouted anyway), but they were a reminder of where we're heading, and the need to re-articulate relationships with non-human forces. I don't know how to do this, which is why I write poems. I'm working in the dark, listening to the echoes: that's also the chthonic work of *zoe*.

NOTES

Bök, Christian. *The Xenotext: Book 1* (Toronto: Coach House Books, 2015).

Braidotti, Rosi. *The Posthuman* (Cambridge: Polity, 2013).

Chapelle, Marie-louise. *Prononcé second* (Paris: Flammarion, 2010).

Haraway, Donna J. *Staying with the Trouble: Making Kin in the Chthulucene* (Durham and London: Duke University Press, 2016).

Huysmans, J. K. *La Bièvre et Saint-Séverin* (Paris: P. V. Stock, 1898).

Perec, Georges. *Species of Spaces and Other Pieces* (London: Penguin Classics, 2008).

– *Tentative d'épuisement d'un lieu parisien* (Paris: Christian Bourgois Editeur, 2008).

Portante, Jean. *In Reality: Selected Poems*, translated by Zoë Skoulding (Bridgend: Seren, 2013).

Pound, Ezra. *An ABC of Reading* (New York: New Directions, 1960).

Rabelais, François. *Gargantua and Pantagruel II*, 1534. http://gallica.bnf.fr accessed 12 February 2017.

Riley, Denise. *Selected Poems* (Hastings: Reality Street Editions, 2000).

Brotchie, Alastair and Harry Mathews. *Oulipo Compendium* (London: Atlas Press, 2005).

Snyder, Gary. *Turtle Island* (New York: New Directions, 1969).

ROSMARIE WALDROP

PHOTO: WALT ODETS

Poet, editor and translator, Rosmarie Waldrop was born in Bavaria in 1935 and studied literature and musicology at the University of Würzburg and the University of Freiburg before immigrating to the United States in the late 1950s. With husband Keith Waldrop, she ran the Burning Deck Press, and has authored over twenty books of her own writing, including poetry, fiction, and essays. Her most recent volume is *Gap Gardening: Selected Poems*, published by New Directions in 2016.

from **LAWN OF EXCLUDED MIDDLE**

When I say I believe that women have a soul and that its substance contains two carbon rings the picture in the foreground makes it difficult to find its application back where the corridors get lost in ritual sacrifice and hidden bleeding. But the four points of the compass are equal on the lawn of the excluded middle where full maturity of meaning takes time the way you eat a fish, morsel by morsel, off the bone. Something that can be held in the mouth, deeply, like darkness by someone blind or the empty space I place at the center of each poem to allow penetration.

All roads lead, but how does a sentence do it? Nothing seems hidden, but it goes by so fast when I should like to see it laid open to view whether the engine resembles combustion so that form becomes its own explanation. We've been taught to apply solar principles, but must find on our own where to look for Rome the way words rally to the blanks between them and thus augment the volume of their resonance.

I wanted to settle down on a surface, a map perhaps, where my near-sightedness might help me see the facts. But grammar is deep. Even though it only describes, it submerges the mind in a maelstrom without discernable bottom, the dimensions of possibles swirling over the fixed edge of nothingness. Like looking into blue eyes all the way through to the blue sky without even a cloudbank or flock of birds to cling to. What are we searching behind the words as if a body of information could not also bruise? It is the skeleton that holds on longest to its native land.

Whenever you're surprised that I should speak your language I am suddenly wearing too many necklaces and breasts, even though feeling does not produce what is felt, and the object of observation is something else again. Not modulating keys, not the splash that makes us take to another element, just my body alarmingly tangible, like furniture that exceeds its function, a shape I cannot get around. The way one suddenly knows the boulder in the road for a boulder, immovable, as if not always there, unmodified by inner hollows or the stray weeds and their dusty green, a solid obstacle with only *trompe-l'oeil* exits toward the subtler body of light accumulating in the distance.

The word "not" seems like a poor expedient to designate all that escapes my understanding like the extra space between us when I press my body against yours, perhaps the distance of desire, which we carry like a skyline and which never allows us to be where we are, as if past and future had their place whereas the present dips and disappears under your feet, so suddenly your stomach is squeezed up into your throat as the plane crashes. This is why some try to stretch their shadow across the gap as future fame while the rest of us take up residence in the falling away of land, even though our nature is closer to water.

I badly wanted a story of my own. As if there were proof in spelling. But what if my experience were the kind of snow that does not accumulate? A piling of instants that did not amount to a dimension? What if wandering within my own limits I came back naked, with features too faint for the mirror, unequal to the demands of the night? In the long run I could not deceive appearances: Days and nights were added without adding up. Nothing to recount in bed before falling asleep. Even memory was not usable, a landscape hillocky with gravitation but without monuments, it did not hold the eye, did not hinder its glide toward the horizon where the prose of the world gives way to the smooth functioning of fear. If the wheel so barely touches the ground the speed must be enormous.

The concept of an inner picture is misleading. Like those on the screen, it takes the outer picture as a model, yet their uses are not more alike than statistics and bodies. Figures, we know, can proceed without any regard for reality, no matter how thin the fabric. True, the missing pieces can be glued in, but if you look for the deep you won't frighten your vertigo away. An ambition to fathom need not hold water. Stay on shore, put on more sweaters, and let the roar of the breakers swallow your urge to scream. If not the clouds themselves, their reflections withdraw with the tide. Then there is the familiar smell of wet sand and seaweed, debris of every kind, including hypodermics, condoms, oozing filth. My outer self comes running on pale legs to claim my share, while my inner picture stands dazed, blinking behind sunglasses, demanding a past that might redeem the present.

I knew that true or false is irrelevant in the pursuit of knowledge which must find its own ways to avoid falling as it moves toward horizons of light. We can't hope to prove gravity from the fact that it tallies with the fall of an apple when the nature of tallying is what Eve's bite called into question. My progress was slowed down by your hand brushing against my breast, just as travel along the optic nerve brakes the rush of light. But then light does not take place, not even in bed. It is like the kind of language that vanishes into communication, as you might into my desire for you. It takes attention focused on the fullness of shadow to give light a body that weighs on the horizon, though without denting its indifference.

It takes wrestling with my whole body for words on the tip of my tongue to be found later, disembodied, on paper. A paradox easily dissolved as any use of language is a passport to the fourth dimension, which allows us to predict our future, matter of body, even rock, thinning to a reflection that I hope outlasts both the supporting mirror and the slide from sign to scissors. Meanwhile, the crossing is difficult, maybe illegal, the documents doubtful, the road through darkness, wet leaves, rotting garbage, people huddled in doorways, The vehicle breaks down, the tenor into song. Again and again, the hand on paper as if tearing the tongue from its root, translating what takes place to what takes time. This, like any fission, may cause a burst of light. A body is consumed more quickly if the temperature accelerates into love. Art takes longer, as the proverb says, but likewise shortens life. We may also get stranded, caught on the barbed wire, muscles torn and useless for the speedway.

Finally I came to prefer the risk of falling to the arrogance of solid ground and placed myself on the thin line of translation, balancing precariously between body harnessed to slowness and categories of electric charge whizzing across fields nobody could stand on. Working the charge against my retina into the cognate red of a geranium I wondered if the direction of translation should be into arithmetic or back into my native silence. Or was this a question like right or left, reversible? And could it be resolved on the nonstandard model of androgyny, sharing out the sensitive zones among the contenders? Meanwhile everyday language is using all its vigor to keep the apple in the habit of falling though the curve of the world no longer fits out flat feet and matter's become too porous to place them on.

from **SPLIT INFINITES**

Pleasure Principle
for Joan Retallack

OF COURSE IT'S NOT EASY to believe in your own dream. The working of instinct near water. Not orchards. Not apples or pears. Not nowadays. I don't know how psychoanalysis has no hesitation on how dark the night can get. The world, which is unfinished, occupying more and more of the sky.

Emotion as unpleasurable tension, the high passage of the moon. The laundry. Sensitivity won't do it. Therefore and quite often we lie down in stubbled fields. The voice of the cicada. Tells nothing.

Any day lies thick in the garden I propose to enter. Then fills with secret rivers that darkness feeds on. Lapsed sense of history. No massacre. The cicadas relentlessly.

It doesn't matter if your feet are small. When you're asleep. The fruit trees enormous. A motor idles in the foreground. If, with quicker travel, things did indeed turn out according to one's wildest. If a child could be born from something not a mother.

The circumstance that the wife occupies the inner room and rarely if ever comes out is called the pleasure principle. In certain societies. Suddenly made clear by the cicadas. The meaning of life, absolutely. Distinguished from the now moonless garden.

And hooded with fabric like mirrors not in use. And like appearance refusing itself. A pleasure that cannot be felt as such to transcend becoming strange.

An orchard in the foreground. With beginnings of unease immediately behind.

from **BLINDSIGHT**

Mallarmé as Philologist, Dying

Even the purest writer is not entirely in his work, we must admit. A saturated white tilts off the page, a ricochet of sense like children heard, not understood. You see the gap between chance breath and the continuous line of the horizon, method to infinite power or out one candle. Anatole *aboli*. *Bibelot* Anatole. Walks down the stairs, one by one, to the bottom of the mirror. It is the lack of self splits his ear. A labyrinth like a sentence. Always, word follows word, to stave off those little deaths. Is he alive?

When he leaves the room, he recaptures a memory called meaning. A matrix where a word is carried by a foreign language. Say "th." Say the whole word: "death." *The Box for Learning English by Yourself and Playing* is broken, the string to push the puppet's tongue between his teeth. "Debt" is not comparable, not part of the body. Throw the dice, throw. Again. If often enough, only everything. Between the teeth.

To track your dream, enter by way of the corridor and comparative grammar. The dream is called work. The corridor leads to Hebrew, which shows how to replace lacking inflection by ideal nakedness. The corridor passes time, so that the girl is cold. When you caress her name, somber and red like an open pomegranate, you slowly descend toward. Stop. The dream insists that meaning, memory, and music are the same. Out of its own lack, it fashions a flesh of vowels, and of consonants a skeleton delicate to dissect. What is a faun to do?

A simple laryngitis. Does not abolish breath. A lacking word, a thought that terrible would vibrate suffocating like an open spasm splits his ear terrible his throat. Geneviève, virgin spasm, vivacious, and beautiful today suffocating. A fan of lacking experiences. For Mademoiselle Mallarmé. It is hot. Wants a book on anatomy, it cannot be too simple: he might place the larynx in the brain. Again. His breath stops, and we are all speechless.

from **DRIVEN TO ABSTRACTION**

By the Waters of Babylon

1

We take language for granted, as we do sitting and weeping. Unfamiliar speech we take for inarticulate gurgling. Filtered through sandbags.

A searchlight beam makes a statement.

The order of the world is so foreign to our subjective interests that we cannot imagine what it is like, says William James. We have to break it. Into histories, art, sciences, or just plain rubble. Then we feel at home.

I could list the parts of the body as in a blason. And how they can get hurt.

2

Unless we recognize a language we do not recognize a man. We wrap entire villages in barbed wire.

My father used to close his eyes and remain as motionless as possible to let his body-image dissolve.

I repeat myself often.

Time has no power over the Id. But heat passes from a warm body to a cold body and not in the reverse direction.

3

Language plays a great part in our life.

There is chaos and void. No man or beast. Not a fly or stalk of ragweed. We think "primal soup," and already there is a world. And fed.

Then somebody thinks "Operation Ivy Cyclone." "Operation Plymouth Rock." "Operation Iron Hammer."

In 2005, in Baghdad, 92% of the people did not have stable electricity, 39% did not have safe drinking water, 25% of children under the age of five were suffering from malnutrition.

4

Whereas the concept of spatial measurement does not conflict with that of spatial order, the concept of succession (bombings?) clashes with the concept of duration (US presence?).

Tanks enter the discussion, and the case for absolute time collapses.

We speak our own language exclusively. It embodies the universal form of human thought and logic.

I toss in my sleep. As do many women.

5

4000 to 6000 civilians have been killed in Fallujah.

It is impossible to describe the fact which corresponds to this sentence, without simply repeating the sentence.

A cat chases a yellow butterfly. My father sneezes.

Unlike the id, the ego, through which alone pleasure becomes real, is subject to time.

6

There used to be harbor where downtown Providence is, a pond full of perch under the civic center, Roger Williams's body under an apple tree.

Where the Sumerian cities of Umma, Umm al-Akareb, Larsa, and Tello were there is now a landscape of craters.

The ultimate origin of the idea of time, it is said, lies in our perception of difference and resemblance.

When I look at the mirror in the morning I see a grey mist. Then it is hard to rescue distinctions.

7

Trenches filled with trash. Sandbags filled with archeological fragments. Men filled with fear.

Language is a network of easily accessed wrong turns.

At the dedication of the Abraham Lincoln Presidential Library and Museum, the President compared his War on Terror with Lincoln's war against slavery.

Sometimes the clouds race along Elmgrove Avenue. Sometimes they hover over city hall.

8

In one version, reality is desperate attacks by a few desperate individuals. In another, we have been in a civil war for a long time.

We place mirrors in our bedrooms. We hope their virtual depth might reflect on our loves.

Greater accuracy in measurement can be obtained by means of atomic and molecular clocks. Implicit is the hypothesis that all atoms of a given element behave in exactly the same way, irrespective of place and epoch.

If I try to say the whole thing in one sentence I say the same thing over and over.

9

My father, from his balcony, looks at astral spaces where the orbiting of a planet, a suicide bombing, and his breath condensing in cold air are equally part of the system.

He wonders whether he must fit his perceptions to the world – which world? – or the world to his perceptions.

50,000 US soldiers in Iraq had no body armor in 2005. The equipment manager had placed it at the same priority level as socks.

Some do not like blood outside the body. Others do not like body counts.

10

In Swan Point Cemetery, there is a gravestone in the form of a little house. With the inscription GONE HOME.

"Assassinated: four clerics, two officials from the Ministry of Defense, the dean of a highschool; killed by bombs: nine National Guards, thirteen civilians, two engineering students. In all, thirty-one dead, forty-two injured, and seventeen abducted. A fairly quiet day here in Baghdad."

The flux of time helps us to forget what was and what can be.

I would prefer to be able to explain the air. The sun. The Adam's apple.

11

Corpses of small children, families lying in pools of blood in their homes. The President promises investigation.

Heine's curse: Nicht gedacht soll seiner werden.

One way of thinking links thoughts with one another in a series, another keeps coming back to always the same spot.

The flux of time is society's most natural ally in maintaining law, order, conformity. We learn that every pleasure is short and are resigned even before society forces us to be so.

12

The spring rain splashes up cones of water from puddles formed by the broken asphalt.

The crimes of US soldiers in Iraq are as inevitable as the crimes committed by soldiers of other imperial armies. It takes many years before it comes to light that they are official policy. 50 years, in the case of No Gun Ri in South Korea.

The aspects of time that were significant for primitive man were repetition and simultaneity. Even in his first conscious awareness of time man sought to transcend, or abolish it.

My writing is nothing but a stutter.

13

Nothing new under the sun. Which comes and goes. When it stood still at the prayer of Joshua, did time nevertheless continue?

I would like to concentrate on the rotation of the earth and the winds it brings about.

Eight months before the invasion, the chief of MI6 reported to Tony Blair that the US was going to "remove Saddam, through military action..." But because "the case was thin, Saddam was not threatening his neighbors, and his WMD capability was less than that of Libya, North Korea or Iran... the intelligence and facts were being fixed around the policy."

Our language seduces us into asking always the same questions. As long as there is a verb "to be" that seems to function in the same way as "to eat" and "to drink", we'll be asking questions of identity, possibility, falsehood, truth.

14

"Well, I knelt down. I said a prayer, stood up, and gunned them all down."

As the physicist Stephen Weinberg said, for good people to do bad things it takes religion.

I suddenly start to wonder at birth, death, sleep, madness, war. As if awakening.

Time helps us to forget, and to forget means to forgive. What should not be forgiven.

15

My father cuts himself shaving. While he looks for a bandaid he thinks of his astral body and if it is bleeding too.

Time is the form of our inner sense, said Kant. And Guyau, that a being who did not desire, did not want anything, would see time shut down in front of him.

Everywhere people wind clocks to prevent this from happening.

The battle of Agincourt was fought in hours, Waterloo in a day, Gettysburg lasted 3 days, the Battle of the Somme four and a half months, Verdun ten, Stalingrad six. There were the Seven- and the Thirty-Years Wars. The President told the West Point cadets: "Iraq is only the beginning."

Providence, 2006

WANTING

Wanting, always, the possibility of this body. Thinking it here. In anxiety. In fear. But wanting to want. The light never to stop.

Caught between wanting and acting. Between language and landscape. Wanting to contain volumes, multitudes. Curves to everywhere. Describing circles of light, flashes of lightning.

Wanting the body visible from head to toe and without secret. A nakedness without debts. Believing it possible. The light as event. Thinking to want to think. As if in response.

Doubting I love while knowing I've wanted to. Thinking to console myself. By describing veins in a block of marble. As if seeing. A reason for seeing.

Fearing to exist without really living. Absence of body within the body. Wanting to be able to suffer. To look at the dark. The mass of night that surrounds. Or is myself.

Thinking of the body. Here, without thinking. Not knowing how to think. Swimming without fatigue. As if without body. In a sea without water. Without end.

THINKING

I don't think I know how to go about it.

I sit at the edge of the water. As if it were the right place for learning to think.

As if it were enough to sway with the current. Or indecision? Stay? Walk away? Give in to the horizontal or a quick push upright? If I can't walk might I yet, like Parkinson patients, be able to dance?

My brain's incessant activity seems fruitless. It can't be thinking. I put it on paper to encounter it outside myself. An obstacle. A wall with a grain, with pores where I might discover a pattern. Then I'm recalled to my body by legs as if pricked by needles.

How can I think when I can't even see, night falling swiftly, shifting around me like water. Can one look at nothing and hope for help?

Is it a matter of rocking with the dark? Monotonously? But I'm speeding or slowing down the long lane where thinking gets lost in layers of dust, failing precision. Failing to see, to embrace. The gulls circling. The vast empty space. Traffic noise borne in on the wind.

Should I take off my clothes, nudity being power? But would I know my body scattered among memories? Impossible to hold in the mind all at once.

If I let the night invade my eyes, all the way to the horizon? As if it had a body? Might I then see the cause of my not seeing?

It might be a beginning.

from **DISSONANCE (IF YOU ARE INTERESTED): COLLECTED ESSAYS**

Why Do I Write Prose Poems
When My True Love Is Verse

I love the way verse refuses to fill up all of the available space of the page, so that each line acknowledges what is *not*.

> [Poetry] is the very art of turnings, toward the white frame of the page, toward the unsung, toward the vacancy made visible, that worldlessness in which our words are couched. (Heather McHugh)[1]

And I love the way poetry's rhythm, maybe its very essence, arises from the tension, the mismatch between line and sentence, between the halt at the "turn" that interrupts the syntactic connection and the meaning's push forward toward completing the sentence.

> Contrary to the received opinion that sees in poetry the locus of an accomplished and perfect fit between sound and meaning, poetry lives, instead, only in their inner disagreement. (Giorgio Agamben)[2]

For the fraction of a moment, this void stops everything. It suspends the assurance of statement to reintroduce uncertainty, possibility, potential. According to Hölderlin, the gap of the caesura, metrical poetry's additional locus of disjunction, blocks the hypnotic enchantment of rhythm and images:

> the caesura (the counter-rhythmic interruption) becomes necessary to block the torrential succession of representations ... in such a way as to make manifest ... representation itself.[3]

A void that shows representation itself. (I would say: language itself.) The silence that makes possible the music.
Or perhaps:

> the shape of thought, the impersonal music of silence hovering over every page like a ghost emptied from a land of shadows. (Russell Edson)[4]

In addition, a bit more tangibly, it lets us feel the magnetic field between the two dimensions, energy's horizontal push becomes dammed up, vertical, orchestral. An aura.
I pursued this void, this numinous showing of language. I tried to exacerbate the tension and disjunction between sentence and line by keeping the lines very short while opening the confines of the

sentence into one quasi-unending flow.

> *In order not to*
> *disperse*
> *I think each movement of*
> *my hand*
> *turns*
> *the page*
> *the interval has all the rights*[5]

But I began to long for complex sentences, for the possibility of digression, for space. The space of a different, less linear movement: a dance of syntax.

The comma stands quite independently in the place where the edges of bodies touch. (Vera Linhartová)[6]

The prose paragraph seemed the right kind of space where form could prove "a center around which, not a box within which" (Ezra Pound).[7]

To write as if leafing through forms of wood I know, trees, books, in an improbably quest of bloom.

I gave up stress for distress, the distress of lacking coordinates, of the unstructured space of prose, the uncharted territory of the page. The excitement and terror of the open. Versus the challenge of closure: in the complete sentence and, extreme, in the proposition.

He wrestled with Sleep like a man reading a strong sentence.
(Robert Duncan)[8]

No. This was not enough tension. Not enough to compensate for the absence of turning, of margin. I must try to move the vacancy and the mismatch from the margin inward.

the empty space I place at the center of each poem to allow penetration

I must cultivate the cuts, discontinuities, ruptures, cracks, fissures, holes, hitches, snags, leaps, shifts of reference, and emptiness inside the semantic dimension. Inside the sentence. Explode its snakelike beauty of movement.

Again speed. A different one. An energy that knots and unknots constellations before they can freeze into a map.

"Gap gardening," I have called it. My main gardening tool is collage. And it is perhaps just another way of talking about poetry as concentrated language. (As Pound and the German language know, dichten=condensare.) Making dense, cutting out steps.

In *The Reproduction of Profiles*, all poems started out from Wittgenstein phrases. Some other phrases come from Mei-mei Berssenbrugge, many from Kafka.

I had mistaken the Tower of Babel for Noah in his Drunkenness.[9]

Displacement, dialog, transformation. We write on a palimpsest. The quotation left intact carries the whole "Description of a Struggle," along with a whiff of the destruction that is the Beatrice of creation.

> In [quotation] is mirrored the angelic tongue in which all words, startled from the idyllic context of meaning, have become mottoes in the book of Creation. (Benjamin)[10]

With a stronger whiff, Wittgenstein's rejection of "the deepest questions" comes to prove "that the deepest rivers are, in fact, no rivers at all."

The displacement matters less to me than the glint of light on the cut, the edges radiating energy. The fragmentary, "torn" nature of the elements. A full quote like the sentence on the Tower of Babel is the exception and functions as a signpost.

Fascination of logical syntax. "If-then." "Because." But I try to undermine the certainty and authority of logic by sliding between frames of reference, especially pitting logic against the body.

The body is, after all, our means to have a world – even to have logic.

The rhetorical theater: a woman addresses her lover?

A dialogue between two sides of one mind?

Dialogue cultivates gaps by definition, by the constant shift of perspective. *Lawn of Excluded Middle*[11] continues to use the rhetorical "you." But in the third volume of the trilogy, *Reluctant Gravities*,[12] I decided to give the second person equal time and weight. This led to the question: do I want the voices to be distinct? Do I for instance give the scientific vocabulary to the male voice, to the female voice the statements about language? But I'm not interested in characters, psychology, or in poetry's traditional "persona" or mask. The voices do not "represent," but frame the synaptic space between them. Except for this constant crossing of this gap they could have been one single voice. This is also why the voices do not always engage with what the other has said, but veer off, pursue their own train of thought and thus enlarge the gap, the tension, mark the cut.

But what has become of sound? When "free verse" took a step away from meter, it was a step away from the oral. The prose poem moves yet farther in this direction. Its sound and rhythm are subtler, less immediate, less "memorable." If it counts, it counts words or sentences rather than stresses or syllables.

Valéry's definition of the poem as "a prolonged hesitation between sound and sense" does not work here. Not the way I think he meant it. My beloved clash of these two (still present in the wordplay) has been displaced. The fissure is now more between sense and sense, sense and syntax, density and intensity.

But there are many kinds of music. Syntax is rhythm, sound in motion. Even if sound does not seem to be in the foreground, it is the body, the materiality of poem. What carries the surface we call mind. It is (mostly) the sound that short-circuits the word's transparency for the signified, which some consider its advantage:

> A symbol which interests us also as an object is distracting.
> (Susanne Langer)[13]

This "distraction" is exactly what poetry worth the name gives us: the word as a thing, palpable, a sensuous, sounding body. The word made flesh. The flesh of a bird, so it can also take wing. Toward the kind of mathematic limit where, to vary Zukofsky, the word approaches both the wordless art of music and the soundless music of silence.

NOTES

[1] McHugh, Heather, quoted by Sharon Dolin, "Broken English," *AWP Chronicle* (December 1996), p. 11.

[2] Agamben. *Idea of Prose*, p. 40.

[3] Hölderlin. "Anmerkungen zum Oedipus," *Sämtliche Werke*, vol. 5, ed. Friedrich Beissner (Stuttgart: Kohlhammer, 1954), p. 214.

[4] Edson, Russell. "Commentary on 'The Tunnel,'" *The Prose Poem* 7 (1998), p. 88.

[5] *The Aggressive Ways of the Casual Stranger* (New York: Random House, 1971), p. 63.

[6] Linhartová, Vera. *Mehrstimmige Zerstreuung*, trans. from the Czech by Dorothea Neumärker (München: Deutscher Taschenbuch Verlag, 1971), p. 142.

[7] Quoted in Creeley. *The Collected Essays* (Berkeley, CA: The University of California Press, 1989), p. 591.

[8] Duncan. "The Structure of Rime" I in *The Opening of the Field* (New York: Grove Press, 1960), p. 12.

[9] New York: New Directions, 1987.

[10] Benjamin. *Reflections*, trans. Edmund Jephcott, ed. Peter Demetz (New York: Harcourt Brace Jovanovich, 1978), p. 269.

[11] New York: Tender Buttons, 1993.

[12] New York: New Directions, 1998.

[13] Langer. *Philosophy in a New Key* (New York: Mentor Books, 1948), p. 61.

JOHN WILKINSON

PHOTO: AUTHOR'S ARCHIVE

JOHN WILKINSON is an English poet and Associate Chair for Creative Writing and Poetics in the Department of English at the University of Chicago. His selected poems, *Schedule of Unrest*, were published by Salt in 2014, and a new collection, *Ghost Nets*, by Omnidawn in 2016. He is joint Principal Investigator for an archival, curatorial and research project on Outsider Writing at neubauercollegium.uchicago.edu/faculty/outsider_writing/. His current scholarly work centres on landscape and abstraction in St Ives and New York painting and poetry.

from **RECKITT'S BLUE**

When gods were young, waves broke stupidly,
The moon wanting merely that.
Let cancel cancel cancel passage,
Term crash: he curves unseated
In fissured air, he first wounds itself,

Snagging holes its ritual   ,
At games, at canoe regatta,
Maybe so but never fret,
Nor   at the break   dumb lacquer
Sun bestows: water cuts and opens,

Hooks shilly-shally   ,
Punched cards or pit divisions,
Stroke follows stroke across the board, tongue
                breakers roll in vast fettle,

Deliver   posturing little gods.
Mere shadows have voracious   spathe
Bodies whistling store – in that smooth
Piano black, a spirit board   .

My house's windows are bricked up.
Shell cracks to the fairer prospect. So it is said.

        *

Soul gathers, more more more abruptness
    plies   ,
                puts it on while strong lobed drag
Growls and resists. Man overboard.
Funnel. Make a paste of soot blood slakes,

Else clapped elbows, clapped knees
In-filled the gap
                trip lash a sampler
To his grading stick, then rile him good
Scarify his plump cheeks, balsa
Dugouts itching to maraud

Fitted GPS truncates
At iron tables in clearings hacked for the purpose.
Felled trees, feathers of the cut wing
Tressing a so sought-after   pleat follows pleat

                        finger-stalls fly the channels!
A complete head rears above the prow in
Its preview of annihilation, scar plan.

I look out for sharp edges, univalent.
I am caught, I am snatched, I am snapped, spoken.

    *

In the outhouse in the straw what goes ahead.
On the enamel lip what goes ahead.
Behind the missing door what   . Emblem
Of covert hopes all know all belong
In twisted hair, a dreadlock, the growling.
Produce the sample. Engineer   conditions.
Bury in the taro patch
Beneath   . Upholstered settle.
Crush on the iron frame string bits
            debasement a greasy slide.
The buttockless stared.
The sealed men's house stood atop its thin poles.
Keys, stamps, mobile phones.
Lumber in the pericardium a pin number accesses,
Neutralising bad thoughts, flicker
Kapkap that rotates on   panels, filigree
Openwork, men with bloodshot eyes, we women
Map their path with soot and blood.
O dark clouds the conch calls,
I shall stunt myself down to the neck so earth blurt.

from **COURSES MATTER-WOVEN**

1

Pressing Emptiness can't adapt to scurryings not audible:
	stopped down mutely to the clay, stern
Vision buoys up still, through cushions
and through influx, a windsock prolapsed in bronze.
		Peewit calls a dipping, dotted course.
		Shining binds the Instrument, analysis
is on a hiding, don't start to think otherwise,
cardboard and tape measures brought for a maquette –

nonetheless a shuffle-deck of feelings slips from cartoon
parameters, each from each, quietly,
		persons run ragged for a stroke
careens just then and there as though it swung against
face-forward, swelling it with what boded ill
beneath the flyover, in the stall underneath straw:
		emaciated palm tree ribs, jutting hips,
 simultaneously these expand and organs hang from them,

human brain even, what activity
can be detected in these? Values *en cocotte*? Whispers
also that everyone agrees they ride on the ability to ruffle
edges whether stuck down or gently nodding.
		Ruffled blue tissue awaits its fruit,
ruffled petals spill their scent, awaiting moths' signature
		Until light interrupts,
lathe-cuts a pattern with its shine and slick, figures out

Vestigial Inwardness, till a notched tape pinches a balloon
to get its reading: that inflicts welts:
		invisible respondents pluck and prod,
harrying a Vision of Humanity,
drawing blood that stains oilily the lacquer dogs slither
over, dogs abound and won't be whipped in, –
		rotates in its collar Liberty, sweet Liberty.
At this the seas roar and the votive gulls hung by threads

pitch sickeningly, even as the broken pack
is drawn off by a smell of meat, mills about within its new
restored form.

In the collar, in the gimbal
spins the human chassis, limbs outstretched and
excruciated in the warp ends of longitude and latitude
picked off from her fingertips, casting
bird coverlets and aeroplanes on predatory mission,

rigged for their remote destinations, brought about.
But she now shrinks within our sights.
But she forms the upside or the downside.
        Birds line up again to test the waters,
sipping at foam.
So she is assembled by numbers.
She kneels in her bracket further bracketed in echoes.
Scurryings and scratches fade, even when the crick throat

gripped in callipers, gasps
across its casing a dashed-off profile moiety while her flip
        upholds a scentless spray of cowslips:
either / or
compounds the Real but what does her cheek press?
        Sung performances fail to
disarray the orange suit or disintegrate the kevlar
before the invisible audience dropping in on this tableau.

6

Just have your footsteps faltering a tactful way off-account.
Any part a set-aside like a meadow drains off pain.
4 hard-boiled eggs rattle in the pan rep Singapore parody
        Liberty, sweet Liberty.
                An orange shell-suit
hangs from its weighed bough.
Conductors with machine-guns among the beads at intersections giggle then stiffing faces,

rotating on their podiums, trained along the shadow edge,
their eyes alert and empty
skin shadow off stone,
        the curve-leg, the straight-leg, the short-leg
stick out to wiggle, majuscules
populate strong light. Loud traffic hushes,
car transporters shrug off cars on the verge, pits
and raw stripes write exercises notarising bone and joint –

Sing it again, Liberty, sweet Liberty, tuned by
       season, beleaguered / *it of it of it* /
footprints of birds in drying concrete, orange leaves
skittering, motor burn fingers, who
       prepares the Involute, horror
then relief conforming song as to her contraterrene;
so also by its crushed possibilities, its crushed possibilities
smell of fire, she shall force forward fiercely

un-elsed, un-othered: eggs rattle in a snag-tooth brake,
concordant reach true temper even as thrust to her knees
       it of it of it, in each case
       a smattering
       regardless of the nettle window,
it of it of it,
despite the collapsed wheat submissions, barley
at this altitude, even as the card melts her name raised,
in metadata lost between formats she shows up

unsorted. By 5 o'clock plucked-up mist starts to crest,
               killer
beats diaphragm the walls, they are unremitting.
             Plausible and tanned a gatekeeper
turns a cheek stripped of its shadow, taps out
       versions of invented Instinct,
             messenger of that
amine for the plucking-up. This inside That that has inside
courses gathering and splaying, matter-woven
       It of it of it –

       leaves commingle,
rucked under bird-lime and snails slick the earth. Starved
children forage
after peg fungi, scrabble through topsoil,
scale along creepers, down chiffon bark, down soft mace.
         In the scaffold
throbs hanging fruit not to harvest. Glowing
wait for their format, wait for the
messenger to bring red catechol so as to interrupt:

It is the dead of day. Commotion stills,
       all companions lie as though comatose from self.
This is a Special Purpose Vehicle and the future swoops
to re-attach their tongues. Then they settle down,

    millions not yet living
speak with one voice. The mining companies
truck in dayworkers who look at first like the ideal match,
yet what does a strip search show.
                        It of it of it.

SCHLUMMERT EIN
    In memory of Sara Wilkinson and for Liz Miles

Eyelids, fall softly, from their gritted corners
        chalk, let it drizzle,
        let the streams flow
thick with a waste glaze, let imagery run off

its surplus of kaolin, choke feed of sediment
        plumed into the blue,
        tulipping its stem.
Cress bunches thickening in shallows, flukes

stinging flank heifers in their shove and jostle
        down a bank, drinking,
        mud caking lips.
Eyelids, fall softly, let me linger interrupted

behind the curtains billowing with images,
        how the unseeable
        sill even so snags, how
the very point lights from behind, thoughts

dispersing into folds slung aloft in sea mist,
        impermissible point
        breaks every motive
falling back behind the eyelids that then fall.

I breathe, I look, I carry forward, I can sense
        the last of you, taking
        walks of air thick with
waste breath your form displaces. O curtain!

O rail! I hate the thick floor beneath, breathe
    over a market quarrel,
    rise over the bass
sawing at its stems to crash down the vault,

let the vault branch recklessly, light-streams
    maze, air's stirring
    carry song back and forth;
I hear your recorder pipe, long for its repeats

giving what-for to earth seeming to attenuate,
    rock is marked
    with your aeolian flow.
Eyelids, fall softly, the cast of their fluttering

fans across the inlet a white shadow, writes
    over deep-set floor
    captivated ripples.
World, gaze out! Rise from a shrouded point.

from **LYRIC POETRY IN EVIL TIMES**

For the past forty years I have sought to write an affectively powerful lyric poetry without the external validation of autobiography. The ambition has been to create in language formal events of thought and feeling as manifest and unarguable as human presence, through a dynamic metaphorical practice derived from my early study of Shelley, and through a densely structured and musical prosody departing from traditional metrics but summoning the history of poetic thought and sound in English. Broadly my poetry has divided into two modes of writing: clustered poems worked as an entity over a long period, and rapid lyrics that emerge out of the gestural vocabulary being developed in the longer, sometimes book-length works. It would be reasonable to ask why my poems have been actuated by so strange an ambition – why not be frankly autobiographical? An autobiographical response could be tried, but more profitable to think about this historical moment, with sociality become measurable, pornographic, fleeting and dissolute / recombinant. Materialism has abandoned the material, and love of clay, wood or vinyl can't compensate. I avow an idol-making out of the material I use, making for the emergence of a unified consciousness and corporeality that feels less like an artifice than do my own name, conferred identity and biography. For that experience to be shared demands intense pressure on the sonic and syntactical stuff of language so that speech happens with no identifiable speaker, and can be felt not only semantically but as charging the body into self-presence. I don't know if this has ever happened for someone reading one of my poems, but it happens for me when I read certain poems – by Denise Riley and W. S. Graham among others.

And like the experience of love itself I feel such an experience as an unasked-for and astonishing reparation. How can that not be true? Is there anything in the world I have not damaged, in my world-shaking human greed and violence and casual everyday collusion? The violated world is covered with a thin scrim of protocols, disguises and distractions. The gratitude I feel in reading a great poem or looking at a great painting floods me, gathers all that scrim into a full substance constituting its adequate respondent, for a moment – one who can "say something back". Well then, what of the concentration camp guard listening to a Beethoven quartet and experiencing a reparation? I don't think this is a closed question, one that can ever go away. I would reframe it by asking how reparation can be made less abstract and mystical, how it can reshape the person in the world, in dailiness, how it can survive the aesthetic experience and break out of the circuit of guilt-atonement-forgiveness.

Such a question returns me to the first person, the lyric cypher.

The death of my sister Sara in 2012 directed me to a more open first-person poetry, adumbrated by an essay I published in *Poetry* in 2015, 'Drift and Pop: On Writing about W. S. Graham'.[1] This essay brings the Cornish upbringing of Sara and me into dialogue with the poetry of W. S. Graham, a poet deeply associated with the landscape and people amidst whom we lived. I have begun to sketch out poems of travel across the Cornish landscape and borderlands (connecting with my earlier book *Down to Earth* which concerns the Mexican / US border), organized around a gypsy or tinker figure and drawing on the walking trope characteristic of Graham's poems as well as the unfolding landscape-abstract paintings of Peter Lanyon and other St Ives artists. The Cornish landscape is marked by depopulation, de-industrialization and the decline of fishing as well as the loss of a native language. Cornwall is a landscape of loss both personal, and (like some other notable tourist destinations) social and cultural. It also offers me some hope of reparation in the familiar rhythms of rowed sea and paced-out land – or in a poultice of its last mined product, china clay (kaolin). I have previously addressed cultural and linguistic devastation in a set of poems in my 2016 book, *Ghost Nets*, prompted by a visit to Lhasa, Tibet; and the title sequence of my previous book, *Reckitt's Blue*, navigates by wave-swell through the shattered and displayed cultures of Papua New Guinea. It seems now that in the light of these preoccupations my work was bound to circle back to Cornwall.

The politics of reparation can be delusory and evil. It seems incredible that in 1937, the year when fascist Italy occupied Abyssinia, Melanie Klein could assert that colonial settlement constituted a reparation for the brutal plunder and murder of a land's people, her metamorphosis of land into good mother dissolving its indigenous population as mere figments, part-objects whose clearing out makes reparation to the maternal land. Tending the soil indeed. Klein reads poems as colonial expeditions, not so far from the mark but hardly an unalloyed good.[2] Colonial expeditions do not always necessitate arms and transports; the digital scrim extracts and discards people's souls from their materials including their art, for the purpose of ready 'manipulation', a term that has ceased to be pejorative. *Reckitt's Blue* is preoccupied by the ethics of appropriation – for neither is appropriation an unalloyed evil, as replacing 'appropriation' by 'translation' should show. (The ultra-radical view that translation into English is invariably a form of colonialist appropriation would condemn English speakers to listen only to their kind, straightjacketed by identity.)

A great poem's reparation restores thinking to rhythm, lucidity to material, self to the maternal body, the history of human labour to language, expedition to exchange, self to the social. And the other way round. It's a lot to ask, but in evil times people are more deeply driven to ask it. I far prefer failure than settling for less, and I like poets who can let their work look ungainly in the attempt. So I trip over my own feet and hope to make a poem that can stand. But what does stand mean? Like Miles Davis says, "When I'm playing, I'm never through. It's unfinished. I like to find a place to leave for someone else to finish it. That's where the high comes in. If I know I left a perfectly good spot for someone else to come in – like, there it is!" So please...

NOTES

[1] John Wilkinson, 'Drift and Pop: On Writing about W.S. Graham', *Poetry* vol. 206, no. 4, July / August 2015, pp. 427-433. On-line at https://www.poetryfoundation.org/poetrymagazine/articles/detail/70238
[2] See 'Love, Guilt and Reparation' in Melanie Klein, *Love, Guilt and Reparation & Other Works 1921-1945*. (New York: Dell Publishing 1977) esp. pp. 333-335.

PHOTO: ROBERT EDGE

JAMES BYRNE is a poet, editor, translator and Senior Lecturer at Edge Hill University. His most recent poetry collections are *Everything Broken Up Dances* (Tupelo, US, 2015) and *White Coins* (Arc Publications, UK, 2015). He is editor of *The Wolf* and, in 2012, co-translated and co-edited *Bones Will Crow: 15 Contemporary Burmese Poets* (Arc Publications, 2012). He is the co-editor of *Voice Recognition: 21 Poets for the 21st Century*, published by Bloodaxe in 2009 and the International Editor for Arc Publications.

ROBERT SHEPPARD is a poet and critic, whose *Complete Twentieth Century Blues* (2008) is published by Salt and whose *History or Sleep: Selected Poems* (2015) is published by Shearsman. His next book will be the collaboratively written anthology of European fictional poets, *Twitters for a Lark*. His most recent critical book is *The Meaning of Form in Contemporary Innovative Poetry* (2016) and his last anthology was *Floating Capital: New Poets from London* (1991). He is Professor of Poetry and Poetics at Edge Hill University.

The editors and the publishers of this anthology thank authors and publishers listed below for their permission to reprint poems and essays from the collections as named, and also those authors whose work is being published here for the first time:

CHARLES BERNSTEIN

'This Line' is from *My Way: Speeches and Poems* (University of Chicago Press, 1999); 'Whose Language' is from *Rough Trades* (Sun & Moon Press, 1991); 'Sunset Sail' is from *Republics of Reality: 1975-1995*, (Sun & Moon Press, 2000); 'Dysraphism' is from *The Sophist* (Sun & Moon Press, 1987); 'Castor Oil' is from *Girly Man* (University of Chicago Press, 2006); 'Preface' is from *Pitch of Poetry* (University of Chicago Press, 2016).

SEAN BONNEY

All material is published by permission of the author.

ANDREA BRADY

'The Fourth Call of Mr Gore', 'All My Sons', 'Queen Bee' & 'Men' are from *The Strong Room* (Crater Press, 2016). 'Poetics' is published by permission of the author.

SOPHIE COLLINS

All material is published by permission of the author.

ALLEN FISHER

I & VI are from *Place*, (Reality Street Editions, 2005); 'Bird Land', 'Bumble Bee' & 'Jitterbug' are from *Gravity as a Consequence of Shape* (Reality Street Editions, 2016). 'The poetics of decoherence and the imperfect fit' is published by permission of the author.

ROBERT FITTERMAN

Extracts from 'This Window' & 'Failure: a Postconceptual Poem' are published by permission of the author.

S. J. FOWLER

'You'll find a bee and sting me with it', 'Looper', 'Bear's attacked me' & 'Atacama', are from *The Guide to Being Bear Aware* (Shearsman, March 2017); 'cob', 'cahoots' & 'tattoos' are from *Minimum Security Prison Dentistry* (anything anymore anywhere, 2011); all other poems are reprinted by permission of the author. 'Poetics' is published by permission of the author.

FORREST GANDER

'A Poetics' is from *A Faithful Existence: reading, memory and transcendence* (Counterpoint, 2000); 'Evaporation, a border history' is from *The Blue Rock Collection* (Salt Publishing, 2004); 'Anniversary' & 'Field Guide to Southern Virginia' are from *Science and Steeple Flower* © 1997 Forrest Gander, reprinted by permission of New Directions Publishing Corp. All poems and poetics are reprinted by permission of the author.

LYN HEJINIAN

'Time of Tyranny' is published by permission of the author. 'Rejection of Closure' was originally publishing in *Writing / talks* ed. Bob Perelman (Southern Illinois University Press, 1985) and in its final form appeared in *The Language of Inquiry* (Berkeley: University of California Press, 2000), and is reprinted by permission of the author.

JOHN JAMES

'Good Old Harry', 'Shakin All Over', 'Stacking' & 'A Theory of Poetry' are from *Collected Poems* (Salt Publishing, 2002); 'A Visitation' is from *Cloud Breaking Sun*, (Oystercatcher Press, 2012). 'Baudelaire at Cébazan' is published by permission of the author and is reprinted from *In Romsey Town* (Equipage, 2011).

TREVOR JOYCE
All material is reprinted from *Selected Poems: 1967-2014*, (Shearsman, 2014) by permission of the author.

BHANU KAPIL
Extracts from *Ban en Banlieue* are reprinted by permission of Nightboat Books, 2015. 'Poetics' is published by permission of the author.

NATHANIEL MACKEY
'Song of the Andoumboulou: 40' is from *Splay Anthem* © 2002 Nathaniel Mackey, reprinted by permission of New Directions Publishing Corp; 'Beginning "We the Migrating They"' is from *Blue Fasa* copyright © 2015 Nathaniel Mackey, reprinted by permission of New Directions Publishing Corp; extract from 'Sound and Sentiment, Sound and Symbol' is from *Callaloo* (1987), reprinted by permission of the author, and is also published in *The Politics of Poetic Form: Poetry and Public Policy*, ed. Charles Bernstein (Roof Books, 1989), with extracts appearing in *Postmodern American Poetry: A Norton Anthology*, ed. Paul Hoover (New York: W. W. Norton & Co., 1994).

DAVID MARRIOTT
'Lorem Ipsum', 'Rhapsode' & 'A Sequel' are from *The Bloods*, (Shearsman, 2011).; 'Else, in Limbo' is from *Hoodoo Voodoo* (Shearsman, 2008); 'Response to Race and the Poetic Avant-Garde' is from *Boston Review*, 2015 and is reprinted by permission of the author.

CHRIS MCCABE
'# 555: george w. bush' & 'A 98p Voicemail Message to Blaise Cendrars' are from *The Hutton Inquiry* (Salt Publishing, 2005); 'Axis is' is from *THE RESTRUCTURE*, (Salt Publishing, 2012); 'Jack Straw' is published by permission of the author; 'A New Way to Pay Old Debts' is from *Speculatrix* (Penned in the Margins, 2014), by permission of Penned in the Margins. 'Changing All that is Metal in Thy House to Gold: The Political as Personal', is published by permission of the author.

GERALDINE MONK
'Pendle', 'The Great Assembly & Feast' & 'Alice Nutter Replies' are from *Pendle Witch-Words*, (Knives Forks and Spoons, 2012); 'Ghost Sonnet 29' & 'Ghost Sonnet 32' are from *Ghost and Other Sonnets* (Salt Publishing, 2009); 'Biscay. Trafalgar. Fitzroy.', 'Faeroes. Southeast Iceland.' & 'Artemis Comes to Tea' are from *They Who Saw The Deep* (Parlor Press LLC, 2016); extract from 'Insubstantial Thoughts on the Transubstantiation Of The Text' is from West House Books / The Paper, 2002.

VALZHYNA MORT
'Jean-Paul Belmondo' & 'Sylt I' are from *Collected Body* (Copper Canyon Press, 2011); 'Maria', 'Psalm 18' & 'Selected Sources for Basic Prosody' are published by permission of the author.

ERÍN MOURE
Extract from 'The Fall' is from *O Cadoiro*, (House of Anansi, 2007); extract from 'O Cadoiro: Postface' is from *Postface to O Cadoiro poems* (House of

Anansi, 2007) [anansi.ca/ocadoiro/postface].

M. NOURBESE PHILIP

Extract from 'Zong!' is from *Zong!* (Wesleyan University Press, 2008); 'Testimony Stoops to Mother Tongue' & extract from 'The Absence of Writing or How I Almost Became a Spy' are from *She Tries Her Tongue, Her Silence Softly Breaks*, (Wesleyan University Press, 2014).

CLAUDIA RANKINE

All material is reprinted from *Citizen: An American Lyric* and is reproduced by permission of Penguin Books Ltd. (London, 2015).

JEROME ROTHENBERG

Extract from 'The Jigoku Zoshi Hells: A Book of Variations' & 'A Note on the Preceding' are from *The Jigoku Zoshi Hells: A Book of Variations* (Argotist Ebooks, 2010).

ZOË SKOULDING

Extract from 'Teint' is from *Teint: For The Bièvre Pour La Bièvre*, (Hafan Books, 2016); 'Underground Rivers: Notes Towards a Zoepoetics' is published by permission from the author.

ROSMARIE WALDROP

Extract from 'Lawn of the Excluded Middle' is from *Curves to the Apple* © 1993 Rosmarie Waldrop, reprinted by permission of New Directions Publishing Corp; 'Pleasure Principle' is from *Split Infinites* (Singing Horse Press, 1999); 'Mallarmé as Philologist, Dying' is from *Blindsight* © 2003 Rosmarie Waldrop, reprinted by permission of New Directions Publishing Corp; 'By the Waters of Babylon' is from *Driven to Abstraction* © 2010 Rosmarie Waldrop, reprinted by permission of New Directions Publishing Corp; 'Wanting' & 'Thinking' are published by permission of the author; 'Why Do I Write Prose Poems / When My True Love Is Verse' is from *Dissonance (if you're interested): Collected Essays* (University of Alabama Press, 2005).

JOHN WILKINSON

Extract from 'Reckitt's Blue' is from *Reckitt's Blue*, (Seagull Books, 2012); extract from 'Courses Matter-Woven' is from *Ghost Nets* (Omnidawn, 2016); 'Schlummert Ein' & extract from *Lyric Poetry in Evil Times* are published by permission of the author.

*

The editors would like to thank the Faculty of English, History & Creative Writing at Edge Hill University; Edge Hill's Corporate Communications team (particularly Roy Bayfield and Natalie McRae); co-Director of Edge Hill University Press, Dr Rodge Glass; the ever-exceptional Tony Ward and Angela Jarman at Arc Publications; the artist Pete Clarke; and all the poets included in this book and their respective publishers. Finally, we would like to acknowledge our wonderful team of interns whose diligence helped the publication process: Bill Bulloch, Jennifer Byrne, Robert Edge, Isabella Casteñeda Godoy, Brendan Quinn and Jessica Tillings.